Wildflowers
OF MONTANA

Donald Anthony Schiemann

2005
Mountain Press Publishing Company
Missoula, Montana

Fourth Printing, April 2013

Library of Congress Cataloging-in-Publication Data
Schiemann, Donald Anthony, 1933-
  Wildflowers of Montana / Donald Anthony Schiemann.
    p. cm.
  Includes bibliographical references and index.
  ISBN 978-0-87842-504-4 (pbk. : alk. paper)
  1. Wild flowers—Montana—Identification. 2. Wild flowers—
Montana—Pictorial works. I. Title.
  QK171.S35 2005

                                    582.13'09786—dc22

PRINTED IN HONG KONG

MP Mountain Press
PUBLISHING COMPANY
P.O. Box 2399 • Missoula, MT 59806 • 406-728-1900
800-234-5308 • info@mtnpress.com
www.mountain-press.com

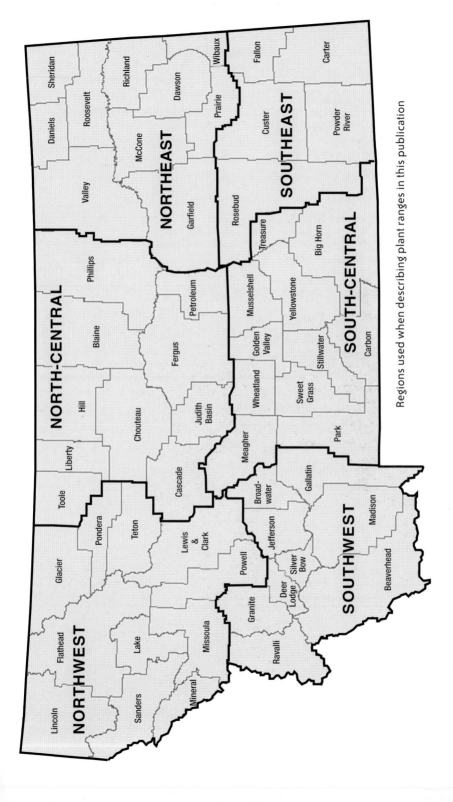

Regions used when describing plant ranges in this publication

Contents

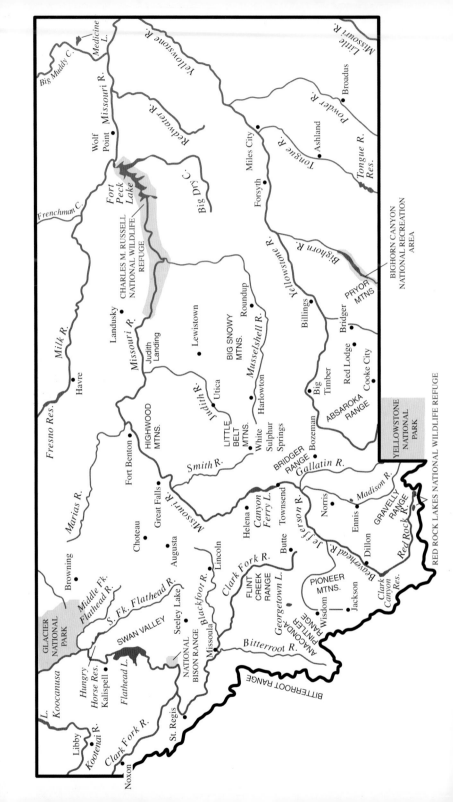

INTRODUCTION

If a Montana wildflower caught your attention because of its beauty or maybe its abundance, and you were interested enough to seek a name, then I sincerely hope I have created a publication that will assist you. I have tried to include Montana's most beautiful and most common wildflowers, as well as examples of less common species. I have also included many of our weeds, some of which are very attractive despite their undesirable qualities. Approximately 2,500 flowering plants grow in Montana. This book features more than 350 species, a large number by any count, but admittedly not comprehensive.

Landscape, Climate, and Vegetation Zones

Everyone who has driven across Montana knows it is an enormous state with a wide range of landscapes, from dry expanses of sagebrush to dense, wet cedar and fir forests. The western third of the state spans the Rocky Mountains and the Continental Divide, with rivers to the west draining into the Columbia River basin and rivers to the east draining predominantly into the Missouri River basin. The eastern two-thirds of the state is treeless plains of short-grass prairie and sagebrush, with the occasional, isolated mountain range rising above the horizon. The elevation ranges from 1,875 feet at the confluence of the Missouri and Yellowstone Rivers on the eastern border of Montana to the 12,799-foot-high summit of Granite Peak in the Beartooth Mountains. The wildflowers are as diverse as the landscape, from pincushion cactus in the dry plains to the glacier lily in alpine meadows.

Climate—measured by yearly temperature and precipitation variations—is an important ecological determinant of the types of plants that will grow in any given location. Montana's climatic range gives rise to five general but distinct vegetation zones—plains, foothills, montane, subalpine, and alpine.

1

The plains vegetation zone generally has grass and sagebrush, with trees only present along waterways and in draws. The foothills vegetation zone is transitional between treeless plains and the forested montane zone. The montane vegetation zone includes the dominantly pine and Douglas fir forests, often interspersed with aspen or larch. The subalpine vegetation zone, transitional between the forested montane zone and the treeless alpine zone, generally has open meadows interspersed with coniferous forests made up of subalpine fir and spruce. The alpine zone is above timberline, so the plants that grow there are low shrubs and herbs that tolerate windy conditions, snow, and cold temperatures. In the Habitat/Range section in the plant descriptions, I include the vegetation zones in which each plant typically occurs.

In a specific area, elevation plays a major factor in determining which vegetation zone you are in; as you climb from the flatlands to the top of a tall mountain, you pass through several different vegetation zones. Within a larger area like Montana, however, elevation is not a good predictor of the vegetation zone. The alpine zone occurs above 9,000 feet in southwest Montana, but begins at about 7,000 feet in Glacier National Park, which is farther north and in a cooler climatic region.

In *Vascular Plants of Montana*, Robert Dorn divided Montana into six regions and listed which regions each plant occurs in. I have used the same six regions (see page iii) and have listed each plant's distribution under the heading Habitat/Range. When a plant was recorded in both the northwest and southwest regions, I listed the distribution as merely *west*, and I used the same method for central and east Montana.

Unlike many field guides, this one doesn't include a blooming time in the plant description. In general, you can assume that the higher in elevation you go, the later in the season the flowers will be blooming. However, flowers bloom much earlier in dry, warm springs compared to those years in which the snow falls late and lingers. In mountainous areas, the time since the snow melted from an area can be a better estimate to blooming time than the actual month.

In the caption to each photograph, I have included the specific location and time of the year that I photographed the wildflower. I hope this will provide a little travel guide to some of the out-of-the-way places of great beauty that exist in Montana. A few alpine wildflowers were photographed along the Beartooth Highway (U.S. 212) at points within Wyoming. Because this is one of the few major roads that reaches the alpine zone, it is an accessible place for finding alpine wildflowers that also occur within Montana.

Plains in the Judith River basin west of Winifred

Plains east of Jordan

Foothills of the Anaconda Range in southwest Montana

Montane zone in the Pryor Mountains east of Bridger

Subalpine vegetation zone along Going-to-the-Sun
Highway in Glacier National Park

Alpine vegetation zone along the Beartooth Highway
between Red Lodge and Cooke City

Plant Names and Book Organization

> *What's in a name? That which we call a rose*
> *By any other name would smell as sweet*
> —WILLIAM SHAKESPEARE,
> Romeo and Juliet

Carolus Linnaeus (1707–78), a Swedish botanist, proposed a scientific nomenclature of plants that endures to this day. Every plant species consists of a two-part scientific name that specifies a genus (capitalized) and species (lowercase). For example, *Helianthus annuus* is the scientific name for common sunflower. Scientific names are often derived from Latin and refer to some particular feature or characteristic of the plant. Genera, each including a few or many species, are grouped into larger divisions called *families*. For example, common sunflower is a member of the sunflower family.

The wildflowers described in this book are first grouped by family in alphabetical order by common family name. Within each family, the plants are organized alphabetically by their scientific names. All identifications for this book were made with the blooming plant, which is not always adequate for identifying a specific species that has been defined by the nature of the fruit or features on the seeds. With these limitations, a few identifications in this book were concluded at the level of genus rather than species. A separate section describes some of the more common flowering shrubs, and these are arranged alphabetically by scientific name but not grouped by family.

Sometimes scientists further divide a species into varieties or subspecies based on consistent, observable differences. I've mentioned a few varieties and subspecies where the distinction is fairly clear-cut, such as petal color, but generally the identification of varieties and subspecies is beyond the scope of this book.

Scientific names can change as new studies and information become available. Some species have two or more scientific names because of disagreement among scientific authorities or because a taxonomic change is slow to be accepted. In this book, I have listed what I consider the most accepted scientific names, and for some species I have also included a second scientific name, called a *synonym*.

Many of us are not scientists, and we choose to communicate with more familiar and easily remembered common names, many of which readily roll off the tongue and are as pretty as the flower they name. Common names are problematic, however, because one species may have five or more different common names, or the same common name may be applied to several different species. In this book, I use the common name that seems most common in Montana. A few other frequently used common names are included in the description. Be forewarned that another field guide may use a different common name for the same species, and you must compare the scientific names to know whether the guides you are using are discussing the same species or not.

Identifying Wildflowers

I identified the wildflowers included in this field guide, at least at first assignment, by the same method most people use: find a picture in a book that looks the same as the flower in the wild. But you'll be able to identify a lot more wildflowers if you learn some of the important characteristics that distinguish one species from another. To identify a wildflower, you need to learn the names of plant parts and how they are arranged and what shapes they come in. In this section I will try to describe the main things to look for when observing a wildflower. A glossary in the back of the book defines the terms.

First, let's look at the stem. If it is woody, even just at the base, the plant is a *shrub* and is included in that section of this guide. If it is not woody, the plant is an herb and falls under the wildflower section of this book. Is the stem square? If so, it is likely in the mint family. Is the plant a vine? If so, it may be in the buttercup, honeysuckle, or pea families. Does the stem contain a milky sap? If so, the plant may be in the dogbane, milkweed, spurge, or sunflower families. Stem height and degree of branching, as well as the presence of prickles, hairs, and glands, can also help identify a plant.

Next, examine the leaves. Leave are either *simple* or *compound*. A compound leaf is divided into leaflets and a simple leaf is not. A compound leaf is *pinnately compound* (leaflets arranged on either side of a stalk), *palmately compound* (leaflets radiating around a common point), or *trifoliate* (three leaflets). It is also important to look at leaf arrangement. Leaves can all be at the base of the plant (*basal leaves*) or on the stem (*stem leaves*) or both. Stem leaves can be arranged *alternate*, *opposite*, or *whorled*. The shapes, margins, and hairiness

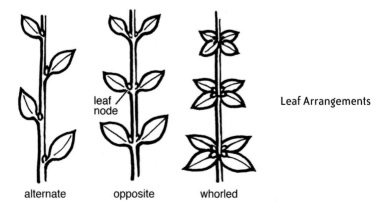

leaf node

Leaf Arrangements

alternate   opposite   whorled

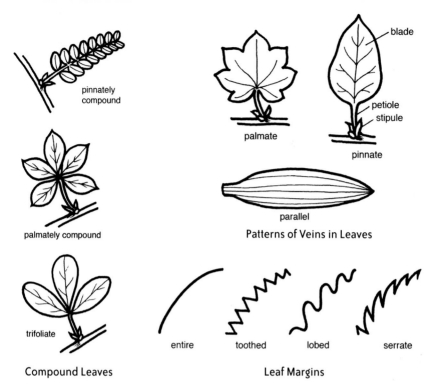

pinnately compound

palmate

blade

petiole

stipule

pinnate

palmately compound

Patterns of Veins in Leaves

parallel

trifoliate

entire   toothed   lobed   serrate

Compound Leaves

Leaf Margins

of leaves vary considerably, even on an individual plant, but you can generally determine whether a leaf margin is toothed or lobed, what the general shape is, and the degree of hairiness on the upper and lower surfaces. The pattern of veins in the leaf can also help in identification.

The flower has several key parts. Let's start with the *petals*, because most of us know what they are. Collectively, the petals are called the *corolla*. The four main things you need to observe about the petals are what color they are, how many there are, whether they are separate or fused at their base, and whether they have a radially symmetrical arrangement or not. The *sepals* are directly below the petals and are usually green, though sometimes they look just like the petals and are called *tepals*. Collectively, the sepals are called the *calyx*.

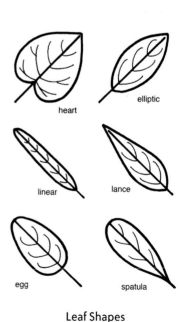

heart

elliptic

linear

lance

egg

spatula

Leaf Shapes

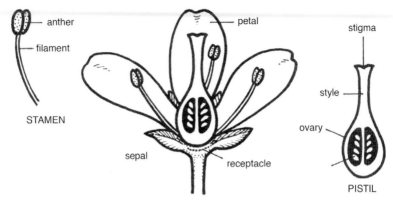

Flower with a Superior Ovary

The female, egg-producing part of a flower is called the *pistil* and the male, pollen-producing part is called the *stamen*. The *ovary*, *style*, and *stigma* make up the pistil and are usually in the flower center. The ovary can be *superior* (above where the petals and sepals join) or *inferior* (below where the petals and sepals join). *Filaments* support the pollen-producing *anthers* that make up the stamens, which usually surround the pistil. It is important to note how many stamens there are and whether they protrude beyond the corolla or not.

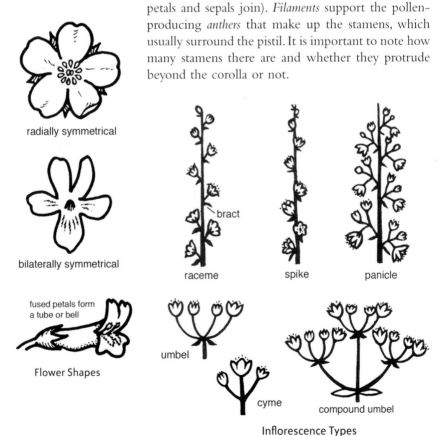

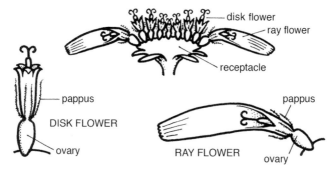

Flower of the Sunflower Family

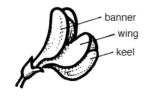

Flower of the Pea Family

Flowers can be solitary or come as a group in several arrangements. A group of flowers is collectively called an *inflorescence*. The main types of inflorescences are *umbels*, *spikes*, *racemes*, *panicles*, and *cymes*.

Some families have such unique flowers that they are easily recognized. Members of the sunflower family usually have petal-like ray flowers surrounding many small disk flowers. Members of the pea family have characteristically pealike flowers that have a banner, keel, and wings.

Photographing Wildflowers

It may be of interest to some readers how I photographed the wildflowers in this book. My first choice of camera was the Nikon F4, and less often the Nikon F90x (sold as N90s in the United States) and the Nikon F100. Most of the pictures were shot with the Nikkor Micro 200mm 1:4D lens, followed by the Nikkor Micro 105mm 1:2.8D lens, and a few with the Nikkor 85mm tilt/shift lens. I occasionally attached an extension tube or a close-up auxiliary lens to these lenses. I sometimes attached a polarizer to reduce reflections and glare. I always use a tripod, the Gitzo G1228 Mountaineer or the Gitzo MK2, both of which are carbon-fiber lightweight tripods. On a few occasions I used a beanbag to steady the camera for very low-profile shots. The film of first choice was Fujichrome Velvia 50, followed by Fujichrome Provia 100F or Kodak E100VS, and, in the last season of photography, Fujichrome Velvia 100F on occasion. A gray card was often used for determining exposure. A shutter cable release was always employed, and the lock-up mirror feature on the F4 camera was utilized occasionally to reduce vibrations at low shutter speeds.

Photographing in direct sunlight can result in undesirable shadows over the flower. Reflectors, silver or gold, were sometimes used to lighten shadowed areas. At other times, holding the Nikon SB-25 or Nikon SB-28 flash unit off camera provided fill-flash. Occasionally, I used two off-camera flash units by attachment to a Stroboframe, a lightweight and compact device for supporting flash units in the field. During the last season, I made a few shots using the Nikon Macro SB-21B, a ring flash unit. The best exposures can be obtained on an overcast day, especially after a rain or with a bit of drizzle that leaves some water drops on the flowers.

Wind is the bane of wildflower photography. A Michigan biology teacher told me that his entire collection of wildflower photos taken one summer in Rocky Mountain National Park was blurred, the consequence of wind that he did not fully appreciate at the time. If you see blurred wildflower pictures in magazines or books, you can usually blame the wind. How can one overcome the annoying effect of wind? First, photograph when there is little or no wind, which usually occurs in early morning and sometimes late in the day. Sometimes a shield of trees and other vegetation will help. Shoot with a high-speed film (which has other problems) so higher shutter speeds are possible. Shoot with flash as the light source. If you are close enough, stabilize the flower by using a Wimberley Plant Clamp ("The Plamp"). My favorite method is to use a hood constructed of polycarbonate, which is a transparent plastic, with the panels joined by transparent tape. This device is cumbersome, especially if you have to carry it for some distance or if used on sloping ground, but it can be quite effective in controlling movement of the wildflowers. I have constructed several of these hoods in different sizes and configurations.

Final Note

I have always walked outdoors and among the wildflowers with a feeling of elation and awe at the beauty that has been entrusted to us. I have photographed all wildflowers in their natural setting, never pulling or cutting one or moving it to another location. Sometimes debris was moved or grasses cut to remove obstructions between the camera and the wildflower. It has always been with some regret that I have left an area disturbed by walking or lying on nearby plants. I hope you too will enjoy our natural world and especially the wildflowers while making as minor an impact as possible on the area of your trespass. Remember, wildflowers can rarely be transplanted with success, so don't try digging them out for planting in your garden. Maybe cutting a few wildflowers that are plentiful can be excused, especially if they bring joy when placed on the table or are used for instruction of children; but be cautious about destroying those wildflowers that are rare or present in low numbers.

Look down, get on your knees if you must, observe closely, and you will enter a world of remarkable beauty, intricate complexity, and infinite astonishment, and it will surely bring to you pleasure and gratitude for being alive in this place. I found it; I hope that my work will help you share it. Remember, too: Sight is a faculty but seeing is an art.

THUMBNAIL IDENTIFICATION GUIDE

Small thumbnail photographs in the following section are grouped by color and other flower features to help you find and quickly identify many wildflowers. Let us assume, for example, that you have found a flower with five yellow petals and wish to know its name. If you do not recognize the family to which the flower belongs, you can turn to the thumbnail section and look at the group of plants that have five yellow petals. Each thumbnail includes the page number that the wildflower appears on. All the wildflowers included in this book are represented in the thumbnails with the exception of easily recognizable plants like cactuses and shrubs. Please appreciate that it is difficult to categorize wildflowers on the basis of a few simple characteristics, and that a single wildflower could be placed in more than one group. In addition, a variety of colors may occur within a single species, and judging intermediate colors is subjective; one person's blue may be another person's lavender. Therefore, you may have to look in more than one group of the thumbnails to find your particular wildflower.

WHITE Five Petals

p. 66–67	p. 206–7	p. 218–19	p. 202–3	p. 222–23

WHITE Five Petals

p. 202–3	p. 212–13	p. 254–55	p. 222–23	p. 206–7

WHITE Five Petals

p. 222–23	p. 204–5	p. 114–15	p. 204–5	p. 48–49

WHITE Five Petals

p. 270–71	p. 214–15	p. 220–21	p. 208–9	p. 120–21

WHITE Five Petals

p. 198–201	p. 210–11	p. 266–67	p. 50–51	p. 196–97

WHITE Five Petals

p. 224–25   p. 224–25   p. 266–67   p. 48–49   p. 230–31

WHITE Four Petals

p. 110–11   p. 86–89   p. 82–83   p. 154–55   p. 154–55

WHITE Four Petals

p. 160–61   p. 142–43   p. 154–55   p. 84–85   p. 154–55

Four Petals | WHITE Three or Six Petals

p. 160–61   p. 130–31   p. 130–33   p. 130–31   p. 130–31

WHITE Three or Six Petals

p. 134–35   p. 138–39   p. 136–37   p. 132–33   p. 140–41

WHITE Three or Six Petals				Many Petals
p. 128–29	p. 128–29	p. 134–35	p. 142–43	p. 264–65

WHITE Many Petals				
p. 254–55	p. 250–51	p. 232–33	p. 246–47	p. 262–63

WHITE Many Petals				
p. 262–63	p. 240–41	p. 242–43	p. 234–35	p. 234–35

WHITE Pealike Flowers				
p. 178–79	p. 184–85	p. 191–92	p. 182–83	p. 182–83

Pealike Flowers	WHITE Funnel- and Bell-shaped Flowers			
p. 178–79	p. 112–13	p. 80–81	p. 136–37	p. 220–21

| p. 120–21 | p. 120–21 | p. 152–53 | p. 224–25 | p. 162–63 |

| p. 100–103 | p. 148–49 | p. 140–41 | p. 64–65 | p. 62–63 |

| p. 136–37 | p. 146–47 | p. 180–81 | p. 138–39 | p. 274–75 |

| p. 170–71 | p. 172–73 | p. 174–75 | p. 172–73 | p. 172–73 |

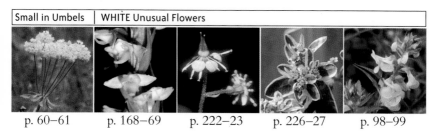

| p. 60–61 | p. 168–69 | p. 222–23 | p. 226–27 | p. 98–99 |

WHITE Unusual

p. 72–73	p. 276–277	p. 98–99	p. 168–69	p. 70–71

WHITE Unusual | **YELLOW Five Petals**

p. 170–71	p. 214–17	p. 46–47	p. 106–7	p. 76–77

YELLOW Five Petals

p. 164–65	p. 212–13	p. 74–75	p. 54–55	p. 270–73

YELLOW Five Petals | **Four Petals**

p. 228–31	p. 218–19	p. 216–17	p. 54–55	p. 158–59

YELLOW Four Petals

p. 88–89	p. 160–61	p. 156–57	p. 156–57	p. 158–59

p. 152–53   p. 134–35   p. 124–25   p. 134–35   p. 236–37

p. 260–61   p. 238–39   p. 238–39   p. 264–65   p. 248–49

p. 252–53   p. 250–51   p. 264–65   p. 242–43   p. 258–59

p. 260–61   p. 76–77   p. 68–69   p. 258–59   p. 232–33

p. 262–63   p. 250–51   p. 254–55   p. 256–57   p. 256–57

Many Petals	YELLOW Pealike Flowers			YELLOW Unusual
p. 248–49	p. 184–85	p. 188–89	p. 192–93	p. 96–97

YELLOW Unusual				
p. 276–77	p. 252–53	p. 226–27	p. 168–69	p. 166–67

YELLOW Unusual				
p. 94–95	p. 260–61	p. 254–55	p. 106–7	p. 90–93

YELLOW Unusual		YELLOW Small Flowers in Ball-like Clusters		
p. 46–47	p. 68–69	p. 174–75	p. 214–15	p. 60–61

YELLOW Small	RED / ORANGE			
p. 60–61	p. 96–97	p. 144–45	p. 90–91	p. 90–93

p. 250–51   p. 232–33   p. 122–23   p. 196–97   p. 136–37

p. 118–19   p. 58–59   p. 166–67   p. 166–67   p. 62–63

p. 98–99   p. 228–29   p. 216–17   p. 76–77   p. 60–61

p. 234–35   p. 228–29   p. 194–95   p. 194–95   p. 66–67

p. 122–23   p. 244–45   p. 194–95   p. 238–39   p. 180–81

Thumbnail Identification Guide   19

p. 204–5   p. 114–15   p. 208–9   p. 204–5   p. 198–99

p. 268–69   p. 116–17   p. 144–45   p. 84–85   p. 156–57

p. 84–85   p. 158–59   p. 82–83   p. 80–81   p. 86–87

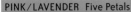

p. 108–109   p. 244–45   p. 210–11   p. 210–11   p. 262–63

p. 238–39   p. 66–67   p. 240–43   p. 252–53   p. 248–249

p. 176–77   p. 178–79   p. 190–91   p. 188–89   p. 190–91

p. 176–77   p. 182–83   p. 188–89   p. 192–93   p. 186–87

p. 274–75   p. 274–75   p. 50–51   p. 272–73   p. 200–201

p. 148–49   p. 150–51   p. 150–51   p. 150–51   p. 148–49

p. 104–5   p. 102–3   p. 104–5   p. 102–3   p. 196–97

PINK/LAVENDER Funnel- and Bell-shaped | PINK/LAVENDER Onion-like Flowers

p. 224–25    p. 112–13    p. 126–27    p. 128–29    p. 126–27

PINK/LAVENDER Unusual

p. 206–7    p. 92–93    p. 96–97    p. 98–99    p. 212–13

PINK/LAVENDER Unusual

p. 120–21    p. 164–65    p. 118–19    p. 146–47    p. 252–53

PINK/LAVENDER Unusual | BLUE/PURPLE Five Petals

p. 180–81    p. 62–63    p. 56–57    p. 58–59    p. 110–11

BLUE/PURPLE Five Petals

p. 52–53    p. 54–55    p. 52–53    p. 268–69    p. 200–201

BLUE/PURPLE Four Petals

p. 108–9   p. 108–9

BLUE/PURPLE Three or Six Petals

p. 124–25   p. 132–33   p. 132–33

Three or Six

p. 124–25

BLUE/PURPLE Pealike Flowers

p. 184–85   p. 186–87   p. 192–93   p. 194–95

BLUE/PURPLE Funnel- and Bell-shaped Flowers

p. 138–39   p. 116–17   p. 70–71   p. 112–13   p. 70–71

BLUE/PURPLE Funnel- and Bell-shaped Flowers

p. 56–57   p. 56–57   p. 104–5   p. 100–103   p. 94–95

Funnel-shaped

BLUE/PURPLE Unusual Flowers

p. 50–51   p. 72–73   p. 88–89   p. 64–65   p. 162–63

Thumbnail Identification Guide   23

⇌ SHRUBS ⇌

Shrubs are woody plants that are smaller than trees and usually represented by a clump of stems. The shrubs described here are arranged alphabetically by genus name.

Serviceberry   *Amelanchier alnifolia*

Serviceberry, also called *saskatoon*, is a bushy shrub up to 20 feet tall, with dark gray or reddish stems. The 1- to 2-inch-long, oval, alternate leaves have petioles and often have toothed margins toward the tips. Showy white or sometimes pinkish, fragrant flowers occur in clusters of a few to many near the end of short branches. Each flower has five elliptical petals that arise from the rim of a flat cup that will mature into a sweet, juicy, dark purple berry. The flower contains twenty yellow stamens and five styles.

Serviceberry, a favorite food of many birds and animals, can be used to make jelly and wine. American Indians stored the berries for food during the winter and also pounded them with meat into pemmican.

HABITAT/RANGE: Found in canyons, on open hillsides, and in open coniferous forests from lowlands to subalpine zones in west, central, and east Montana.

Kinnikinnick   *Arctostaphylos uva-ursi*

Kinnikinnick, also called *bearberry*, forms low, dense mats no more than 6 inches tall even though the woody, reddish stems may be 10 feet long. The evergreen leaves are about 1 inch long, broader near the blunt tip, and shiny and waxy. The pink or sometimes white flowers, clustered in racemes at the tip of the branches, have five lobes that are fused into a urn-shaped structure with a small opening that faces downward.

The bright red berries, which persist throughout winter, are edible and often eaten by bears.

HABITAT/RANGE: Prefers open woods or forest edges and also dry banks and alpine slopes in west, central, and southeast Montana.

Silver Sagebrush   *Artemisia cana*

Silver sagebrush, one of twenty-two *Artemisia* species reported in Montana, is a highly branched leafy shrub, 12 to 28 inches tall, with white shredding bark. Older plants appear twisted. The numerous alternate leaves have silvery hairs on both sides. The linear leaves, $\frac{3}{8}$ to $1\frac{1}{4}$ inches long, usually have entire margins and are stalkless and pointed at both ends. The numerous flower heads, hidden by the leafy upper stems, contain five to twenty flowers that are compacted into the upper leaf axils.

Meriwether Lewis collected a specimen of silver sagebrush in 1804. Various sagebrush extracts were used by American Indians for medicinal purposes, but sagebrush can cause allergic reactions, so their use is not recommended.

HABITAT/RANGE: Inhabits the plains and mountain valleys across Montana.

Serviceberry in early May along U.S. 89 just south of Belt

Kinnikinnick in early June at the base of the
Beartooth Highway south of Red Lodge

Silver sagebrush in early July in
Bighorn Canyon National Recreation
Area in south-central Montana

Oregon Grape

Berberis repens
Mahonia repens

Oregon grape is a low, spreading evergreen shrub less than 1 foot tall. The glossy, pinnately compound, alternate leaves are hollylike, with five to seven spine-tipped, broad leaflets per stem. Clusters of small, yellow flowers are arranged in narrow racemes at the end of the stems. Six petals and six similar sepals are each arranged in two whorls, the petals are slightly shorter than the sepals. Three small bracts lie below the sepals. Six stamens are attached to the base of the petals and will move toward the single style if touched. The flowers mature into grapelike clusters of blue berries that have a chalky coating.

The tart berries of Oregon grape have been used in jellies and wine. The American Indians used the yellow inner bark as a dye, and also for several medicinal purposes. An alkaloid in the sap has demonstrated antibiotic activity against a variety of microbes.

HABITAT/RANGE: Found in many places varying from dense to open forests and low to medium elevations in west, central, and southeast Montana.

Buckbrush

Ceanothus velutinus

Buckbrush, a sprawling evergreen shrub, is 2 to 5 feet tall, with smooth, thick, dark green leaves that are broadly oval, 2 to 4 inches long, and shiny and sticky above and pale below. The leaves are alternate and have fine teeth on the margins and three prominent veins. Another common name, _snowbrush_, refers to the tight clusters of white, strongly fragrant flowers on the branch ends. Each flower has five separate petals, five sepals, and five stamens.

The seeds of buckbrush, which may lie dormant in the soil for hundreds of years, require heat to germinate; the presence of this shrub often indicates that fire has passed through the area.

HABITAT/RANGE: Grows on moist to semimoist soils in open forests or on forest borders from the foothills to montane zones in west and central Montana.

Mountain-mahogany

Cercocarpus ledifolius

Mountain-mahogany, an intricately branched shrub, is 2 to 6 feet tall and has gray bark. The leathery, linear leaves, with margins that are folded under, are clustered at nodes along the stems. Tiny flowers with five green to brown sepals and no petals grow singly or in clusters along the branches.

HABITAT/RANGE: Grows in open areas across southern Montana.

Oregon grape in June at the Harpers Lake
Fishing Access just north of the junction
of Montana 83 and Montana 200

Oregon grape at Miner Lakes
west of Jackson

One of many mountain-mahogany in
Bear Trap Canyon on the Madison
River east of Norris

Buckbrush in late June in the Swan Valley
north of Seeley Lake

Rabbitbrush

Chrysothamnus nauseosus
Ericameria nauseosa

Rabbitbrush is a densely branched, aromatic shrub with 1- to 5-foot-tall stems that grow in a round, compact arrangement and look silvery because they are covered with white, woolly hairs. The leaves, about 1 to 3 inches long, are narrow and grayish green. The flower heads, which contain about five tiny, yellow disk flowers, are arranged in dense clusters at the tips of the branches, resembling whisk brooms. The bracts overlap like shingles on a roof, distinguishing this shrub from gray horsebrush (*Tetradymia canescens*).

One common name, *rubber rabbitbrush*, refers to the presence of latex; the plant has been used as chewing gum. American Indians burned the branches to smoke animal hides and also used them to cover sweat lodges and floors.

HABITAT/RANGE: Grows in dry open places on grasslands and among sagebrush from the plains and valleys up to montane forests across Montana.

Red-osier Dogwood

Cornus stolonifera
C. sericea

The many stems of red-osier dogwood form a spreading clump or thicket, usually 3 to 8 feet tall but sometimes reaching 15 feet. The distinctive reddish bark is more apparent on young growth and in autumn and winter. The entire, pointed leaves, 1 to 3 inches in length and about two-thirds as wide, are held opposite on the stem by short petioles, and have five to seven pairs of prominent parallel veins. The small white flowers are arranged in flat-topped clusters. Each flower has four small sepals, four oval-shaped spreading petals, four stamens, and a club-shaped pistil.

HABITAT/RANGE: Prefers moist soils along streambanks, in wet areas, and in meadows from valleys up to timberline across Montana.

River Hawthorn

Crataegus douglasii
C. rivularis

River hawthorn, also called *black hawthorn*, is the most common of the four *Crataegus* species in Montana. Hawthorns are distinguished by their stout, straight or curved thorns on the branches. River hawthorn may reach 14 or more feet with scaly gray branches that have sharp, straight or slightly curved, 1-inch thorns. The alternate, egg-shaped, glossy, leathery leaves are dark green, sharply toothed, and often lobed at the tip. The cup-shaped flowers have five white or pinkish, rounded petals and ten to twenty stamens, and are arranged in showy, flat-topped racemes.

The edible though not very tasty berries are eaten by birds and small animals. Shrikes sometimes cache captured prey on the thorns.

HABITAT/RANGE: Grows on dry to moist soils in river bottoms, in meadows, and along forest borders from valleys and canyons to mountain foothills in west, central, and southeast Montana.

Rabbitbrush in mid-July near Hells Creek State Park on the south side of Fort Peck Lake

Red-osier dogwood in early June along a stream near Painted Rocks Lake southwest of Sula

River hawthorn in late May near Crystal Lake in the Big Snowy Mountains near Lewistown

Mountain Spray   *Holodiscus discolor*

Mountain spray, also called *oceanspray*, has reddish gray, highly branched stems that grow 3 to 9 feet tall. The arching branches, bending under the weight of the abundant flowers, hold slightly lobed, finely toothed, 2- to 3-inch-long leaves that are green above and silvery below due to a coat of soft woolly hair. The tiny, cream-colored flowers have five petals and are arranged in hanging, pyramid-like clusters on the ends of branches, resembling ocean spray.

Meriwether Lewis collected this plant in Idaho in 1806. American Indians used the flexible branches of mountain spray for making various tools.

HABITAT/RANGE: Prefers rocky soils in open areas, woodlands, and brushy slopes in montane zones in west Montana.

Swamp Laurel   *Kalmia microphylla*
                                                   K. polifolia

Swamp laurel, also called *alpine laurel*, is a low-lying shrub that grows up to 8 inches tall. It spreads over the ground and roots where branches touch. The opposite, oval-shaped leaves have turned-under margins, a leathery texture, and are dark green above but grayish on the underside. Several saucer-shaped, bright pink flowers occur at stem tips, each supported by a long, slender, red stalk. The anthers of the stamens reside in little pockets, creating bumps on the closed flower. When the opened flower is bumped, such as by a visiting insect, the stamens spring upright and release their pollen.

HABITAT/RANGE: Prefers wet areas and meadows and is more common in subalpine and alpine zones in west and south-central Montana.

Trapper's Tea   *Ledum glandulosum*

Trapper's tea, also called *Labrador tea*, is an erect evergreen shrub that grows 2 to 5 feet tall. The alternate leaves are ½ to 2½ inches long, spaced closely on the stem, elliptic to oval in shape, dark green on the upper surface, and pale with tiny golden glands and short white hairs beneath. The white flowers are arranged in dense, umbrella-shaped clusters at the tips of the branches. Each flower has five spreading petals and eight to twelve protruding stamens that are hairy near the base.

Trapper's tea is poisonous to livestock, especially sheep, and toxic to humans; nonetheless, the plant has been used to prepare a tea. Long boiling reportedly destroys the toxic alkaloids, but the tea causes drowsiness, frequent urination, intestinal upsets, and other more serious ailments.

HABITAT/RANGE: Grows in wet areas and acidic soils in wet forests and along streams usually located just below subalpine zones in west and central Montana.

Mountain spray in mid-July in a woody area along Montana 135 east of St. Regis

Swamp laurel in early July along the west end of the Beartooth Highway between Red Lodge and Cooke City

Trapper's tea in late June along Hungry Horse Reservoir east of Kalispell

Red Twinberry   *Lonicera utahensis*

Red twinberry, also called *Utah honeysuckle*, is a 2- to 5-foot-tall shrub with pale green, smooth, oval leaves that are whitish below. Two white, creamy, or yellowish trumpet-shaped flowers, sometimes tinged with red, hang on stems that join at a leaf axil. The tube of each flower has a prominent nectar-filled knob. Another common species of twinberry, **(L. involucrata)**, differs from red twinberry by the presence of two pairs of conspicuous dark red or purple bracts.

HABITAT/RANGE: Prefers moist soils in open coniferous forests at montane to subalpine zones in west and north-central Montana.

Fool's Huckleberry   *Menziesia ferruginea*

Fool's huckleberry, also called *false azalea*, resembles huckleberries (*Vaccinium* species). The difference lies in the ovary—fool's huckleberry has a superior ovary that matures into a capsule, whereas huckleberries have inferior ovaries that mature into berries. Fool's huckleberry is 3 to 7 feet tall with sticky, egg-shaped to elliptical, alternate leaves that are clustered at branch ends. The leaves have fine-toothed margins and a midvein that forms a small white tip. Urn-shaped, long-stalked, yellowish or rust-colored flowers occur in clusters at the base of new twigs.

HABITAT/RANGE: Prefers moist soils in wet areas and along streams in coniferous forests at low to high elevations in west and central Montana.

Mountain Lover   *Paxistima myrsinites*

Mountain lover, also called *mountain box*, is a dense, evergreen, 8- to 25-inch-tall shrub with four-sided, reddish brown, branched stems. The glossy, thick, opposite leaves are sharply toothed and elliptic to oval. Tiny, dark red, fragrant, four-petaled flowers emerge from the axils of the stalkless leaves.

Lewis and Clark collected specimens of mountain lover at the mouth of the Columbia River in 1805 and in Idaho in 1806.

HABITAT/RANGE: Inhabits moist open to somewhat dense forests or open sites from the foothills to subalpine zones in west Montana.

Mockorange   *Philadelpus lewisii*

Mockorange, also known as *syringa*, is a spreading, densely branched shrub that grows 4 to 10 feet tall. Older stems shed reddish brown bark, revealing a gray bark beneath. The elliptic or lance-shaped leaves, 1 to 3 inches long with short stems, occur in opposite pairs and have entire or serrated margins. The flowers, which smell like orange blossoms, are arranged in clusters, each having four white petals, four styles, and many conspicuous yellow stamens.

The species name of this shrub was selected in 1814 to honor Meriwether Lewis, who collected specimens in Idaho and western Montana in 1806.

HABITAT/RANGE: Found on medium-dry to moist soils along streams, rocky hillsides, and open forests in west and central Montana.

Red twinberry in mid-June along a wooded trail near Crystal Lake in the Big Snowy Mountains near Lewistown

Fool's huckleberry in late June at Lake Alva in the Swan Valley north of Seeley Lake

Mountain lover in early June at the forest border along Road 486 north of Columbia Falls

Mockorange in late June near a small pond on the National Bison Range west of St. Ignatius

Pink Mountain Heather   *Phyllodoce empetriformis*

Pink mountain heather, a mat-forming shrub with striking dark red flowers, has wiry stems covered with closely spaced, stiff, needlelike leaves, much like those of evergreens. The bell-shaped flowers are arranged in umbels near the tips of the low branches. The flowers are held on thin, reddish, hairy stalks. The pistils extend beyond the petals, but the stamens do not.

> HABITAT/RANGE: Grows on moist open meadows and slopes in alpine and subalpine zones in west and south-central Montana.

Ninebark   *Physocarpus malvaceus*

Ninebark, a 2- to 6-foot-tall shrub, is characterized by bark that shreds from the stems in many layers, once believed to be nine in number. The maple-like leaves are palmately divided with three shallow lobes and are toothed on the margins. The white, saucer-shaped, stalked flowers surround a cuplike hypanthium and are arranged in spherical clusters on twig ends. The center of the flower appears brownish yellow and contains many long stamens.

Meriwether Lewis collected a specimen of ninebark along the Columbia River during the Lewis and Clark Expedition of 1804–1806.

> HABITAT/RANGE: Prefers dry to moist open woods and sunny hillsides from the valleys to lower subalpine zones in west and central Montana.

Shrubby Cinquefoil   *Potentilla fruticosa*

Shrubby cinquefoil, a highly branched, 1- to 4-foot-tall shrub, has smooth, reddish brown, peeling bark on twisted stems. The pinnately compound leaves have five narrow, linear, entire leaflets and alternate on the stem. Long silky hairs on the leaves and stipules impart a grayish green hue. Numerous bright yellow, saucer-shaped flowers arise singly from leaf axils. Each flower, enclosed by five sepal-like bracts, has five petals and many stamens and pistils.

> HABITAT/RANGE: Prefers wet and cool habitats in meadows, on foothills, and in open woods across Montana.

Wild Plum   *Prunus americana*

Wild plum often grows in dense thickets 4 to 15 feet tall. The branches have grayish bark and twigs with narrow, thornlike tips. The elliptical or egg-shaped, alternate leaves are 1 to 4 inches long, pointed at the tip and rounded at the base, with sharp, forward-pointing teeth on the margins. One to four stalked flowers, which open before the leaves, emerge from the tip of smooth spur branches in flat-topped inflorescences. Each flower has five white petals, five sepals, and twenty or more stamens.

> HABITAT/RANGE: Grows along streams and wet ditches from the plains and valleys to the foothills in northwest, south-central, and east Montana.

Pink mountain heather in early July at the west end of the Beartooth Highway between Red Lodge and Cooke City

Ninebark in mid-June in Gallatin Canyon south of Bozeman

Shrubby cinquefoil in late June near Georgetown Lake west of Anaconda

Wild plum in early May along U.S. 212 west of Ashland

Chokecherry   *Prunus virginiana*

Chokecherry, a shrub to small tree, grows 3 to 15 feet tall. The oval, finely toothed, and pointed leaves, rounded at the base and widest just above their middle, are stalked and alternate. Two or three conspicuous reddish glands are located at the base of the leaf blade. Numerous whitish or cream–colored, saucer–shaped flowers are arranged in a dense, cylindrical, 2- to 6-inch-long raceme.

The dark red to black cherries that appear in the late summer are edible but tart and create a dry mouth. With added sugar the berries make a delicious jam or jelly.

> HABITAT/RANGE: Found on dry to moist soils in sunny valleys, on foothills, and along waterways from the plains to montane zones in west, central, and east Montana.

Alder Buckthorn   *Rhamnus alnifolia*

Alder buckthorn, an erect and spreading shrub, is 2 to 5 feet tall, with grayish, hairy branches that turn darker with age. The rather thick, alternate, short-stalked leaves are 2 to 4 inches long, egg-shaped to elliptic in shape, and have five to seven prominent side veins. The leaves have toothed margins and stipules. Two to five small, greenish yellow, bowl-shaped flowers are arranged in clusters in the lower leaf axils. Each flower has five sepals and no petals. A related species found in the far northwest corner of Montana, **cascara (*R. purshiana*)** is a much larger plant, more like a tree, and has ten to twelve side veins in the leaves and eight to forty flowers in clusters.

The berries, and also the bark, of *Rhamnus* species have a strong purgative effect and have been used as laxatives for many years. Because of the plant's toxicity, it is inadvisable to use branches of buckthorns for roasting hot dogs.

> HABITAT/RANGE: Prefers moist to wet shady areas in the foothills and lower mountain valleys up to montane zones in west Montana.

Golden Currant   *Ribes aureum*

Golden currant, a 3-foot-tall shrub with smooth, spineless stems, has wide, three-lobed leaves, and each lobe may again be divided. The leaves have a wedge-shaped base and a few teeth and hairs. The foliage turns rose or red in fall when the red or black berries mature. Five to eighteen golden yellow to reddish, fragrant flowers are arranged in a long inflorescence that sometimes extends above the leaves. The five yellow, spreading, petal-like sepals of the smooth calyx are larger than the petals.

American Indians ate the tart berries and used them for treating ailments. A specimen of golden currant was collected by Meriwether Lewis in 1805 at Three Forks.

> HABITAT/RANGE: Grows in drained but moist sites along streams or on the plains and foothills across Montana.

okecherry in mid-June on the National
Bison Range west of St. Ignatius

Alder buckthorn in early June along a small stream
near Road 486 north of Columbia Falls

olden currant in mid-May
ong the Madison River at Bear
ap Canyon east of Norris

Wax Currant   *Ribes cereum*

Wax currant, also called *squaw current*, is 2 to 6 feet tall, with sticky hairs but no thorns. The alternate, three- to five-lobed, toothed leaves are round or oval. The tube-shaped, pink to whitish flowers are about ½ inch long and arranged in clusters from short side branches. Petals of the flower are inserted inside a five-lobed calyx tube.

The berries of wax currant are edible but the insipid taste would discourage all but the very hungry.

HABITAT/RANGE: Prefers moist to dry soils on hills, slopes, and open prairies and clearings from the foothills to montane zones across Montana.

White-stemmed Gooseberry   *Ribes inerme*

White-stemmed gooseberry, a sprawling, prickly shrub, grows about 5 feet tall. The grayish, flaky, mostly smooth stems bear both prickles and spines. The five-lobed leaves are hairless on the surface but have hairs on the toothed margins. The white to pink, funnel-shaped flowers have green to purplish, spreading calyx lobes. Long stamens project well past the petals.

The edible but tart berries of white-stemmed gooseberry have been used to make jelly.

HABITAT/RANGE: Found on moist shaded ground in foothills and montane forests in west Montana.

Mountain Gooseberry   *Ribes montigenum*

Mountain gooseberry is a 3-foot-tall, branching and spreading shrub with bristly sharp spines at stem nodes. The toothed leaves are three- to five-lobed and have a glandular surface covered with fine hairs. Three to eight small, greenish yellow or pinkish, saucer-shaped flowers droop from leaf axils.

HABITAT/RANGE: Prefers rocky soils from montane to alpine zones in southwest and south-central Montana.

Sticky Currant   *Ribes viscosissimum*

Sticky currant is usually less than 6 feet tall, with spineless, stiff, spreading and sprawling branches. The leaves are palmately veined, have three to five shallowly toothed lobes, and like the stems, have sticky glandular hairs that give the plant a somewhat disagreeable odor. Six to twelve greenish to yellowish white flowers, often tinged with pink, are clustered at the branch ends in racemes. The five sepals and five petals spread from the tube to form an opening like a bell. The pointed calyx lobes are greenish white and tinged with pink. The stamens are equal in length to the petals.

HABITAT/RANGE: Found in dry or moist openings and woods, especially following a fire, from montane to subalpine zones in west and central Montana.

ax currant in mid-May in Bear Trap Canyon
on the Madison River east of Norris

White-stemmed gooseberry in
mid-May in Bear Trap Canyon on
the Madison River east of Norris

Mountain gooseberry in early July at
Hyalite Reservoir just south of Bozeman

Sticky currant in late June
near Swan Lake

Wood's Rose   *Rosa woodsii*

Wood's rose, a branched and spiny shrub, grows 3 to 6 feet tall. The compound, alternate leaves have three to nine toothed leaflets. Two sharp spines, sometimes curved with thick bases, are located at the base of each leaf, and smaller spines are located between the leaves. The pinkish to reddish flowers occur singly or in clusters at the ends of lateral branches. Each flower has five showy petals, five green sepals, and numerous stamens and pistils.

The ripe fruits, called *rose hips*, are rich in vitamin C and were eaten by American Indians. The plant also has a variety of medicinal uses.

HABITAT/RANGE: Prefers moist soils along streambanks, ponds, and hillsides from the plains to montane forests in west, central, and east Montana.

Thimbleberry   *Rubus parviflorus*

Thimbleberry belongs to the same genus as raspberry and blackberry, but it lacks spines on the stems and has large, palmately lobed, toothed leaves up to 10 inches wide. The crowded stems are usually 2 to 4 feet tall, but may reach 6 to 10 feet. A few to several white flowers, about 2 inches wide, are attached to the stem tip.

The fruit of thimbleberry resembles a raspberry with a tart flavor that varies with season and habitat. The berries are consumed by many animals, including grizzly bears, who will then leave red-stained droppings. The leaves and roots were used by American Indians to prepare teas for relieving diarrhea and calming the stomach.

HABITAT/RANGE: Found in open to dense forests from low to subalpine zones in west, central, and southeast Montana.

Black Elderberry   *Sambucus racemosa*

Black elderberry, a highly branched, 3- to 10-foot-tall shrub, has a strong smell. The reddish stems are brittle and pithy. The leaves are pinnately compound with five to seventeen lance-shaped leaflets that have sharp teeth on the margins. The tiny white or cream-colored flowers are arranged in round-topped clusters.

The edible berries have been used to make pies and jelly, but uncooked fruit may cause nausea.

HABITAT/RANGE: Prefers moist soils on streambanks and in forest openings from the foothills to montane and subalpine zones in west, central, and southeast Montana.

Wood's rose
in mid-June in
Sluice Boxes State
Park, which is
west of U.S. 89
and southeast
of Great Falls

Thimbleberry
in late June on
the east side of
Swan Lake

Black elderberry
in early June
along the Rocky
Mountain Front
west of Choteau

Greasewood   *Sarcobatus vermiculatus*

Greasewood, a thorny 3- to 7-foot-tall shrub with white bark, has numerous succulent, green leaves that distinguish it from gray sagebrushes (*Artemisia* species). The linear leaves are alternate on the stem and round or triangular in cross section. Inconspicuous male and female flowers are separate but located on the same plant. The male flower is a cone-shaped structure attached to the ends of the stems. The cone holds the tiny yellowish green or rose-colored flowers arranged in a spiral along a spike. The smaller numbers of female flowers occupy a shorter spike located singly in leaf axils.

Greasewood is able to grow on salty soils because it can deposit the salts in its tissue; you can detect a salty taste in its leaves. The plant can be poisonous for livestock.

HABITAT/RANGE: Prefers dry alkaline salt flats across Montana where groundwater is available to its deep roots. It is more common in southern counties of the state.

Buffaloberry   *Shepherdia canadensis*

Buffaloberry, also called *soapberry* and *soopolallie*, is a bushy, thornless shrub with opposite leaves. It usually grows 3 to 6 feet tall but may reach 12 feet. The closed leaves, which open after the flowers appear, are shaped like an arrowhead pointing skyward and covered with brownish scales and hairs. The upper surface of the open leaves is bright green and veined. The small unisexual flowers, located in leaf axils, have four yellowish sepals and no petals.

The bright red berries, which appear in late summer and fall, are not considered tasty or even edible. However, American Indians developed a taste for a foamy mixture they prepared by whipping the berries in water.

HABITAT/RANGE: Common from valleys to subalpine forests throughout Montana.

Cascade Mountain Ash   *Sorbus scopulina*

Cascade mountain ash, a 3- to 16-foot-tall shrub with several erect, reddish brown branches, is the more common of two species of mountain ash that are likely to be encountered in the wild in Montana. Both species have alternate, pinnately divided leaves with finely toothed leaflets. **Sitka mountain ash (*S. sitchensis*)** differs in having seven to eleven egg-shaped, blunt-tipped leaflets instead of the eleven to seventeen lance-shaped, pointed leaflets of Cascade mountain ash. The tiny white to cream-colored flowers of Cascade mountain ash have oval petals and are arranged in flat-topped, crowded clusters that are 3 to 6 inches wide.

The bitter, mealy berries are rich in vitamin C and can be eaten raw, cooked, or dried.

HABITAT/RANGE: Found along streams and in wet meadows, canyons, and open or cutover forests from 4,000 to 5,500 feet elevation in west and central Montana.

Greasewood in early July in Big Horn National Recreation Area in south-central Montana

Top right: Buffaloberry with open flowers and closed ones in mid-May in Hyalite Canyon south of Bozeman
Bottom right: Open, veined leaves of buffaloberry

Cascade mountain ash in late June on Stemple Pass south of Lincoln

Birchleaf Spiraea · *Spiraea betulifolia*

Birchleaf spiraea is a low shrub with stems that are hardly woody. The 10- to 24-inch-tall stems bear alternate, egg-shaped leaves, usually wider above their middle, that have irregular sharp teeth on the upper margin, similar to birch tree leaves. The small, off-white, fragrant, saucer-shaped flowers are arranged in a flat-topped cluster in which the outer flowers bloom first. Each flower has five tiny petals and twenty-five to fifty long stamens.

HABITAT/RANGE: Grows in woods, often forming a dense forest floor cover, from valleys to upper subalpine zones in west and central Montana.

Steeplebush · *Spiraea douglasii*

Steeplebush, also called *pink spiraea* and *Douglas spiraea*, has 2- to 6-foot-tall stems with shiny, smooth, oval leaves. Masses of tiny pink to bright rose flowers are arranged in a pyramid-like inflorescence that resembles a steeple. Each minute flower contains five petals.

HABITAT/RANGE: Grows on wet and boggy soils along streambanks or lakeshores at low to subalpine zones in northwest Montana.

Gray Horsebrush · *Tetradymia canescens*

Gray horsebrush is a low, rounded, 1- to 3-foot-tall shrub with highly branched stems that are brittle and covered with short woolly hairs. The lower parts of the stems are woody and leafless, while upper stems bear narrow alternate leaves. Each of the numerous yellow flower heads, which cover the plant top, are borne on short stalks and consist of four slender disk flowers surrounded by four hairy, whitish, tangled bracts.

HABITAT/RANGE: Grows on dry soils on plains and mountain foothills up to montane zones in west, central, and northeast Montana.

Big Huckleberry · *Vaccinium membranaceum*

Big huckleberry is one of eight *Vaccinium* species found in Montana and one of the tallest, growing up to 4 feet or more. The older stems have shredding gray bark, and the young twigs have thin ridges. The smooth, egg-shaped, alternate leaves have fine teeth on the margins and a pointed tip. A single inconspicuous, yellowish pink, urn-shaped flower hangs from the leaf axil.

The dark purple, juicy berries, a favorite food of grizzly and black bears, are well-known to Montanans, who invade the forests of northwest Montana in late summer to pick them. The crop varies each year, and in some years there are not enough berries to go around, forcing bears to seek alternative foods in human communities.

HABITAT/RANGE: Prefers sandy or gravelly, dry or moist soils and is sometimes the predominant understory plant in montane coniferous forests in west and central Montana.

Birchleaf spiraea in a wooded area along Montana 135 east of St. Regis

Gray horsebrush in late July along Call Road at the northeast corner of the Gravelly Range south of Ennis

Steeplebush in mid-July in a swampy area bordering a lake north of Noxon

Big huckleberry in early June north of Columbia Falls
Inset: The nearly mature berry on July 1 along Lake McDonald in Glacier National Park

ARUM FAMILY   Araceae

Members of the arum family, one of only four monocot families in this book, have mostly basal leaves. Small flowers are crowded in a fleshy spike, which is usually associated with a modified leaf. The collective calyx and corolla has four or six lobes. There are four or six stamens, one pistil usually without a style, and a superior ovary.

Skunk Cabbage   *Lysichitum americanum*

The stems of skunk cabbage are underground, from which large cabbage-like leaves develop after the flowers begin blooming. The corncob-like stalk is 8 to 20 inches tall, bearing hundreds of small yellow flowers. The bright yellow hood is a bract that emerges from wet soil and then opens to reveal the stalk.

When in bloom, its skunklike odor attracts flies, which pollinate the flowers. Despite the odor, bears and elk eat skunk cabbage. The entire plant is edible, and its bitter taste can be reduced by boiling or drying.

HABITAT/RANGE: Grows in wet swampy areas in woods at low elevations in northwest Montana.

BLAZING-STAR FAMILY   Loasaceae

Plants in the blazing-star family, represented in Montana by a single genus with seven species, have barbed or stinging hairs, causing the foliage to stick onto any passing animal or foreign object. The flowers usually have five petals with numerous stamens and one pistil on an inferior ovary.

Blazing Star   *Mentzelia laevicaulis*

Blazing star, also called *smooth-stemmed eveningstar*, is a short-lived perennial with five long, brilliant lemon yellow petals that collectively flare into a star. The narrower, shorter sepals alternate with the petals. The numerous long, yellow stamens, the outer ones often flattened, give the flower its blazing appearance. The 12- to 40-inch-long, sturdy, whitish stems bear alternate leaves, those at the base deeply lobed, and those above stalkless and less divided. The stems and leaves are covered with hair that imparts a sandpaper-like feel.

Some American Indians used the seeds of blazing star for making a mash to add to soups or stews, and chewed the roots to relieve thirst. The Cheyenne Indians used the roots for treating earache and arthritis, and viral diseases like measles and smallpox.

HABITAT/RANGE: Found on dry soils on gravelly sagebrush plains from valleys to montane zones in west, central, and northeast Montana. Often grows on road banks and highway shoulders.

A dense patch of skunk cabbage in early May at the
southeast corner of Flathead Lake east of Polson

Blazing star flowers in late July in an open dry area along Montana 48 near Anaconda

BORAGE FAMILY   Boraginaceae

Members of this rather large family, represented by seventeen genera in Montana and sometimes called the forget-me-not family, are distinguished by the coiled inflorescence that uncurls as the flowers mature. The five petals are united in a narrow tube with five spreading lobes at the top. The pistil is superior with a single style and one or two stigmas.

❧ Cryptantha *Cryptantha* species ❧

In addition to the common name *cryptantha*, members of this genus, with thirteen species reported in Montana, are sometimes referred to as *miner's candle* or *white forget-me-nots*. Some species are extremely difficult to distinguish from one another. Most, but not all, cryptanthas are small plants, less than 18 inches tall, with narrow leaves and coarse or bristly hairs. Flowers are arranged in a series of coiled narrow branches, or sometimes singly in leaf axils. The white flowers with yellow throats, or occasionally yellow flowers, are small and inconspicuous. The five spreading petals are fused at the base into a tube and are somewhat hidden by hairy sepals.

Miner's Candle   *Cryptantha celosioides*

Miner's candle, a biennial or short-lived perennial, has a single tall, unbranched stem that is 4 to 20 inches tall. Basal leaves are often spoon-shaped, widening at the tip into a spatula shape. White stiff hairs cover the stem, leaves, and sepals. Small white flowers, about ½ inch across the upper part of the corolla, have spreading petals with five lobes, and arise from leafy bracts over most of the length of the stem. The white flowers are tubular at the base and have a yellow throat.

> HABITAT/RANGE: Prefers dry soils in fields, on mesas, and on mountain foothills from low to montane zones in west, central, and east Montana.

Yellow-eye Cryptanth   *Cryptantha flavoculata*

Yellow-eye cryptanth has one to several slender hairy stems that are 4 to 16 inches tall. The leaves are 1 to 4 inches long, linear to spatula-shaped, and covered with hairs. The short white corolla tube is 0.2 inch or more in length, longer than the calyx. The flower has five spreading petals and a prominent yellow throat or "eye."

> HABITAT/RANGE: Yellow-eye cryptanth is a rare wildflower reported in only one county in Montana—Carbon County.

Miner's candle in late May at Tongue River Reservoir State Park in south-central Montana

Yellow-eye cryptanth in early May in Bighorn Canyon National Recreation Area

Bristly Cryptantha

Cryptantha interrupta
C. spiculifera

Bristly cryptantha is similar to miner's candle (*C. celosioides*), but the flowers are slightly smaller, only 0.2 to 0.4 inch across the upper part of the corolla. A tuft of lance-shaped, broadly pointed or rounded leaves, sometimes indented, occurs at the base of the 4- to 20-inch-tall stem. The small white flowers are arranged in a congested inflorescence. The petals are fused at the base into a tube and display five spreading lobes.

HABITAT/RANGE: Found on dry, sandy or clay soils among sagebrush, on plains or hillsides, and in grasslands from low to high elevations in west, central, and east Montana.

Hound's Tongue

Cynoglossum officinale

Hound's tongue has a single 1- to 3-foot-tall stem that bears numerous lance-shaped, hairy leaves that have a vein pattern resembling a dog's tongue. The lower leaves, which feel like velvet to the touch, may be 1 foot long. The upper leaves are smaller, are without stalks, and clasp the stem. Small, dull reddish purple, funnel-shaped flowers with five spreading lobes form slightly coiled racemes at the top of the stem. The mature flower forms four nutlike fruits covered with barbed spines that will catch on the hair of passing animals.

Hound's tongue may cause skin reactions and contains alkaloids that affect the central nervous system and cause liver damage and cancer. Hound's tongue contains allantoin, which has been used to treat skin and intestinal ulcers, and heliosupine, an alkaloid used for relief of hemorrhoids.

HABITAT/RANGE: Introduced from Europe, this common weed has spread across North America and is found on dry, sandy, disturbed soils, such as roadsides and overgrazed pastures, across Montana.

Blueweed

Echium vulgare

Blueweed is a bristly perennial with 2- to 3-foot-tall stems. The narrow, elliptical basal leaves, also covered with long stiff hairs that are swollen at their base, are about 8 inches long and held on stalks. The stem leaves are shorter and stalkless. The blue, funnel-shaped corolla has five unequal lobes. The short-stalked flowers are arranged in short spikes along one side of the stem, the spikes together forming a long cluster of flowers. Each flower has five sepals, five petals, five protruding stamens, and one hairy pistil.

HABITAT/RANGE: Blueweed, an introduced plant from Europe, grows in fields, in overgrazed pastures, and along roadsides, but normally does not grow along with cultivated crops. Reported in northwest Montana.

Bristly cryptantha in late May among sagebrush bordering Ruby Reservoir south of Alder

Hound's tongue in mid-June in the
Highwood Mountains east of Great Falls

Blueweed in mid-July in a
field west of Thompson Falls

Alpine Forget-me-not   *Eritrichium nanum*

Alpine forget-me-not, a low perennial, has stems 4 inches or less in height and leaves with long, woolly hairs that form a tuft at the leaf tips. The pale green leaves, more numerous at the base, form a dense cushion or mat. The pale to deep blue flowers, with yellow or white centers, have five petals that are fused at their base to form a small tube. A related species, *E. howardii*, has obscured silvery-hairy leaves without a terminal tuft or fringe.

The genus name *Eritrichium* comes from Greek and means "wool" or "hair," while the species name *nanum* means "very small" or "dwarf."

HABITAT/RANGE: Found on open rocky slopes at alpine zones in west and central regions of Montana.

Many-flowered Stickseed   *Hackelia floribunda*

Although the flowers of stickseeds resemble, and are often called, *forget-me-nots*, the latter plants are placed in an entirely different genus (*Myosotis*). Generally, stickseeds are taller plants and have prickles on the nutlike fruits. Many-flowered stickseed has a 1- to 3-foot-tall stem and long, hairy leaves with petioles on the basal leaves but none on the smaller upper leaves. Each stem has clusters of small, pale blue, funnel-shaped flowers on stalks that droop as the flowers mature. The corolla is a short tube with five spreading lobes and a yellow center. Five small stamens are attached inside the tube and below the yellow center. The mature pistil will produce four nutlets, each with several rows of barbed spines on the margins. Many-flowered stickseed is a biennial or a short-lived perennial. A similar wildflower, **western stickseed (*Lappula redowskii*)**, is more common than many-flowered stickseed and is distinguished by being smaller and having a single row of prickles on the nutlet.

HABITAT/RANGE: Found on wet soils in meadows and on streambanks from the foothills to subalpine zones in west, south-central, and northeast Montana.

Blue Stickseed   *Hackelia micrantha*

Blue stickseed, also called by the more alluring name *forget-me-not*, has stems that may reach 3 feet tall. Both the stem and leaves of this perennial are covered with stiff hairs. The lower, alternate, sharp-pointed, lance-shaped leaves are supported by long petioles, whereas the smaller stem leaves are stalkless. The small, round, sky blue to lavender flowers mature to prickly nutlets that attach to clothing and animal fur when contacted. The prickles occur on both the margins and the body of the nutlet.

HABITAT/RANGE: Found on dry meadows and sometimes in open forests from the foothills to lower montane zones in west and central Montana.

Alpine forget-me-not in late June along the Beartooth Highway
between Red Lodge and Cooke City

Many-flowered stickseed in mid-June in the
Highwood Mountains east of Great Falls

Blue stickseed in late June along the
Boulder River south of Big Timber

Western Stickseed
Lappula redowskii
L. occidentalis

Western stickseed is 6 to 16 inches tall with simple or branched stems and narrow, oblong to linear, somewhat blunt-tipped leaves. Numerous small blue to nearly white flowers emerge from small bracts and open in elongated terminal racemes. Segments of the calyx are narrow and lance-shaped and just shorter than the corolla tube. Western stickseed is distinguished from many-flowered stickseed (*Hackelia floribunda*) by being smaller and not having a curved or drooping fruit stalk.

HABITAT/RANGE: Prefers dry hillsides and valleys and is common on roadsides and disturbed soils across Montana.

Yellow Gromwell
Lithospermum incisum

Yellow gromwell has leafy, hairy stems that are 4 to 12 inches tall and grow in a clump. The narrow, alternate dark green leaves are up to 3 inches long, have entire margins, and small hairs pressed close to the surface. The bright yellow, trumpet-shaped flowers emerge from the axils of the upper leaves. Each flower has a long, thin corolla tube with five spreading and ruffled lobes that are covered with fine hairs. Yellow gromwell resembles other flowers in the borage family but can be distinguished by its rather large, bright yellow flower with fringed lobes.

The stems, leaves, and roots of this perennial have been used to make teas with stimulating effects. Western Indians cooked the roots for food.

HABITAT/RANGE: Found on dry soils in meadows, open forests, and plains from the foothills to montane zones in west, central, and east Montana.

Western Gromwell
Lithospermum ruderale

Western gromwell is a bushy plant that grows to 10 to 20 inches tall. The many unbranched, hairy stems bear numerous narrow, stalkless, hairy, dark green leaves that are about 4 inches long but are smaller near the base of the stem. The tiny, pale yellow flowers grow in small clusters from the axils of the upper leaves, which partially hide the flowers. Each flower has five petals fused at the bottom into a small tube and spreading at the top into five lobes.

The roots of gromwell contain a purple dye. *Puccoon*, another common name, is an Indian word referring to a plant containing a dye. Some American Indians used the cooked roots of gromwell as a food, or to make a tea for controlling internal bleeding, treating skin and eye problems, and as a contraceptive. The chewed plant was blown into the face to keep someone awake.

HABITAT/RANGE: Adapted to a number of habitats ranging from warm dry plains to rich soils on grasslands and open forests up to montane zones in west and central Montana.

Western stickseed in mid-June at the base of the Pryor Mountains east of Bridger

Yellow gromwell in early May at Tongue River Reservoir State Park in south-central Montana

Inset: Western gromwell in early July at the mouth of Gallatin Canyon south of Bozeman

Western gromwell in early June at the Harpers Lake Fishing Access near the junction of Montana 83 and Montana 200

🌿 Bluebells *Mertensia* species 🌿

Eight species of *Mertensia* have been reported in Montana. The leaves of blue-bells are alternate and have entire margins. All bluebells have funnel-shaped, drooping or erect clusters of blue flowers located in the axils of terminal leaves. The foliage is usually hairy. Flower petals are fused for most of their length and are much longer than the calyx.

Alpine Bluebells   *Mertensia alpina*

The erect, 2- to 10-inch-tall stems of alpine bluebells bear mostly smooth, hairless, lance-shaped leaves that lack conspicuous side veins. The bell-shaped, blue flowers are wider than long. The petals flare abruptly from short basal tubes that are approximately the same length as the floral tube. The anthers are completely enclosed within the tube and not clearly visible in the throat.

HABITAT/RANGE: Found in drained meadows and on open rocky soils at subalpine and alpine zones in west and central Montana.

Mountain Bluebells   *Mertensia ciliata*

Mountain bluebells grows in patches with numerous 1- to 3-foot-tall stems bearing egg-shaped basal leaves on long petioles and smaller, stemless, elliptical leaves higher up. The leaves are slightly hairy or have a fringe along the margin. The blue, tubular flowers hang in clusters from the top of the stems. Mature flowers turn pink, and a style protrudes from the bell. Mountain bluebells resembles **tall bluebells (*M. paniculata*)**, found in western Montana, but differs in having the bell of the corolla shorter or equal to the tube and having leaves that are usually not pointed.

HABITAT/RANGE: Prefers moist areas in aspen groves and along streambanks from montane to alpine zones in west and central Montana.

Leafy Bluebells   *Mertensia oblongifolia*

Leafy bluebells grows less than 1 foot tall. The numerous basal leaves are elliptic to lance-shaped with a well-developed petiole. Stem leaves are also numerous but smaller in size. The light blue, tubular flowers are smooth inside and arranged in drooping clusters at the ends of unbranched stems.

Green bluebells (*M. lanceolata*) resembles leafy bluebells but the leaves are more elliptical. The erect leafy stems are usually less than 16 inches high and support a cluster of long blue flowers with a bell that is only slightly shorter than the tube.

Small bluebells (*M. oblongiflora*) differs from leafy bluebells by the presence of basal leaves and a corolla tube that is 2 to 4 times rather than 1.3 to 2 times longer than the bell.

HABITAT/RANGE: Leafy bluebells is common in a variety of habitats across Montana. Green bluebells grows on open rocky soils at moderate to high elevations east of the Continental Divide.

Alpine bluebells in early July at high elevation along the Beartooth Highway between Red Lodge and Cooke City

Mountain bluebells in late June along Goose Creek in Bozeman Pass east of Bozeman

Leafy bluebells in late May in an open area near the base of the Beartooth Highway south of Red Lodge

Green bluebells in early July near Fairy Lake in the Bridger Range near Bozeman

Obscure Bluebells *Mertensia viridis*

Obscure bluebells has multiple, 6- to 12-inch-tall stems bearing thick, bluish leaves. The basal leaves are elliptic to lance-shaped and have long petioles. Stem leaves are smaller and stalkless. This plant resembles leafy bluebells (*M. oblongifolia*) but has a flower limb only slightly shorter rather than conspicuously shorter than the tube. In addition, obscure bluebells has a ring of long hair near the base of the blue corolla tube. Filaments are attached near the throat of the corolla, and the anthers project beyond the throat.

> HABITAT/RANGE: Common on mountain and alpine slopes and ridges in west and central Montana.

Woods Forget-me-not *Myosotis alpestris*
Myosotis sylvatica var. *alpestris*

Woods forget-me-not resembles alpine forget-me-not (*Eritrichium nanum*) and the stickseeds (*Hackelia* and *Lappula* species). It usually has deeper blue flowers than the European cultivated plant (*Myosotis sylvatica* var. *sylvatica*), but some taxonomists consider woods forget-me-not to be a variety of *M. sylvatica*. The erect, tufted stems of woods forget-me-not are 4 to 10 inches tall. The alternate, lance- to spoon-shaped basal leaves are covered with long soft hairs and have petioles, whereas the smaller stem leaves are stalkless. The flowers have a short basal tube that opens into five spreading lobes that have red, white, or yellow rings at their centers.

> HABITAT/RANGE: Prefers moist soils on open meadows and slopes from subalpine to alpine zones in west and central Montana.

BROOMRAPE FAMILY Orobanchaceae

This small family, represented by a single genus with four species in Montana, includes some unusual plants that have no green leaves and derive their nutrition by parasitism on the roots of other plants. The leaves consist of scales that alternate on the stem. Solitary, bilaterally symmetrical flowers are located in leaf or bract axils. The calyx has four or five lobes, and the corolla has five lobes. The tube of the corolla is usually curved.

Clustered Broomrape *Orobanche fasciculata*

The thick, fleshy stems of clustered broomrape are 2 to 7 inches tall but are partly located beneath the ground. The stems of this annual are covered with small bractlike leaves and each supports two to six flower heads on stalks that originate in the leaf axils. The yellow to purplish stems, leaves, and flowers are covered with sticky hairs. The petals are fused into a funnel-shaped, curved tube with five lobes.

> HABITAT/RANGE: Found on prairies and in the foothills, often parasitizing sagebrush, across Montana.

Obscure bluebells in early June in the Castle Mountains near Lennep

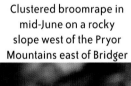

Clustered broomrape in mid-June on a rocky slope west of the Pryor Mountains east of Bridger

Woods forget-me-not in mid-June along West Rosebud Road southwest of Roscoe

BUCKWHEAT FAMILY   Polygonaceae

Members of the buckwheat family, represented in Montana by five genera, have flowers with small showy sepals and no petals. The stems are usually enlarged at the nodes, with a papery sheath at the base of the petiole. These plants are divided into two groups, knotweeds and buckwheats. Knotweed flowers are grouped in dense clusters, each flower containing five sepals. Buckwheats have six sepals in two whorls of three, and flowers in dense umbels.

Yellow Buckwheat   *Eriogonum flavum*

The woolly stems of yellow buckwheat are 2 to 8 inches long but are somewhat prostrate in large flat mats up to 12 inches wide. The 2- to 3-inch-long leaves are crowded mostly at the base of the stem and have woolly hair below but are less hairy above. A whorl of leaflike bracts is attached to the stem just below the flowers, which are arranged in an umbel. Each bright yellow or rose-tinged flower is held on a long stalk that terminates in a cuplike bract. The yellow, petal-like sepals are woolly on the underside.

  HABITAT/RANGE: Found on open rocky and gravelly soils from valleys to alpine zones in west, central, and east Montana.

Cushion Buckwheat   *Eriogonum ovalifolium*

Cushion buckwheat lacks leaves and bracts on the 6- to 12-inch-tall stem. The small, egg-shaped or nearly round basal leaves form mats that may reach 12 to 16 inches wide. Both the stems and leaves are covered with white, woolly hair. Each flower in the cluster at the top of the stem has six petal-like sepals, the outer three oval-shaped and the inner three shaped like a spatula. The flowers may be white, purple, or yellow, turning to burgundy as the flowers age.

  HABITAT/RANGE: Found in dry open areas in forests or among sagebrush from the plains to subalpine zones in west and central Montana.

Sulfur Buckwheat   *Eriogonum umbellatum*

The lance- or spatula-shaped basal leaves of sulfur buckwheat are grouped in flat mats and are green on top with a woolly, silvery gray surface on the bottom. The straight, leafless, woolly stems are 2 to 12 inches tall, ending with a whorl of leafy bracts located just below the flowers. The tiny flowers are arranged in an umbel, each flower on a long thin stalk attached within a bract that has three to ten lobes turned downward and arranged in a cup shape. The creamy white to yellow petal-like sepals are smooth on the back and have a red or purple tinge.

  HABITAT/RANGE: Found on grassy slopes and in open forests in west and central Montana.

Yellow buckwheat in mid-June along Montana 200 west of Montana 83

Cushion buckwheat in early July in the Gravelly Range south of Ennis

Top left: Unopened flowers of sulfur buckwheat in mid-June at Battle Ridge in the Gallatin National Forest north of Bozeman

Bottom left and right: Sulfur buckwheat in mid-July in the Pioneer Mountains south of Wise

Water Smartweed   *Polygonum amphibium*

Water smartweed, included in the knotweed group of the buckwheat family, is an aquatic or semiaquatic perennial found on muddy ponds, on mud flats, or in shallow water. A prostrate or erect stem may grow up to 7 feet long, with floating, oval leaves, and a terminal, unbranched spike of tiny pink or rose-colored flowers. Water smartweed grows quickly and can cover a shallow pond by late summer. Ducks are very fond of the seeds of this plant.

> HABITAT/RANGE: Found across Montana in ponds and marshes with permanent water.

American Bistort   *Polygonum bistortoides*

American bistort has narrow, tapered basal leaves with long petioles, whereas the stem leaves are small and lance-shaped and lack petioles. The flowers are small, white to pinkish, and clustered in a raceme at the tip of the stem. The white stamens extend beyond the sepals so that the flower cluster looks like a brush.

The leaves of American bistort are edible but tart, similar to rhubarb, but can be sweetened for jam. The roots are said to taste something like almonds or water chestnuts but are sometimes bitter because of tannic acid content; eaten raw they can cause intestinal upset. American Indians ate the roots raw or in stews and soups and ground flour from dried leaves and seeds.

> HABITAT/RANGE: Common in shady woods, along streambanks, and in alpine meadows in west and central Montana.

Mountain Sorrel   *Rumex paucifolius*

Mountain sorrel, also called *sheep sorrel* and *few-leaved dock*, has large elliptic or lance-shaped leaves that taper at the base. The plant is 6 to 28 inches tall, standing higher than most surrounding vegetation. The small, pale to deep red, unisexual flowers are arranged in a loose, spikelike inflorescence on the upper half of the hairless stem.

> HABITAT/RANGE: Prefers wet grasslands and mountain meadows from montane to alpine zones in west, central, and northeast Montana.

Water smartweed at Cliff Lake south of U.S. 287 near the intersection with Montana 87 and west of Quake Lake

Field of American bistort in early July in the Gravelly Range south of Ennis

Inset: American bistort in late June near Fairy Lake in the Gallatin National Forest just north of Bozeman

Mountain sorrel in mid-July in a high mountain meadow in the Gravelly Range south of Ennis

BUTTERCUP FAMILY   Ranunculaceae

This large family, represented by fourteen genera in Montana, includes members that are related to fossils that lived shortly after flowering plants first appeared more than 100 million years ago. The family's lengthy evolution may be the reason it includes a number of wildflowers that lack any obvious features in common. The family's primitive characteristics include the absence of fusion of floral parts and the presence of numerous stamens and pistils. Another important characteristic of this family is a dome or cone-shaped receptacle.

Blue Monkshood   *Aconitum columbianum*

Blue monkshood, also called *Columbian monkshood* and *aconite*, is a conspicuous and unique perennial, the only representative of the genus *Aconitum* found in Montana. The stem of blue monkshood is 3 to 7 feet high, with numerous palmately divided, toothed leaves. The petal-like sepals are blue to deep purple, the upper ones forming a hood with a pointed beak. Two spreading, fan-shaped sepals occur on each side of the flower. The five small petals are mostly hidden by the conspicuous sepals. A variety with a yellow flower grows in the Bitterroot Valley.

Aconitum comes from Greek *akoniton*, meaning "leopard poison." Species in this genus contain toxic alkaloids in the seeds and roots, and blue monkshood has been implicated in livestock poisonings. Herbalists have applied plant extracts topically for easing local pain.

HABITAT/RANGE: Blue monkshood grows in moist woods or on streambanks or forest borders at low to subalpine zones in west Montana.

Baneberry   *Actaea rubra*

The stem of baneberry is 1 to 3 feet tall, bearing basal leaves that clasp the stem and a few large compound stem leaves that are repeatedly divided into nine or more toothed leaflets, each ¾ to 3½ inches long. Twenty-five or more small white flowers are grouped in tight, spherical racemes. The flowers have three to five whitish, petal-like sepals that drop off when the flower opens, five to ten tiny cream-colored petals that also drop off early, numerous stamens on long filaments, and a single style. When the flower is mature, white or red berries are present that retain the dark stigma, which gives the berry the appearance of a *doll's eye*, a common name sometimes applied to this perennial.

Bane means "poison" or "death." The berries of baneberry are poisonous and can cause severe intestinal inflammation. Although no deaths have been reported in the United States, there are reports of European children fatally poisoned by related *Actaea* species that grow there.

HABITAT/RANGE: Common in wet forested areas, under trees and shrubs, and along streams in west and central Montana.

e monkshood
mid-July in Giant
dars Preserve
r Bull Lake
thwest of Libby

A patch of baneberry in late June
der trees in Red Rock Lakes National
Wildlife Refuge east of Monida

Drummond's Anemone
Anemone drummondii
A. lithophila

Drummond's anemone has 4- to 10-inch-tall stems that bear cloverlike basal leaves, each leaflet divided into three narrow segments, on long petioles. A whorl of stalkless leaves is located at the middle of the stem. Each stem supports one white flower that is often tinged with blue, green, or lavender on the back of the sepals. Short, straight hairs cover the underside of the sepals and also the leaves and stems.

HABITAT/RANGE: Found in meadows and on rocky slopes from subalpine to alpine zones in west and central Montana.

Cliff Anemone
Anemone multifida

Cliff anemone has a cluster of long-petioled basal leaves from which arise several 8- to 20-inch-long, hairy stems. The leaves are divided into three or more lance-shaped lobes. A whorl of leaves that resembles those at the base is located about halfway up the stem. From the axis of the whorl originate one to three flower stalks, which may bear a smaller whorl of leaves or bracts, topped by a single flower. The flower has five to nine sepals that range from cream to yellow to red, with combinations of these colors sometimes occurring on one plant.

HABITAT/RANGE: Prefers dry to moist soils in sunny areas but can be found in a wide range of habitats from foothills to alpine zones in west, central, and northeast Montana.

Pasqueflower
Anemone nuttalliana
Anemone patens, Pulsatilla patens

Pasqueflower, also called *prairie crocus* and *windflower*, has a hairy, 12- to 16-inch-tall stem bearing a single purple or bluish lavender flower. The basal leaves have 2- to 4-inch-long stalks with blades that are divided into many narrow segments. Just below the flower is a whorl of three bracts. The cup-shaped, 1- to 2-inch-wide flower has five to seven sepals but no petals. Soft hairs line the outer surface of the sepals, and long, silky, straight hairs cover the entire plant. Inside the silky cup are numerous yellow stamens and many pistils, each with a single style that, on maturity, will produce a featherlike fruit that looks like a lion's beard. Pasqueflower is often confused with sugarbowls (*Clematis hirsutissima*), a flower distinguished by numerous opposite leaves on the stem and no basal leaves.

American Indians used pasqueflower for many medicinal purposes, the benefits deriving in part from a volatile oil that acts as an irritant and is potentially very toxic.

HABITAT/RANGE: Pasqueflower, sometimes pushing through the snow as early as late March, is common in well-drained prairies and mountain meadows of west, central, and east Montana.

Drummond's anemone in early June in open woods on Ear Mountain west of Choteau

Cliff anemone in early June at the Suce Creek Trailhead in Paradise Valley, south of Livingston

Pasqueflower on May 1 near East Rosebud Lake west of Red Lodge

Yellow Columbine　　　　　　　*Aquilegia flavescens*

The stems of yellow columbine are 8 to 30 inches tall, with basal compound leaves that are divided into three sets of three thin leaflets per leaf. The stem bears a few reduced leaves or bracts. Vigorous plants may branch several times, but others, especially in alpine areas, may have only a single stem. Each flower has five cream-colored petals that open wide in front and taper behind into yellow spurs that curve inward. The five petal-like sepals are yellow but often show some pink.

Columbine comes from the Latin *columbinus*, meaning "dovelike," a reference to the resemblance of the blades of the petal-like sepals to flying doves. Yellow columbine has been used for a variety of medicinal purposes, though it is potentially very toxic, particularly the seeds and roots. Dried roots placed on the skin will cause perspiration.

HABITAT/RANGE: Common on moist meadows, along streams, and from montane woods to alpine slopes in west and central Montana.

Marsh Marigold　　　　　　　*Caltha leptosepala*

Marsh marigold, also called *elkslip*, is a small perennial with a pinkish, 1- to 8-inch-tall stem and a cluster of heart-shaped basal leaves with wavy or coarsely toothed margins. The shiny, dark green leaves are longer than wide and rounded at their tip. There are no stem leaves. The single buttercup-like flowers are 1 to 2 inches wide and lack petals but have five to twelve petal-like white sepals. Each flower contains many yellow stamens.

Marsh marigold has a bitter taste and is believed to be poisonous to cattle, although it is eaten by elk without any ill effects.

HABITAT/RANGE: Forms dense mats over subalpine and alpine meadows that are flooded during the spring thaw, often emerging through the melting snow, in west and south-central Montana.

Yellow columbine in late June at Crystal Lake in the Big Snowy Mountains near Lewistown

Marsh marigold in late June in a wet area along U.S. 212 west of Cooke City

Rock Clematis   *Clematis columbiana*

Rock clematis, also called *Columbia virgin's bower*, is a semiwoody, creeping or climbing vine that may reach 10 to 12 feet long and often drapes itself over stumps and fallen trees. The compound leaves have three separated leaflets that in turn have leaflets that are lance-shaped and have indentations on the margins. The 1½- to 2½-inch-wide, solitary, pale blue or purple flowers are supported on long stalks that arise fro–m the leaf axils. Each flower is composed of four, and sometimes five, pointed nodding sepals but no petals. Numerous white or yellow stamens crowd the interior of the flower and, with the pistils, form a white or greenish mound. The ovary styles will enlarge on maturity and form a feathery plume for disseminating seeds. A related species, **western virgin's bower (*C. occidentalis*)** has only three leaflets whereas rock clematis has six or nine in each compound leaf. Some taxonomists include both species in *C. occidentalis*.

HABITAT/RANGE: Common in dry to moist soils of woods and thickets at forest edges from valleys to subalpine zones in west and central Montana.

Sugarbowls   *Clematis hirsutissima*

Sugarbowls, also called *vase flower* and *leatherflower*, is a sturdy perennial with 1- to 2-foot-tall hairy stems and lacy leaves that are deeply divided into fingerlike segments that also have a silver, hairy covering. Each stem bears a single, nodding, cup-shaped flower resembling a sugarbowl. The flowers have no petals but are composed of four sepals that are dark blue or purple on the inside and a pale or grayish purple on the outside. The tips of the finely haired sepals flare out and reveal many yellow stamens and pistils in the throat of the flower. The styles on the ovary will on maturity form feathery plumes nearly 2 inches long. Sugarbowls may be confused with pasqueflower (*Anemone nuttalliana*), but that flower blooms earlier and does not have opposite stem leaves.

HABITAT/RANGE: Grows on dry soils on prairies and in open woods in west and central Montana.

White Virgin's Bower   *Clematis ligusticifolia*

White virgin's bower is a climbing, semiwoody vine that grows up to 20 feet long, often forming dense mats over fences, shrubs, and small trees. The leaves are pinnately compound with five to seven egg-shaped or lance-shaped, coarsely toothed, stalked leaflets. The cream-colored flowers arise from leaf axils and are arranged in an open, pyramid-shaped, branched inflorescence. The flowers have no petals but contain four to six petal-like, showy sepals, along with several flattened stamens. Male and female parts occur in separate flowers.

HABITAT/RANGE: Found along streams or from sagebrush plains to forest borders and along railways and in riparian habitats in west, central, and northeast Montana.

Rock clematis
in mid-June at
Crystal Lake in
the Big Snowy
Mountains south
of Lewistown

Sugarbowls in early
June in an open
area bordering the
forest at the Suce
Creek Trailhead in
Paradise Valley

White virgin's
bower in early
July growing
over shrubs
along Wolf
Creek north
of Helena

🦎 Larkspur *Delphinium* species 🦎

Eleven species of *Delphinium* have been reported in Montana. The stems of larkspurs are erect and have basal leaves, palmately divided into narrow segments, and a few smaller stem leaves. The flowers are arranged in terminal, simple or compound racemes. Larkspurs have bilaterally symmetrical flowers with five conspicuous petal-like sepals and four smaller petals, two broad lower purple ones and two upper white or blue ones with purple lines. The upper sepal of the flower extends into a long spur, a very unique and prominent characteristic of all larkspurs.

Larkspurs contain many toxic alkaloids that can cause skin reactions and affect the nervous and respiratory systems. The plants are poisonous for cattle if eaten in large amounts. Sheep are more tolerant of the plant's toxicity.

Low Larkspur   *Delphinium bicolor*

Low larkspur rarely exceeds 16 inches in height. The palmately compound leaves are mostly basal and are divided into narrow segments. One to fifteen rather dark blue to purple flowers occur on each stem. The upper petals are white with blue lines. The five sepals are spread wide, with the upper one extended backward into a long conical spur. Low larkspur resembles **upland larkspur (*D. nuttalianum*)**, but that species has a notch in each of the two small lower petals that overlap the two unequal but larger sepals.

A subspecies, **Geyer larkspur (*D. bicolor* ssp. *calcicola*)** is 1 to 2 feet tall, with fine hairs on the lower part of the stems, and bears many prominently hairy leaves often dissected into linear segments. The upper petals of the flowers are whitish with blue tips but lack prominent purple or blue lines. The sepals are mostly flared. Both lower and upper flower stalks are nearly equal in length, and about as long as the flowers. The brilliant blue flowers bloom in early summer.

> HABITAT/RANGE: Found on grassy prairies, on meadows, and in ponderosa pine forests up to subalpine zones in west, central, and east Montana.

Tall Larkspur   *Delphinium occidentale*

Tall larkspur reaches heights of 3 to 6 feet. The leaves are palmate and divided into five to seven hairy, lance- or diamond-shaped lobes. A cluster of pale blue, white-streaked flowers is attached along the upper part of the stem by short stalks. The flowers have five sepals that look like petals. The uppermost sepal extends backward to form a hollow spur.

> HABITAT/RANGE: Common in areas that have adequate but not excessive moisture throughout the season, such as mountain meadows or streambanks, in west and central Montana.

Low larkspur in mid-June near Miner Lakes west of Jackson

Geyer larkspur in mid-June east of
Bridger in south-central Montana

Tall larkspur, showing a white
color variation, in mid-July on
Stemple Pass Road south of Lincoln
and northwest of Helena

🌿 Buttercup *Ranunculus* species 🌿

Thirty species of *Ranunculus* have been reported in Montana. A few are aquatic, but most are terrestrial. Most buttercups have five yellow petals and look similar enough that species identification is difficult and often requires the mature fruit as well as the flowering plant. Basal leaves of terrestrial buttercups have long petioles, and the stem leaves are simple to compound and alternate. Flowers occur alone or as a few in an open inflorescence. Each flower has five separated, greenish sepals and five separated petals, and a few to many stamens and pistils. The shiny, reflective surface of the petals is one helpful feature for distinguishing buttercups from other five-petaled, yellow flowers.

Tall Buttercup   *Ranunculus acris*

The hollow, erect, and usually hairy stems of tall buttercup are 1 to 3 feet tall and branched and spreading. The long-stalked basal leaves are up to 12 inches long, are sparsely covered with long hairs, alternate on the stem, and are deeply divided into three to five lobes, which are in turn further divided into narrow pointed segments. Stem leaves of this perennial have short petioles and are three-lobed. The open inflorescence has few to many saucer-shaped flowers, each held on a long stalk and having five broad and bright yellow petals and much shorter, spreading, greenish hairy sepals.

> HABITAT/RANGE: Found on moist or well-drained, and often disturbed, soils of fields and meadows from the plains to the foothills in west and central Montana. It has become a serious pest on some irrigated hay meadows.

White Water Buttercup   *Ranunculus aquatilis*

The brownish stems and threadlike leaves of white water buttercup form dense masses of submersed growth in water with white flowers floating on the surface. The finely divided leaves are supported on a limp petiole. Each flower is about ½ inch in diameter, having five to ten petals, five sepals, and ten to fifteen stamens and pistils.

> HABITAT/RANGE: Common along streambanks where the water is shallow and slow flowing in west, central, and east Montana.

Yellow Water Buttercup   *Ranunculus flabellaris*

Yellow water buttercup, an aquatic perennial, has two different types of leaves: the submersed leaves are divided into many linear segments, and the smaller floating leaves have three to five lobed and toothed, fan-shaped segments. The floating, branched stems are hollow, with roots occurring at the nodes. One to seven stalked, yellow flowers are arranged in an open terminal inflorescence. Each flower has five to six yellow petals that are longer than the sepals.

> HABITAT/RANGE: Found in wet, muddy, or semiaquatic environments in west Montana.

Tall buttercup in mid-July in the Swan Valley north of Seeley Lake

White water buttercup in late June on the National Bison Range, which is west of St. Ignatius

Yellow water buttercup in mid-July in a pond along U.S. 89 north of Browning

Sagebrush Buttercup   *Ranunculus glaberrimus*

Sagebrush buttercup, also called *early buttercup*, is a low-growing perennial, only 2 to 8 inches tall, with mostly basal leaves on long petioles. The oval or elliptical, fleshy leaf blades are simple, but stem leaves may have three lobes. Five shiny, waxy, bright yellow petals that turn white with age form a cup around the numerous yellow stamens that surround a mound of greenish yellow pistils. Five shorter sepals below the petals have a purplish tinge.

Sagebrush buttercup is one of the first flowers in spring, blooming just as the snow cover begins to disappear. Blue grouse eat sagebrush buttercup, and probably other wildlife eat it when seeking food in early spring.

HABITAT/RANGE: Common from prairies to pine woods in west, central, and east Montana.

Western Meadowrue   *Thalictrum occidentale*

The erect stems of this perennial are up to 3 feet tall. The compound leaves are located mostly on the thin stem, rather than at the base, and are divided into at least twenty-seven or more rounded, three-lobed leaflets. The flowers are clustered at the top of the stem in branched inflorescences. The flowers lack petals and are composed of purplish-tinged, greenish sepals that form tiny umbrellas over the flower parts. The male and female flowers are borne on separate plants. The male flower is more conspicuous, with a mass of pendulous, yellow, tassel-like stamens that quiver with even a slight breeze. The female flowers are a cluster of naked ovaries resembling the heads of snakes.

HABITAT/RANGE: Common in woods and meadows that are dry at least part of the season from montane to subalpine zones in west and central Montana.

Globeflower   *Trollius laxus*

The smooth stems of globeflower are 4 to 16 inches tall, bearing basal leaves on long stalks that clasp the stems and alternate leaves on short stalks higher on the stem. All the leaves are palmately divided into five lobes that are deeply toothed. Each stem bears a single flower having no petals but five to nine pale yellow sepals that fade to creamy white. Each flower has many yellow stamens, the outer ones flattened and lacking anthers. This perennial herb may sometimes be mistaken for marsh marigold (*Caltha leptosepala*) because it grows in the same habitat and blooms at the same time, but marsh marigold has heart-shaped leaves that are not divided.

Globeflower, like many buttercups, contains a sap that can irritate and blister the skin. The flower blooms in early spring in areas receiving runoff from melting snow.

HABITAT/RANGE: Found on wet soils in meadows and along streambanks from montane and subalpine forests to alpine zones in west and south-central Montana.

gebrush buttercup in late April
ong Battle Ridge in the Gallatin
tional Forest north of Bozeman

Globeflowers in late June in front of receding snow along U.S. 212 between Cooke City and Yellowstone National Park

Male flowers of western meadowrue in late June at Flint Creek on the north side of Georgetown Lake

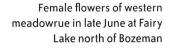

Female flowers of western meadowrue in late June at Fairy Lake north of Bozeman

CACTUS FAMILY   Cactaceae

It is not difficult to identify a cactus, but there are great variations in size, shape, and structure among members of this family, with three genera represented in Montana. These mostly leafless herbs or shrubs have flat or needlelike spines. The large, showy, brightly colored flowers have many petals and stamens and no stalks. The succulent stems have raised ribs or nipples. Cacti contain a thin, watery juice; this ability to store water helps them survive hot, dry environments.

Pincushion Cactus   *Coryphantha missouriensis*

Pincushion cactus, also called *nipple cactus*, is a low, round, globe-shaped, stemless plant less than 2 inches tall, with spines that protrude from small tubercles on the main body of the plant. The flowers are about 1 inch long with many lance-shaped petals that are greenish yellow, sometimes having a red tinge. It resembles cushion cactus (*C. vivipara*), but that plant has reddish purple flowers.

HABITAT/RANGE: Found on dry deserts and plains and in valleys and foothills, and more likely to occur east of the Rocky Mountains in west, central, and northeast Montana.

Cushion Cactus   *Coryphantha vivipara*

Cushion cactus, also called *ball cactus*, has a barrel-shaped stem growing singly or in mounds. The ½-inch-long spines are in clusters; three to ten spines in the center are colored on the tip and surrounded by twelve to forty shorter, white ones. The bright reddish purple, funnel-shaped, waxy flowers have many short, pointed petals.

HABITAT/RANGE: Prefers dry, rocky, or sandy soils in desert valleys and mountain foothills in southwest, central, and east Montana.

Plains Prickly Pear   *Opuntia polyacantha*

The succulent, jointed, flat stems of plains prickly pear grow in a mound 3 to 6 inches high and often reaching 10 feet across. The needle-sharp spines are 2 to 3 inches long, growing in bundles of about ten from woolly nodes on the stem. The flowers are 2 to 3 inches wide and vary from lemon yellow to peach. A red coloration is rare in Montana.

The fruits as well as the fleshy stems are edible.

HABITAT/RANGE: Plains prickly pear grows most often on sandy and poor gravelly soils as an occasional plant, but overgrazing by cattle can break the plant into segments that will take root so that eventually many plants cover a wide area. Common on the dry soils of west, central, and east Montana.

Pincushion cactus in late May in Bighorn Canyon National Recreation Area in south-central Montana

Cushion cactus in early June; specific location in Montana not recorded

Plains prickly pear in mid-June on an open, sandy, dry field east of Fort Benton

Inset: Sweat bees, members of a group of insects that visit only one or a few species of plants, pollinating prickly pear cacti

CAPER FAMILY Capparidaceae

Members of this family, represented by just two genera in Montana, have mostly alternate, palmately compound leaves. The white, yellow, or pink to purple flowers occur alone or in racemes. There are four sepals, four separate petals, and six to sixteen stamens usually much longer than the petals. The superior ovary has a single style.

Rocky Mountain Beeplant *Cleome serrulata*

Rocky Mountain beeplant, an annual, grows from 1 to 3 feet tall, with stems that are hairless or with sparse, long hairs. The compound leaves are alternate and divided into three lance-shaped, entire leaflets that are longer than the petioles. The pink to reddish purple flowers have four separate petals and are arranged in racemes. Each flower has four sepals, united at the base, and six stamens. Conspicuous pink filaments of the stamens extend far beyond the length of the petals. The fruits are beanlike, single-celled capsules with several seeds. A similar species, **yellow beeplant (C. *lutea*)**, has smaller flowers, yellow petals, and three to seven leaflets.

When Rocky Mountain beeplant is in bloom, it secretes large amounts of nectar, attracting bees and flies.

HABITAT/RANGE: Prefers disturbed or barren soils along roadsides and on overgrazed lands on the plains, foothills, and montane zones in west, central, and east Montana. Yellow beeplant has been reported only in Carbon and Big Horn Counties.

DOGBANE FAMILY Apocynaceae

Members of the dogbane family, represented by just one genus in Montana, have stems that contain a milky sap. Most of the members have simple, opposite leaves. The flowers have five somewhat fused petals, forming a corolla with a distinct tube or funnel. Anthers are sometimes gathered about the stigma. The pistil is superior.

Spreading Dogbane *Apocynum androsaemifolium*

Spreading dogbane is an 8- to 20-inch-tall, bushy perennial with branched stems that contain a milky sap. The short-stalked, drooping, opposite leaves are smooth, oval to oblong, and usually hairy on the lower surface. Small white or pink, bell-shaped flowers with five-lobed corollas originate from the axils of the terminal leaves on the branches. White flowers often have red stripes on the inside of the corolla.

The name *Apocynum* comes from Greek, meaning "noxious to dogs." The plant is poisonous, and animals avoid it because of its bad taste. American Indians used fibers from the stems of this plant to make cord.

HABITAT/RANGE: Prefers well-drained or dry soils on warm open hillsides in coniferous forests, or fields and meadows, from low to subalpine zones in west, central, and southeast Montana.

Rocky Mountain beeplant
in early September along
Baxter Lane in Bozeman

Spreading dogbane in late June on the east side of Swan Lake southeast of Bigfork

DOGWOOD FAMILY   Cornaceae

Most of the members of the dogwood family are trees and shrubs, but a few are herbs. Only two species in one genus are found in Montana: bunchberry (*Cornus Canadensis*), an herb, and red-osier dogwood (*C. stolonifera*), a shrub (see **Shrubs**). Leaves of dogwoods are opposite or whorled, entire, and have conspicuous veins. Small greenish yellow or whitish flowers grow in clusters and often with showy bracts. Flower parts are in fours—four petals and four sepals, either of which may be lacking. The compound pistil usually has a single style.

Bunchberry   *Cornus canadensis*

Bunchberry is a low perennial that spreads by underground stems, often forming dense patches. Four to six leaves are arranged in a whorl at the top of the stem; the largest leaf is about 3 inches long. What appear to be petals are in fact four white bracts. The tiny flowers form a head with purple dots in the center of these bracts, each flower having four sepals and the same number of petals and stamens, all parts attaching to the top of the ovary.

The red berries are edible but the flavor is not favored by everyone. Unripe berries may cause stomach pains and diarrhea. Bunchberries have been used in puddings, preserves, syrups, and jellies. The berries have anti-inflammatory benefits and have been used to treat headaches, intestinal problems, rashes, and burns.

HABITAT/RANGE: Prefers moist woods from lowlands to alpine zones in west, central, and southeast Montana.

EVENING-PRIMROSE FAMILY   Onagraceae

Wildflowers in the evening-primrose family, represented by nine genera in Montana, have showy flowers that are arranged in branched clusters or as single flowers in racemes or spikes. The leaves are usually opposite. Flower parts are typically in fours—four petals, four sepals, eight stamens, and four compartments in the ovary, which is inferior. A narrow tube, called a hypanthium, is very long in some species and located at the top of the ovary, supporting the flower parts at its mouth. The stamens, twice or equal to the number of calyx lobes, are inserted just above the ovary. The compound pistil has four stigmas.

Clarkia   *Clarkia pulchella*

Clarkia, also called *elkhorns*, has such unique blossoms that this annual will not be confused with any other species in Montana. The finely hairy stem of clarkia, frequently drooping or supported by other vegetation, is 4 to 20 inches long. Long, linear leaves with entire margins alternate along the stem. Only a few terminal, deep rose to lavender flowers are present on each

Bunchberry in early July along Moose Creek in the
Little Belt Mountains north of White Sulphur Springs

n. All floral parts are in fours—four
e-lobed petals about 1 inch long
h a narrow base, four sepals fused on
side, four fertile stamens, four non-
ile stamens, and a stigma with four
e white lobes.

his genus is named after William
rk of the Lewis and Clark Expe-
on. Meriwether Lewis collected a
cimen of this plant on the return
in 1806.

ABITAT/RANGE: Prefers dry sandy or
ravelly soils in open areas, especially
rassy hillsides, of forests or sagebrush
om the foothills to alpine zones in west
ontana.

Clarkia in mid-June on Waterworks Hill
on the outskirts of Missoula

Fireweed
Epilobium angustifolium

Fireweed is a conspicuous wildflower; the unbranched, leafy stems reach 4 to 6 feet tall, terminating in a showy, many-flowered inflorescence. The 4- to 6-inch-long, linear or lance-shaped leaves alternate on the lower part of the stem. The leaves are lighter colored beneath and have prominent veins. The pink to magenta flowers have four irregularly spaced petals. The bloom opens first at the base of the long spike, while new buds droop from above.

Fireweed, common across southern Canada and the northern United States, is a favorite forage of bears and other animals. The roots have been used as a boiled herb, and the shoots are said to resemble asparagus and the leaves spinach. The greens have been eaten raw or cooked and used to prepare teas, but some find that they have a laxative effect. The plant is rich in vitamins A and C and has been widely used in medicine for anti-inflammatory benefits, treating candidiasis, diarrhea, asthma, and skin sores. Some American Indian tribes used fiber from fireweed for making cord and fishnets.

Although fireweed is the most conspicuous and most readily identifiable *Epilobium* species in Montana, many others grow here. They are generally called *willow-herbs* because of their willowlike leaves. Some are low-growing herbs with erect stems. The white to rosy purple flowers have four lobed petals.

HABITAT/RANGE: Fireweed is one of the first plants to colonize burned areas in moist habitats; it spreads rapidly by seed and underground stems. Common on disturbed soils in cool habitats along highways and open woods in west, central, and east Montana.

Scarlet Gaura
Gaura coccinea

Scarlet gaura is also called *butterfly weed*, but this perennial is not related to the butterfly weed (*Asclepias* species) of the milkweed family that attracts butterflies. The weak, branching stem of scarlet gaura is 8 to 24 inches long, crowded with lance-shaped leaves that are smaller on the upper part of the stem and have shallow teeth. The stems bear a dense spike of flowers with four petals. Each flower has four sepals that bend sharply backward, and eight stamens that are shorter than the style.

Individual flowers bloom for less than twenty-four hours. The flower opens in the evening and its white petals attract pollinating, night-flying moths. The following morning the petals turn pink or red, and the flower closes before evening.

The name *Gaura* comes from the Greek *gauros,* meaning "superb" or "proud." Scarlet gaura has been used for various medicinal purposes, including treatment of pain, burns, and rheumatism. Dakota Indians chewed this plant and rubbed it on their hands before pursuing horses.

HABITAT/RANGE: Prefers dry and sandy soils of grasslands and sagebrush areas on the plains, valleys, and foothills throughout Montana but is more common east of the Rocky Mountains.

A willow-herb in mid-July along a small stream in the
Lewis and Clark National Forest west of Augusta

Fireweed in mid-July in the Swan Valley
north of Seeley Lake

Scarlet gaura in early June at the Otter Creek
Fishing Access on the north side of the
Yellowstone River near Big Timber

🦎 Evening Primrose *Oenothera* species 🦎

Seven species of the genus *Oenothera* occur in Montana, four with white flowers and three with yellow flowers. Evening primroses have mostly leafless stems, with clustered or alternate, lance-shaped or pinnately divided basal leaves. The showy white or yellow flowers have four petals, four sepals, and eight stamens. White flowers fade to pink and yellow to orange or reddish. The long, slender hypanthium is very prominent and appears to be part of the stem. The stigma is cross-shaped with four lobes. The flowers open in late afternoon or evening, are pollinated by night-flying insects, and close during bright sunlight the following day. *Oenothera* means "wine-scented," a reference to the use of the roots of evening primrose for making wine.

Prairie Evening Primrose   *Oenothera albicaulis*

Prairie evening primrose, also called *white-stemmed evening primrose*, has white stems that are 4 to 20 inches long but spread horizontally in a circle from the root, so this annual appears short. Basal leaves are arranged in a rosette and the stem leaves are alternate. The basal leaves, about 4 inches long, are elliptical and entire or somewhat lobed below, whereas stem leaves are more deeply segmented. The flowers open from drooping buds near sunset and remain open for several days, during which the white heart-shaped petals turn pink. Each flower emerges from a leaf axil and has four backward-bending sepals, four petals, and eight stamens. The style is elongate, and the tip of the stigma has four lobes.

> HABITAT/RANGE: Prefers sandy soils and grassy plains in northwest, central, and east Montana, but is most likely to be found in south-central and southeast parts of the state.

Gumbo Evening Primrose   *Oenothera caespitosa*

Gumbo evening primrose, also called *desert evening primrose* and *tufted evening primrose*, is a stemless perennial with long linear leaves that are clustered in a crude basal rosette. The bluish green leaves have short petioles, are slightly toothed or have wavy margins, and are winged near their base. The heart-shaped flowers are 2 to 3½ inches wide and have four lobed petals and a tube that is 1 to 5 inches long. The flowers open late in the day and turn pink after pollination by nocturnal insects. Four large sepals bend backward at their tips. The hypanthium tube is flared in a way that it resembles a stalk, although the flowers are in fact stalkless.

Crushed roots were used by American Indians for treating skin lesions. Meriwether Lewis collected a specimen of this wildflower on the expedition's return trip in 1806.

> HABITAT/RANGE: Prefers dry open sites and clay soils, known as "gumbo" in eastern Montana, on slopes and roadsides from the plains to subalpine zones in west, central, and east Montana.

Prairie evening primrose in late May in a dry sagebrush area south and southeast of Forsyth

Gumbo evening primrose in early June along a roadside west of Augusta

Hooker's Evening Primrose

Oenothera hookeri
O. elata

The stem of Hooker's evening primrose, usually unbranched, is 1 to 4 feet tall. The numerous narrow leaves are 6 to 12 inches long, but smaller toward the top of the stem. The yellow flowers, which turn orange or purplish with age and drop off early, are 2 to 3 inches wide and arranged in a raceme interspersed with bracts. A 1- to 2-inch-long calyx tube that may look like a stem supports each flower. The flower has four broad petals and eight stamens that differ in length.

HABITAT/RANGE: Found on road banks, open slopes, or moist prairies and plains at low elevations in Montana.

Pale Evening Primrose

Oenothera pallida

Pale evening primrose has reddish, semiwoody stems that are up to 20 inches long and are usually erect but sometimes collapse onto the ground. The leaves are narrow, linear, and often toothed on the margins. The flowers open from pink buds in late afternoon and last only one day. The flowers are about 1½ inches wide, emerging from leaf axils, and have four white petals that turn pinkish after pollination and have some yellow at their base.

HABITAT/RANGE: Prefers sandy soils of stable dunes, gravelly slopes, and sagebrush areas in southwest, south-central, and northeast Montana.

FIGWORT FAMILY

Scrophulariaceae

The large figwort family, sometimes called the snapdragon family, is represented by twenty-two genera in Montana. The leaves are mostly opposite or whorled. The often showy flowers are bilaterally symmetrical with four or five fused sepals and four or five petals fused into a tube with upper and lower lips. The upper lip is entire or two-lobed, and the lower lip is often three-lobed and spreading. There are two, four, or five stamens, and when five are present, one is sterile and different in appearance.

Wyoming Kittentails

Besseya wyomingensis

Wyoming kittentails is a 3- to 10-inch-tall perennial with egg-shaped basal leaves on long petioles and small, finely toothed stem leaves that are stalkless and alternate. The small flowers are arranged in a dense spike at the top of the single stem. The flowers have no petals but have two hairy sepals and two long stamens with reddish purple filaments that confer the prominent color. This wildflower could be confused with some species of *Synthyris*, also called *kittentails* and members of the figwort family.

HABITAT/RANGE: Grows on dry soils from the plains to foothills and alpine zones, blooming soon after the snow melts, in west, central, and southeast Montana.

oker's evening primrose in early July
n the Charles M. Russell Trail along
the Judith River south of Utica

Pale evening primrose on an early mid-July morning
on a sandy roadside bank west of Augusta

Wyoming kittentails on
May 1 in Bear Creek Canyon
in the Gallatin National
Forest south of Bozeman

❧ Paintbrush *Castilleja* species ❦

Most Montanans will readily identify a plant in the genus *Castilleja* as "Indian paintbrush," but twenty-two different species occur in the state. Hybridization occurs between species, complicating identification. The recognizable "flower" is actually brightly colored calyxes, leafy bracts, and sometimes upper leaves. Ten species in Montana have red or purplish bracts and the remainder have bracts that are usually yellowish or greenish but occasionally purplish or reddish. Paintbrushes usually have several stems, bearing alternate stalkless leaves. The true flowers, borne in terminal spikelike inflorescences, are rather inconspicuous. The corolla has five petals fused below into a tube but separated above into two lips, the upper lip extended into a long beak and the shorter, three-lobed lower lip tucked under it. Each flower holds four stamens. The calyx has four sepals that are also fused at their base.

Paintbrushes are somewhat parasitic in that they draw water and some nutrients from nearby plants, usually sagebrush or grasses, by using short side branches from their roots. For this reason paintbrushes cannot be transplanted or easily grown from seed.

Harsh Paintbrush   *Castilleja hispida*

The 8- to 24-inch-tall stems of harsh paintbrush have long hairs. The lower stem leaves are small and entire, whereas the upper alternate leaves are divided at the tip into three to five (or five to seven) lobes. The middle lobe of the leaf is broad and rounded, whereas the lateral lobes are narrow and pointed. The upper leaves are sometimes yellowish but usually, along with the sepals and bracts, are deep red or scarlet. Lobes on the calyx have blunt tips. The corolla is reddish green, with the upper hood-shaped part of the flower equal in length to the fused part, or tube.

> HABITAT/RANGE: Found on hills and dry open woods at montane zones in west Montana.

Wyoming Paintbrush   *Castilleja linariaefolia*

The state flower of Wyoming, this paintbrush differs from many others found in Montana by the shape of the leaves, which are grasslike and divided into narrow segments near the end. The stems are 8 to 32 inches tall. Leaflike bracts provide a bright scarlet color, while the tubular two-lipped flower is yellowish green. The bracts, located below the corolla, have one or two pairs of segmented lobes.

> HABITAT/RANGE: Found on dry soils in the steppe, or in riparian and moist habitats, from the foothills to montane zones in west and central Montana.

A yellow paintbrush in mid-June in the Pryor Mountains east of Bridger

Harsh paintbrush in mid-June along the west side of Hungry Horse Reservoir in northwest Montana

Wyoming paintbrush in early May in an open field west of Bridger

Yellowish Paintbrush   *Castilleja lutescens*

Yellowish paintbrush grows with many 12- to 20-inch-tall, unbranched stems covered with stiff short hairs and bearing narrow, lance-shaped leaves with mostly entire margins. A pair of short lobes may be present on the upper leaves. The bracts are yellowish or sometimes greenish. The calyx has two long, pointed lobes that are shallowly divided into two lobes with pointed tips. The yellow corolla is just a bit longer than the calyx. The hood-shaped flower part is much shorter than the floral tube.

HABITAT/RANGE: Found on grasslands and in open coniferous forests in west and central Montana.

Common Paintbrush   *Castilleja miniata*

Common paintbrush reaches a height of 1 to 3 feet, taller than most paintbrushes. The stem bears entire, narrow, lance-shaped leaves; upper leaves may have narrow lobes. Bright red, scarlet, or reddish orange sepals and bracts attract immediate attention. The greenish, red-tipped petals in the corolla are not very obvious because they do not extend beyond the colorful leafy bracts.

HABITAT/RANGE: One of the more common and widespread paintbrushes in Montana, common paintbrush prefers moist soils in meadows and along streams from montane to subalpine zones in west and central Montana.

Great Plains Paintbrush   *Castilleja sessiliflora*

Great Plains paintbrush, called by many other names, including *downy paintcup*, may not be recognized at first as a paintbrush. The clustered stems are 4 to 12 inches tall and covered with shaggy hairs. The lower leaves on the stem are linear and the upper ones have a pair of narrow lobes. The corolla consists of a long curved tube, longer than the narrow three- to five-lobed greenish bracts that are tinged with pink or red and covered with fine hairs. The flowers vary from pink to purple or pinkish green to yellowish green, or a combination of these.

HABITAT/RANGE: Prefers dry rocky hills and open sandy prairies among pine and juniper trees in south-central and east Montana.

Yellowish paintbrush on June 1 on a forest border adjacent to Montana 83 just south of Salmon Lake

Great Plains paintbrush in late May at Tongue River Reservoir State Park in south-central Montana

Common paintbrush in late June in the Flint Creek Range northeast of Georgetown Lake

Blue-eyed Mary   *Collinsia parviflora*

Blue-eyed Mary, an easily overlooked annual, is one of the smallest wildflowers in Montana. The delicate, slender, and widely branched stem is usually about 5 inches tall but may grow to 12 inches. The narrow, lance-shaped, purple-tinged leaves, usually reddish purple below, have an entire margin, are sparsely hairy, and are located opposite on the stem except in the flower axils, where they might be whorled. The pale to deep blue flowers, with some white on the upper lips, are held on weak stalks and occur singly or in whorls in leaf axils. Each tiny flower, less than ¼ inch long, has a brownish lavender calyx, a two-lobed upper lip, and a three-lobed lower lip, and contains four stamens.

The genus name of this flower honors Zacheus Collins (1764–1831), a Philadelphia botanist, and the species name means "small flowered."

HABITAT/RANGE: Found on stony slopes and rocky disturbed soils near trees and along roads in a variety of habitats from valleys to subalpine zones in west and central Montana.

Dalmatian Toadflax   *Linaria dalmatica*

Dalmatian toadflax has a 1- to 3-foot-tall stem that is woody at the base. The grayish green, alternate leaves, with a fine powdery surface, are egg-shaped with a sharp tip, and clasp the stem at their base. The bright yellow flowers, which resemble snapdragons with an orange beard in the throat, are arranged in a long raceme on one or several branches. The flower tube has five lobes, two upper and three lower. A thin spur, which contains nectar, extends from the base of the flower tube. Dalmatian toadflax resembles butter-and-eggs (*Linaria vulgaris*), another non-native, but differs in having larger leaves that clasp the stem.

HABITAT/RANGE: An invasive noxious weed from the Mediterranean region, dalmatian toadflax prefers disturbed soils along roads and on sagebrush flats from the foothills to montane zones in west, central, and northeast Montana.

Butter-and-eggs   *Linaria vulgaris*

The non-native butter-and-eggs, also called *common toadflax*, grows in patches and can be weedy. The 8- to 32-inch-tall stem of butter-and-eggs bears many simple, linear, stalkless, grayish green leaves that alternate. The light to bright yellow flowers with hairy orange patches at their throats are arranged in dense spikes. Each flower has five petals, the three lower ones projecting backward and the two upper ones bending forward. The 1- to 1½-inch-long corolla ends in a long spur that projects backward.

It has been said that a tea prepared with butter-and-eggs is an effective treatment of skin rashes and constipation.

HABITAT/RANGE: Introduced from Eurasia, butter-and-eggs grows on open, disturbed soils such as roadsides and waste areas in west, central, and southeast Montana.

Blue-eyed Mary in early May in the
Bitterroot Mountains west of Woodside

Dalmatian toadflax in late June along
U.S. 89 south of Gardiner

Butter-and-eggs in early July near the Charles M.
Russell Trail along the Judith River south of Utica

Yellow Monkeyflower   *Mimulus guttatus*

Yellow monkeyflower varies from a low annual with creeping stems no higher than 2 inches to a bushy perennial that may reach 3 feet tall. The egg- or lance-shaped leaves, with sharp teeth on the margins, are arranged opposite on hollow stems. The flowers are held on slender stalks that arise from upper leaf axils. The yellow corolla is 1 to 2 inches long, the fused petals forming a tube with two upper and three lower lobes. The lower lip has maroon spots and two ridges extending back into the hair-lined throat. The fused sepals form a green calyx that is ridged and toothed, with the upper tooth being longest, a distinguishing feature of this wildflower.

Meriwether Lewis collected this species in 1806 along the Blackfoot River.

HABITAT/RANGE: Found on wet soils along streams, springs, and lakes at low to high elevations in west and central Montana.

Lewis's Monkeyflower   *Mimulus lewisii*

Lewis's monkeyflower resembles yellow monkeyflower (*M. guttatus*) except that the flowers are pink to rosy red rather than yellow. The clustered stems may be reclining or upright, reaching heights of 1 to 3 feet and forming a large mass. The sticky, hairy, lance-shaped leaves are 1 to 4 inches long, unevenly toothed or plain on the edges, and arranged opposite on the stems. The red corolla forms a tube with a hair-lined throat that has two yellow patches and darker reddish lines near the opening.

This wildflower was named to honor Meriwether Lewis, who is credited with collecting the first described specimen. Hummingbirds seek its nectar and are dusted with pollen from the anthers.

HABITAT/RANGE: Prefers wet soils along streams, ponds, and seepage areas in valleys and on mountains in west and central Montana.

Thin-leaved Owl Clover   *Orthocarpus tenuifolius*

Thin-leaved owl clover, a small annual with single or occasionally branched stems, is 4 to 16 inches tall. Lower leaves are narrow and entire, while those higher on the stem are divided into three to five narrow segments. The numerous upper leaves overlap, transforming into bracts in the floral spike. The yellow flowers, often purple-tipped, are arranged in a dense spike and are separated by pinkish purple bracts. The fused petals form a two-lipped tube, the upper lip hoodlike and the lower lip usually swelled and bearing three tiny, toothlike projections. Owl clover may resemble some yellow paintbrushes; however, in paintbrushes the upper lip of the corolla is much larger than the lower lip. In addition, the yellow petals of owl-clover are conspicuous, whereas it is the bracts of paintbrushes that confer their distinctive color.

Meriwether Lewis collected a specimen of this wildflower in 1806 near Lolo.

HABITAT/RANGE: Prefers moderately dry soils of grassy prairies and valleys but grows up to subalpine zones in west and central Montana.

Yellow monkeyflower in late June along the East River Road south of Livingston

Thin-leaved owl clover in mid-June on the National Bison Range west of St. Ignatius

Lewis's monkeyflower in late July near the base of the Beartooth Highway south of Red Lodge

Coiled Lousewort   *Pedicularis contorta*

Coiled lousewort, also called *alpine fernleaf,* occurs in solitary clumps. The 6- to 24-inch-tall leafy stems bear pinnately compound, fernlike basal leaves with toothed leaflets, and smaller alternate stem leaves that reduce to bracts among the flowers. The stems and leaves are often tinged with maroon. The white or cream-colored flowers are in an open raceme on the upper half of the stems, resembling lit candles from a distance. The upper lip of the flower curves sideways and downward like a sickle and ends above the wide lower lip.

HABITAT/RANGE: Grows on dry, open, rocky slopes and moist meadows at subalpine and alpine zones in west and central Montana.

Elephanthead   *Pedicularis groenlandica*

Elephanthead resembles a miniature pink elephant with big drooping ears and a long curved trunk. The unbranched, reddish purple stem is 6 to 20 inches tall with mostly basal fernlike leaves that are narrow and pinnately divided. The pink to purple or red flowers are arranged in a dense raceme.

Meriwether Lewis collected a specimen of elephanthead in 1806 along the Blackfoot River.

HABITAT/RANGE: Found in wet meadows and grassy fields along streams from montane to subalpine zones in west and central Montana.

Parry's Lousewort   *Pedicularis parryi* var. *purpurea*

Parry's lousewort in Montana is *P. parryi* var. *purpurea,* which differs from *P. parryi* var. *parryi* by having purple rather than yellow flowers. The 4- to 8-inch-tall stems are surrounded at the base by many fernlike leaves. A few smaller leaves are located on the stem. The calyx is covered with long entangled hairs. The flower bracts are divided. The hood of the purple corolla is cone-shaped at the tip, with a beak.

Louseworts are parasitic plants that cannot be easily grown when removed from their natural habitat.

HABITAT/RANGE: Found on open slopes and meadows from middle to high elevations in southwest and central Montana.

Parrot's Beak   *Pedicularis racemosa*

Parrot's beak, also called *sickletop lousewort,* resembles coiled lousewort (*P. contorta*), but that species has pinnately compound, fernlike leaves. The 6- to 20-inch-tall, clustered stems of parrot's beak bear lance-shaped, double-toothed, simple leaves on short petioles. The white flowers, sometimes tinged with pink, have a wide, three-lobed lower lip and a sickle-shaped upper lip that is curved downward into a distinct beak.

HABITAT/RANGE: Found in a variety of habitats including wet and dry meadows, rocky slopes, and open forests at montane to subalpine zones in west and central Montana.

Coiled lousewort in late June near Road 279 east of Lincoln

Elephanthead in early July along Moose Creek in the Little Belt Mountains north of White Sulphur Springs

rry's lousewort in early June in a shaded ood in the Gravelly Range south of Ennis

Parrot's beak in mid-July around Fairy Lake in the Bridger Range north of Bozeman

🦎 Penstemon *Penstemon* species 🦎

Penstemon is the largest genus of flowering plants endemic to North America, with twenty-nine species in Montana. With the exception of a few unique species, most penstemons are difficult to identify, particularly those with blue to lavender or purple flowers. The leaves of these perennials usually occur in opposite pairs. All penstemons have tubular corollas with five petals fused at the base and three lobes on the lower lip and two lobes on the upper lip. The cuplike calyx is composed of five sepals that are shorter than the petals. The flowers of penstemons have four fertile stamens plus a nonfertile one called a *staminode*, which is often hairy, thus earning the common name *beardtongue*.

Alberta Penstemon   *Penstemon albertinus*

Alberta penstemon is 6 to 12 inches tall, with clustered stems. Some of the opposite, smooth and hairless, lance- to egg-shaped basal leaves have tiny irregular teeth. Lower leaves are stalked, while upper leaves are narrower and stalkless. Many bright blue or pinkish, funnel-shaped flowers with paler throats are arranged in whorls in upper leaf axils.

A similar species, **Wilcox's penstemon (*P. wilcoxii*)** hybridizes with Alberta penstemon. One of the tallest penstemons in Montana, it has slender, 16- to 40-inch-tall stems that are smooth or finely haired below the inflorescence. The smooth leaves have toothed margins and clasp the stem at their base. Bright blue to purple flowers are located on divided branches that occur along a central axis. The flower tube is ½ to 1 inch long.

Meriwether Lewis collected a specimen of Wilcox's penstemon in eastern Idaho in 1806.

HABITAT/RANGE: Alberta penstemon prefers dry open or rocky areas from the valleys to foothills and subalpine forests in west Montana. Wilcox's penstemon grows on similar sites in northwest Montana.

White Beardtongue   *Penstemon albidus*

Easy to identify because of its white color, white beardtongue has a wide distribution in the Great Plains. The stems are 6 to 16 inches tall. Both the stems and leaves have tiny rough hairs that feel like sandpaper. The lower leaves have petioles and are lance-shaped, whereas the upper leaves are linear with entire margins. The white to pale lavender, funnel-shaped flowers have a narrow throat and five fused petals that flare into lobes: the two upper lobes bend backward. Purple lines are present on the lower inside surface of the corolla throat. The nonfertile stamen is covered with yellow hairs.

HABITAT/RANGE: Grows on gravelly or sandy prairies, grasslands, plains, hills, and slopes in central and east Montana, and rarely in the northwest.

Top left: Wilcox's penstemon in early June south of Montana 37 and east of Libby

Top right: Alberta penstemon in mid-June along Hungry Horse Reservoir east of Kalispell

Bottom: White beardtongue in mid-June near Road 236 north of Judith Landing on the Missouri River

Yellow Penstemon   *Penstemon confertus*

Yellow penstemon has one or a few mostly hairless stems that are 8 to 20 inches tall. Basal leaves are arranged in a rosette and are mostly elliptical on short petioles. The stem leaves are lance-shaped and stalkless or clasping, becoming smaller with the inflorescence. The light yellow to cream–colored flowers are arranged in dense clusters emerging from leaf axils and encircling the stem. The corolla includes hairless anthers that are purple on the outside.

HABITAT/RANGE: Found on moist soils in west and north-central Montana.

Blue Penstemon   *Penstemon cyaneus*

The smooth, 12- to 26-inch-tall stems of blue penstemon are sometimes covered with a waxy powder. The smooth, thick, opposite leaves are lance- or egg-shaped. The basal leaves form a rosette and have short petioles, whereas the upper leaves are stalkless and clasp the stem. The bilaterally symmetrical flowers are clustered along the upper part of the stem. The large blue corolla is up to 2 inches long. The inner surface is lighter colored and hairless except for the sterile, yellow-bearded stamen in the throat. The hairless sepals are broad and tapered or rounded at the tip.

HABITAT/RANGE: Found in patches on disturbed soils along roadsides, and on open plains with sagebrush, from the foothills to montane zones in southwest and south-central Montana.

Fuzzytongue Penstemon   *Penstemon eriantherus*

Fuzzytongue penstemon stands out among the many penstemons because of its wide-open, hairy throat with an extended sterile stamen covered with yellow hairs—the "fuzzytongue." The 5- to 15-inch-tall stems bear hairy, narrow leaves that may be toothed. The flower color varies from pale lavender to deep violet. The three lower lobes have purplish veins, serving as guidelines for pollinating insects seeking the flower's nectar.

HABITAT/RANGE: Prefers dry and rocky soils of plains and sagebrush slopes on the foothills and lower mountains in west, central, and east Montana.

Larchleaf Penstemon   *Penstemon laricifolius*

Larchleaf penstemon, a low, mat-forming perennial, has distinctive needle-shaped leaves, similar to a larch tree (*Larix* species). The pale lavender to purple or pink flowers are arranged in an open raceme or panicle at the ends of the many stems. The funnel-shaped flower is smooth on the outside but finely haired on the lower lip. The sterile stamen has short yellow hairs over the front portion.

HABITAT/RANGE: Prefers dry rocky soils on the plains and foothills in Carbon and Big Horn Counties in south-central Montana.

Top left: Yellow
penstemon in late
June in an open wet
area along Montana 83
south of Swan Lake

Top right: Blue
penstemon in early
July on a roadside at
low elevation in the
Gravelly Range
south of Ennis

Fuzzytongue
penstemon in late
May at Bighorn
Canyon National
Recreation Area
in south-central
Montana

Archleaf
penstemon
in mid-June
in Bighorn
Canyon National
Recreation Area
in south-central
Montana

Lyall's Beardtongue   *Penstemon lyallii*

The 12- to 32-inch-tall stems of Lyall's beardtongue bear numerous distinctive leaves. They are opposite and 1 to 5 inches long, and occur only on the stems. Short glandular hairs are present on the upper stem, flower stalks, and sepals, giving a silvery and silky appearance to this perennial. The pale lavender flowers are arranged in a short dense spike. The interior of the petal tube varies from white to blue or violet and has two ridges on the tongue that are covered with hairs. The outside of the tube is smooth. The banner has a white to pale yellow central stripe. The sepals are narrow, glandular, entire, and pointed.

The species name honors David Lyall (1817–1895), a surgeon and naturalist from Scotland who was surveying the boundary between British Columbia and the United States when he collected a specimen of this penstemon in the Rocky Mountains in 1862.

HABITAT/RANGE: Grows on steep rocky outcrops and streamsides from montane to alpine zones in northwest Montana.

Shining Penstemon   *Penstemon nitidus*

Shining penstemon, also called *wax-leaved penstemon*, blooms in May, earlier than all other penstemons. The 4- to 12-inch-tall stems bear distinctive thick, fleshy, broadly lance- or egg-shaped leaves that have a whitish or bluish cast due to a removable waxy substance on the surface. The lower entire-margined leaves have petioles, whereas the broader stem leaves are stalkless. The entire plant, including the anthers of the four fertile stamens, is smooth and hairless. The sterile stamen is covered with long, bright yellow hair, contrasting with the bright blue flower.

HABITAT/RANGE: Found on grasslands, talus slopes, and other rocky and sparsely vegetated soils, including roadsides, from the plains to the foothills in west, central, and east Montana.

Small-flowered Penstemon   *Penstemon procerus*

Small-flowered penstemon has numerous small flowers crowded into distinct whorls. Several slender, smooth stems, usually less than 16 inches tall, grow in a mat, each bearing several pairs of bright green, opposite, entire, and stalkless leaves. The intense blue to purple or sometimes cream-colored flowers are supported by short stalks that arise from leaf axils.

HABITAT/RANGE: Found in mountain meadows and in open forests on drained slopes from valleys to alpine zones in west and central Montana.

Lyall's beardtongue on July 1 on a vertical stone wall along
Going-to-the-Sun Highway in Glacier National Park

Bottom left:
Small-flowered
penstemon on
July 1 near St.
Mary's Lake
in Glacier
National Park

Bottom right:
Shining
penstemon in
late May on a
rocky roadside
of U.S. 12 east of
Townsend

Yellow Rattle   *Rhinanthus crista-galli*

Yellow rattle, an annual, has a single erect, 6- to 24-inch-tall stem with widely spaced pale green, lance-shaped, opposite leaves. The firm, rough leaves have sharp teeth, are stalkless, and are 1 to 2½ inches long. The unusual yellow flower protrudes from a flat, inflated, veined, green calyx that has four pointed lobes. Pairs of flowers arise from the axils of upper leaflike bracts. The corolla, which is barely visible, is two-lipped; the upper lip hoodlike and often with two white side lobes, and the shorter lower lip with three lobes. Each flower contains four stamens.

HABITAT/RANGE: Prefers moist to dry open fields and meadows, and especially disturbed soils, from the foothills to montane zones in northwest Montana.

Common Mullein   *Verbascum thapsus*

Common mullein, also called *woolly mullein*, is not likely to go unnoticed in the second year of its biennial life cycle when it grows a hairy, erect stem that may reach 6 or 7 feet tall. Only a basal rosette of thick long leaves represents the plant in the first year of growth. Leaves alternate on the stem in the second year. The stalked saucer-shaped flowers are arranged in a long open spike at the top of the stem. The dark brown stems of the dead plants are visible throughout the winter, protruding above the surface of the snow. Two species of mullein occur in Montana: common mullein (*V. thapsus*), and **moth mullein (*V. blattaria*)**. Common mullein, the more common, differs in being densely covered with long hairs and a congested spike of yellow flowers, whereas moth mullein is only hairy on the top surface of the leaves and the light yellow to white flowers are arranged in a more open spike.

Common mullein and moth mullein were introduced into North America from Eurasia. Deer and elk eat the plants, and many birds eat the seeds. Mullein was used by Dioscorides, a Greek physician, for treating a variety of medical problems. In recent times the plant has been used to treat respiratory complaints and wounds, and administered as a sedative.

HABITAT/RANGE: Common mullein grows in large numbers on disturbed dry sandy soils in valleys, foothills, and montane forests in west, central, and east Montana. Moth mullein occurs in the west, north-central, and northeast regions of the state.

Yellow rattle in mid-June on the National Bison Range west of St. Ignatius

Common mullein in late July near Red Rock Lakes National Wildlife Refuge west of West Yellowstone

American Speedwell   *Veronica americana*

The sprawling stem of American speedwell may be 40 inches long, emerging from horizontal stems called *rhizomes*. The opposite leaves, usually with three to five pairs on each stem, are all on short petioles and are oval to lance-shaped, sharply pointed, and with a few teeth or nearly entire margins. Both the stem and leaves lack hairs. The blue or pale violet, saucer-shaped flowers are on thin stalks that arise from upper leaf axils in branched inflorescences. Four flat petals with dark veins are partially fused at the base. The petals differ in shape: the top one is widest and the bottom one is smallest. A white eye is often present in the center of the petals. The base of two widely separated stamens is fused with the petals.

> HABITAT/RANGE: Confined to wet soils in marshes, along streams, and in ditches at low to middle elevations in west and central Montana.

Cusick's Speedwell   *Veronica cusickii*

Cusick's speedwell, a small delicate perennial, has erect, unbranched stems that grow 4 to 8 inches tall in clusters. The simple, opposite, egg-shaped, 1-inch-long leaves with entire margins clasp the stem and are half as wide as long. The bluish violet flowers are arranged in a raceme at the stem top. Each flower has four petals, the lower three smaller, and the upper one the largest because it is actually two fused petals. There are four sepals and two stamens, the latter fused to the petals. The style, about $\frac{1}{4}$ inch long, is a thin projection from the pistil, which is located between two shorter stamens.

> HABITAT/RANGE: Prefers moist soils in meadows and on hillsides in subalpine to sometimes timberline zones in west Montana.

Alpine Speedwell   *Veronica wormskjoldii*

This slender, erect perennial has an unbranched, 2- to 12-inch-tall stem covered with short hairs. The short, egg-shaped to oblong leaves, usually smooth but sometimes with silky hairs, are opposite and stalkless. Deep blue, short-stalked flowers are arranged in a tight, rounded head at the top of the stem.

> HABITAT/RANGE: Found on moist soils in open areas and often along streams at subalpine and alpine zones in west and central Montana.

American speedwell in mid-July along a small stream east of U.S. 89 in the Little Belt Mountains northeast of White Sulphur Springs

Bottom left: Cusick's speedwell on July 1 along Lake McDonald in Glacier National Park

Bottom right: Alpine speedwell in early July near Hyalite Reservoir south of Bozeman

FLAX FAMILY   Linaceae

Members of the flax family, represented in Montana by a single genus with four species, have flowers with sepals, petals, stamens, and a pistil—all parts attached directly to the end of the flower stalk. Showy petals, which usually fall quickly, are separate from each other. Five sepals are either separated or joined at the base. The five to ten or more fertile stamens are usually joined at the base and often separated by infertile stamens. The pistil may have five to ten styles that are usually free. Leaves are simple and entire.

Wild Blue Flax   *Linum perenne*
                                        L. lewisii

The slender, mostly branched stems of wild blue flax are up to 2 feet tall, often extending above grasses. The narrow, short, alternate leaves are spaced close together. The bright blue flowers, which open a few at a time, have five broad petals that are 1 to 2 inches in diameter. Each flower has five stamens and five styles, which are longer than the stamens.

> HABITAT/RANGE: Found on drained soils of prairies and meadows and on grassy foothills and subalpine slopes in west, central, and east Montana.

GENTIAN FAMILY   Gentianaceae

Members of the gentian family, represented in Montana by seven genera, have showy flowers with four or five petals that are fused into a tube or bell-shaped structure that is usually five-lobed. The number of stamens equal the number of petals and alternate with them in the corolla. The pistil is superior and has none or a simple style and a two-lobed stigma. Stem leaves are usually opposite and lack petioles.

Green Gentian   *Frasera speciosa*

Green gentian, also called *monument plant*, begins its life with a vegetative phase that lasts for twenty to sixty years. During this phase the plant grows a rosette of large basal leaves, the number increasing each year. Finally, it erupts with a 2- to 5-foot-tall stalk bearing numerous flowers that last one season, leaving a dried stalk as the only evidence of its remarkable life.

Look for striking purple dots on the four greenish white petals and pinkish hairs on two large nectar glands located near the base of each petal. The prominent green ovary sits in the center of four long stamens. Each flower includes four sepals and four narrow bracts. Flower stems arise from the axils of the leaves. The stem leaves, arranged in tiers of whorls with three to five leaves each, are very large at the base and smaller at the top of the thick, unbranched stem.

> HABITAT/RANGE: Prefers dry to moist soils on grasslands and meadows and in open forests from valleys to subalpine zones in west and central Montana.

Wild blue flax in early June in Corbley Gulch near Springhill northeast of Belgrade

Green gentian in late July near Fairy Lake in the Bridger Range north of Bozeman

Pleated Gentian

Gentiana affinis
Pneumonanthe affinis

Pleated gentian has 6- to 15-inch-tall stems that bear several opposite, entire, lance-shaped, stalkless leaves. Several to many flowers emerge from the tips of the stems or in the upper leaf axils. The blue to indigo, cylindrical flowers have membranous, pleated folds between the five lobed petals. Greenish spots cover the upper surface of the petals, visible only when the flower opens in bright sunlight. Pleated gentian resembles **explorer's gentian (***Gentiana calycosa***)**, but has narrower pointed leaves and slightly smaller, more numerous flowers crowded in clusters.

The genus of this wildflower, *Gentiana*, was named after King Gentius of Illyria, an ancient country of the Adriatic. He first described the plant's medicinal properties, which included treatment of digestive disorders, a benefit sought by American Indians and early settlers.

HABITAT/RANGE: Prefers moist soils in wet meadows and along streambanks at subalpine zones in west and central Montana.

Arctic Gentian

Gentiana algida

One or more 8-inch-tall stems rise from a basal rosette of linear or narrowly lance-shaped leaves about 5 inches long. Five petals, separated by pleats that are nearly as long as the petals, are fused into a tube, the typical shape of a gentian. The 1½- to 2-inch-long corolla is greenish white to pale yellowish with purple or blue streaks.

Arctic gentian has a bitter taste and in large amounts can cause intestinal upset; however, the plant has long been used for treating what it purportedly causes. The species name *algida* comes from the Latin word *algidus,* meaning "cold."

HABITAT/RANGE: Prefers moist subalpine to alpine tundra and meadows in south-central and southwest Montana.

Northern Gentian

Gentianella amarella
Gentiana amarella

The often branching, usually hairless stems of northern gentian are 2 to 18 inches tall, with opposite, stalkless, narrow, pointed basal and stem leaves. The upright trumpet-shaped flowers arise from upper leaf axils. The flowers have four or five flared petal lobes that vary from purplish blue to greenish yellow or sometimes white. There is a feathery fringe just inside the throat of the flower. The calyx of the flower has five pointed lobes.

HABITAT/RANGE: Prefers moist sandy soils in sloughs, mountains meadows, forest borders, and streambanks at alpine to subalpine zones in west and central Montana.

Pleated gentian in late July on the northeast side of the Gravelly Range south of Ennis

Bottom right: Northern gentian in late
June northeast of Seeley Lake

ottom left: Arctic gentian in early August along the
rtooth Highway between Red Lodge and Cooke City

GERANIUM FAMILY   Geraniaceae

The geranium family, represented by just two genera in Montana, includes only a few species of wildflowers, identifiable by alternate or opposite leaves that are palmately divided into three to five major segments, and pistils that develop on maturity into a long "beak." Geranium comes from the Greek word *geranos*, meaning "crane," referring to this beaklike structure. The leaves of most geraniums have a distinctive aroma. The flowers are normally conspicuous and are usually constructed with five petals and five free or united sepals. The number of stamens is two to three times the number of petals and some may be sterile.

Crane's-bill   *Erodium cicutarium*

Also called *filaree* and *stork's-bill*, crane's-bill is a mat-forming annual with hairy, somewhat reddish, 2- to 12-inch-long stems that arise from a flat rosette of pinnately compound, fernlike leaves. Opposite stem leaves are attached at swollen nodes. Two to ten small, bright pink flowers, $\frac{1}{4}$ to $\frac{1}{2}$ inch in diameter, are arranged in clusters on long leafless stalks that arise from leaf axils. Each flower has five petals, five bristle-tipped sepals, and ten stamens, five of which are sterile.

Crane's-bill takes its name from the shape of the seed pod, which resembles the head of a stork with its downward-pointing bill. Crane's-bill was introduced from Europe and is sometimes so widespread it has been called a weed—one with a very pretty flower!

HABITAT/RANGE: Found on clearings, disturbed soils, open fields, and dry plains or moist soils from valleys to foothills in west, central, and northeast Montana.

White Geranium   *Geranium richardsonii*

White geranium may reach a height of $2\frac{1}{2}$ feet. Most of the leaves are basal on long petioles, but a few small leaves are present on the stem. The large, palmately divided leaves have five to seven deeply divided segments that are coarsely toothed on their edges. The five white or pinkish petals are hairy on the inner part of the upper side, with distinctive purplish veins. Flower stalks are covered with purplish-tipped glandular hairs. White geranium may hybridize with other species and make identification difficult. Hybridization with sticky geranium (*G. viscosissimum*) produces a plant with pink instead of red flowers.

The species name honors Sir John Richardson (1787-1842), an English surgeon and botanist who served as physician on three different expeditions to the Arctic.

HABITAT/RANGE: Prefers partially shaded areas in woods from low to montane and subalpine zones in west and central Montana.

Crane's-bill in mid-June
on the National Bison
Range west of St. Ignatius

White geranium in late June in an open
wooded area along Battle Ridge in the Gallatin
National Forest north of Bozeman

Sticky Geranium — *Geranium viscosissimum*

The slightly hairy multiple stems of sticky geranium may reach 3 feet tall, bearing mostly basal palmate leaves that are deeply divided into five to seven segments having sharp irregular teeth along the edges. The brilliant flowers have five broad petals, hairy on the inner surface, varying from pinkish lavender to violet or purple and having dark reddish purple veins. When the petals fall off, the stigma and style elongate into a 1-inch-long structure that resembles the bill of a crane. Glandular hairs on the sepals and leaf stems make the plant sticky, exuding a substance that has a geranium-like aroma.

HABITAT/RANGE: Found in meadows or open woods from foothills to subalpine zones in west and central Montana.

HAREBELL FAMILY — Campanulaceae

The harebell family, sometimes called the *bluebell* or *bellflower family*, is characterized by bell-shaped flowers that may be blue, lavender, or even white. The corolla of the flower has five petals fused into a tube with five lobes. Each flower has five sepals and five stamens attached to the top of an inferior ovary. Flowers are usually arranged in racemes, sometimes in cymes or with several in the axils of the bracts of a raceme. Leaves are usually alternate and mostly simple. The stems contain a milky juice.

Common Harebell — *Campanula rotundifolia*

Harebell, also called *scotch harebell* and *bluebell*, may grow to a height of 20 inches but may be only a few inches tall at alpine elevations. Basal leaves are round and usually wither when this perennial is in bloom. The stem leaves are long, very narrow, and alternate. A milky juice exudes from broken leaves. Many bell-shaped, bluish violet, nodding flowers, with five lobes that bend back, hang on thin stalks along the slender stem. Only a single large flower may be present on plants growing at high elevations. The style is nearly as long as the petals.

HABITAT/RANGE: Adapted to a variety of habitats from lowland meadows to alpine slopes, preferring dry or well-drained soils in west, central, and east Montana.

Sticky geranium in early July along Moose Creek east
of U.S. 191 in Gallatin Canyon south of Bozeman

Common harebell in mid-July at Pintler Lake in the Anaconda Range north of Wisdom

HEATH FAMILY   Ericaceae

The heath family, sometimes called the *wintergreen family* and represented by seventeen genera in Montana, includes some rather unusual appearing but attractive wildflowers, although most members are shrubs and a few are trees. See **Shrubs** for kinnikinnick (*Arctostaphylos uva-ursi*), big huckleberry (*Vaccinium membranaceum*), swamp laurel (*Kalmia microphylla*), and pink mountain heather (*Phyllodoce empetriformis*). Members have urn-shaped, open funnel-shaped, or flared brightly colored flowers with parts mostly in fives—five petals, five sepals, ten stamens, and five compartments in the ovary. The pistil has a single delicate style and stigma. The evergreen leaves are leathery, simple, and usually alternate on the stem.

Pipsissewa   *Chimaphila umbellata*

Pipsissewa, also called *prince's pine*, is a low, evergreen semishrub, usually less than 1 foot tall and woody only near its base. The leathery, waxy leaves with toothed edges are arranged in whorls along the stem. The nodding, saucer-shaped flowers have five pink to rose-colored, separated petals and ten stamens surrounding a conspicuous green ovary. A related species that grows in western Montana, **little pipsissewa (C. menziesii)**, differs in being shorter and having smaller leaves.

Pipsissewa has been used to flavor candy, root beer, and beer—uses that have resulted in overcollecting. The leaves and berries are edible, and the stems and roots have been used to make tea. American Indians used the plant for a variety of medicinal purposes, and sometimes dried the leaves for smoking.

HABITAT/RANGE: Found in coniferous forests and on subalpine slopes that are moist early in the season and dry later on in west and central Montana.

Pinedrops   *Pterospora andromedea*

Pinedrops demonstrates the versatility and diversity in plant design among the wildflowers—this perennial has no chlorophyll and obtains nutrients from fungi that survive on the dead and decaying plant material on forest floors. Pinedrops grows as a solitary or with just a few unbranched stems that reach 3 feet tall. Reddish brown scales, not leaves, cover the hairy, sticky, and fleshy stem. Bell-shaped, yellow flowers on curved stalks hang downward from the stem in an open raceme. The flower petals are united into a vase-shaped structure with spreading lips at the opening.

HABITAT/RANGE: Found alone or with a few close neighbors in montane to subalpine coniferous forests in west, central, and southeast Montana.

Pipsissewa in early August at Crystal Lake in the Big Snowy Mountains near Lewistown

Pinedrops in mid-July in the backwoods of the Swan Valley north of Seeley Lake

Pink Pyrola   *Pyrola asarifolia*

The leafless stem of pink pyrola is 6 to 12 inches tall, with a basal rosette of shiny, green, round, leathery leaves about 1 to 3 inches in diameter. The pink to purplish flowers face downward in a long, narrow raceme. A conspicuous long green style hangs beyond the petals, curving upward like an elephant's trunk.

Pyrola comes from Latin, meaning "pear," a reference to the shape of the leaves of this wildflower.

HABITAT/RANGE: Prefers moist soils in shaded woods and near springs from the plains to mountains up to 9,000 feet in west and central Montana.

Green-flowered Wintergreen   *Pyrola chlorantha*

The erect stem of green-flowered wintergreen, an inconspicuous perennial, is 4 to 10 inches tall, with mostly round to egg-shaped basal leaves that are sometimes toothed on the margins. The leaves are held on long petioles and are a darker green on the lower surface. Two to eight flowers are arranged in a raceme at the end of the stem. Each downward-facing flower has greenish white to yellowish green petals. The style of the flower protrudes beyond the petals and curves downward. *Wintergreen*, a common name for all *Pyrola* species, refers to the persistent nature of the leaves into winter.

HABITAT/RANGE: Prefers moist and humus-rich soils in shady montane to subalpine forests in west and central Montana.

One-sided Wintergreen   *Pyrola secunda*

One-sided wintergreen, also called *sidebells pyrola*, has unbranched, 2- to 6-inch-tall stems. Egg-shaped or elliptic, alternate leaves, which crowd the lower stem, are bright green, shiny, and usually toothed on the margins. Six to twenty small, bell-shaped, greenish white flowers hang from one side of the upper part of the stem, bending it downward. A long straight style with a blunt stigma extends beyond the corolla of each flower.

HABITAT/RANGE: Prefers moist coniferous forests from montane to subalpine zones in west and south-central Montana.

Wood Nymph   *Pyrola uniflora*
                                           Moneses uniflora

It is easy to overlook wood nymph, also called *one-flowered wintergreen*, because a single, nodding flower blooms at the end of a short stem no more than 6 inches tall. A whorl of shiny, round, veined, toothed, evergreen leaves grow at the base of the stem. Five petals with wavy margins are spread around a very prominent green ovary with five lobes. Ten stamens with terminal pores on their anthers and swollen bases surround the ovary. The flowers have a very faint pleasant odor.

HABITAT/RANGE: Common on moist soils in coniferous forests at low to middle elevations in west and central Montana.

Pink pyrola in early July along Moose Creek in the Little Belt Mountains north of White Sulphur Springs

Green-flowered wintergreen in late July along Flint Creek Road east of Georgetown Lake

One-sided wintergreen in late July near Georgetown Lake west of Anaconda

Wood nymph in late July near the base of the Beartooth Highway south of Red Lodge

HONEYSUCKLE FAMILY   Caprifoliaceae

Most of the plants included in the honeysuckle family, represented in Montana by five genera, are shrubs or woody vines. See **Shrubs** for black elderberry (*Sambucus racemosa*) and red twinberry (*Lonicera utahensis*). The opposite leaves are simple or pinnately divided. The flowers, arranged in a branched or forked cluster, have five petals that are fused into the shape of a funnel or trumpet. Each flower has five sepals and usually five stamens, equal to the number of corolla lobes. The pistil is compound with one or no style, one to five small, often lobed stigmas, and an inferior ovary. The calyx has four or usually five lobes on the rim of a floral cup that completely encloses the ovary.

Twinflower   *Linnaea borealis*

Twinflower is trailing woody vine that spreads over the ground surface, often creating large carpets of flowers over the forest floor. Short stems arise at nodes along these branches, bearing small, egg-shaped, opposite leaves that sometimes have a few shallow teeth along the margins of the outer half of the leaf. The flower stem is about 4 inches high, split at the top into two slender stalks that support nodding, bell-shaped, pink or lavender flowers with hairy throats.

> HABITAT/RANGE: Found in cool moist coniferous forests, woods, and thickets in west, central, and southeast Montana.

Orange Honeysuckle   *Lonicera ciliosa*

Orange honeysuckle, also called *trumpet honeysuckle*, is a vine that climbs 15 to 30 feet over other trees, shrubs, or fences. The broadly oval leaves, opposite on the stem and hairless except along the edges, are dark green above and whitish below. The pair of leaves below the flower is fused and wrapped around the stem. A cluster of showy, orangish yellow or orangish red, trumpet-shaped flowers are 1 inch or more long and supported by a single stem that is cradled within the upper leaves.

> HABITAT/RANGE: Prefers moist soils on hillsides, in canyons, and in open or deep woods at low to middle elevations in northwest Montana.

Twinflower in late June
northeast of Swan Lake

Orange honeysuckle in late June on the east side of Swan Lake southeast of Bigfork

IRIS FAMILY   Iridaceae

Members of the iris family are monocots and may be confused with members of the lily family, but lilies have six stamens. The narrow basal leaves of irises are folded lengthwise, resembling grass, and enfold younger leaves. The often showy, radially symmetrical flowers, located at the terminal end of the stem or in panicles, have three petal-like sepals, three petals, three stamens, and a single style that is usually three-lobed with three and sometimes six stigmas. Two bracts below the flower are usually papery or dried when the flower is mature. The family is represented by two genera in Montana.

Rocky Mountain Iris   *Iris missouriensis*

Rocky Mountain iris, also called *Missouri iris* and *blueflag*, has 8- to 24-inch-tall stems with two or more long, narrow, parallel-veined basal leaves. Each of the clumped stems bears two to four pale to dark blue flowers with purple stripes. Three petal-like sepals, with purple lines and yellow center stripes, bend backward and downward. The three narrower petals are erect.

Meriwether Lewis collected this wildflower in 1806 near Ovando. The roots and young shoots of Rocky Mountain iris are toxic, causing a burning sensation, difficult breathing, vomiting, and diarrhea. Some individuals demonstrate allergic skin reactions to the plant. American Indians used the roots for treating toothache.

HABITAT/RANGE: Prefers moist or marshy soils on open plains and meadows at lower elevations in west and central Montana.

Yellow Iris   *Iris pseudacorus*

Yellow iris, a species introduced from Europe that escaped cultivation, stands about 3 feet tall and grows in shallow water. The broad leaves are stiff and pointed. Showy pale to bright yellow, three-parted flowers, about 4 inches wide, sometimes have purple markings.

HABITAT/RANGE: Grows in areas with permanent shallow water along the shores of streams and ponds and in roadside ditches, often with cattails (*Typha* species), in west Montana.

Blue-eyed Grass   *Sisyrinchium angustifolium*
                                                  S. montanum

Blue-eyed grass has a flat stem that is usually 4 to 10 inches tall but can be taller. The stiff, grasslike basal leaves are shorter than the stem and folded lengthwise. One to five starlike flowers occur on each stem in an umbel. Each flower has six pale to dark blue finely pointed petal-like sepals that arise from a short tube with a yellow center and yellow anthers. Two long, pointed leaflike bracts that are unequal in length are located below the flowers.

HABITAT/RANGE: Found on grassy meadows or in open sites that are moist to moderately dry from the plains to subalpine zones in west, central, and northeast Montana.

Rocky Mountain iris in late June at Red Rock Lakes National
Wildlife Refuge west of West Yellowstone

Yellow iris in early June in a pond at Lee Metcalf
National Wildlife Refuge near Stevensville

Blue-eyed grass in early
June west of Augusta

LILY FAMILY   Liliaceae

The lily family, represented by twenty-four genera in Montana, includes many familiar plants such as onions, lilies, and asparagus. Most members of the lily family have fleshy leaves with parallel veins running from the base to the tip. The flowers have three petals and three petal-like sepals, often arranged in two circles. The flowers are often showy but sometimes small and inconspicuous. Flowers may be solitary or arranged in spikes, racemes, or panicles.

Short-styled Onion   *Allium brevistylum*

Short-styled onion has a 10- to 20-inch-tall stem that flattens near the top and does not bend like that of nodding onion (*A. cernuum*). Several shorter, flat, grasslike leaves arise from the base of the stem. The erect cluster of pink to rose-purple flowers are supported by stalks that join at their bottom like an inverted umbrella. Papery, united bracts enclose the juncture of the flower stalks with the stem. The petals and petal-like sepals are longer than the style and stamens, inspiring the name *short-styled onion*.

Short-styled onion is edible, with an onion or garlic odor, and is eaten by many wild animals, including bear and elk.

HABITAT/RANGE: Found on wet soils in meadows, along streams, and on wooded slopes from montane to subalpine zones in west and central Montana.

Nodding Onion   *Allium cernuum*

The smooth, round, leafless stems of nodding onion are 6 to 20 inches tall, with three to seven 2- to 10-inch-long, grasslike, flat or concave leaves that emerge from the base of the stem. The tip of the stem is crooked where it holds the distinctive nodding head of white or pinkish flowers that hang on slender stalks, resembling a starburst. Each flower has three petals, three petal-like sepals, and six prominent yellow-tipped stamens that protrude beyond the petals and sepals.

Nodding onion is edible, with an onion taste. Wildlife feed on the bulbs and leaves in spring, and when dairy cows eat it, their milk develops an onion flavor.

HABITAT/RANGE: Prefers moist to well-drained soils on open hillsides, grasslands, and sagebrush steppes from the foothills to subalpine zones in west, central, and southeast Montana.

Short-styled onion in late June along Battle Ridge
in the Bridger Range north of Bozeman

Nodding onion
in late July in the
Pioneer Mountains
south of Wise River

Geyer's Onion   *Allium geyeri*

Geyer's onion has a 4- to 20-inch-tall stem and three or more grasslike basal leaves, slightly shorter than the stems, which have parallel veins. The flowers are arranged in a cluster with two to three papery bracts. The six stamens in each flower are shorter than the pointed petals and petal-like sepals, which are usually pink but sometimes white. Geyer's onion has two varieties: *A. geyeri* var. *tenerum* grows in the central Rocky Mountains, and among its long-stalked flowers are stalkless, egg-shaped bulbs that sprout after falling to the ground, providing an asexual form of reproduction. *A. geyeri* var. *geyeri* lacks the asexual bulbs.

American Indians used the leaves and bulbs as food, eaten raw or cooked.

HABITAT/RANGE: Found in wet meadows and along streams from the foothills to alpine zones in west, central, and southeast Montana.

Chives   *Allium schoenoprasum*

Chives, also called *Siberian chives*, has a round, hollow, 8- to 18-inch-tall stem and usually two round, alternate leaves that wrap around the stem base. The dense flower head may contain as many as thirty bell-shaped, pink or rose-colored flowers on short stems, each consisting of three petals and three petal-like sepals that are lance-shaped and flare outward a bit at their tips.

The leaves, bulbs, and flower heads of chives are edible and can be used like the domestic plant. Be careful not to confuse the bulbs with those of the deadly mountain death camas (*Zigadenus elegans*), which can be distinguished by the absence of an onion aroma.

HABITAT/RANGE: Prefers moist to wet soils in meadows and open areas from valleys to alpine zones in west and south-central Montana.

Textile Onion   *Allium textile*

Textile onion, also called *prairie onion*, has several erect stems that are 3 to 10 inches tall and arise from a buried bulb. Two to four narrow, folded, threadlike leaves have a strong odor and taste of onion. Five to fifty-four white flowers, sometimes pale pink with deep purple lines, are arranged in a tight cluster at the top of the stem, and papery bracts enclose the base of the cluster. Each flower has three petals and three sepals.

Meriwether Lewis described textile onion in his journal in 1805, noting that the cooked bulbs were quite "agreeable." Various medicinal properties have been attributed to textile onion, including antimicrobial activities. The bulbs have long been used for treating indigestion and were once believed to cure sexual impotency.

HABITAT/RANGE: Grows in a variety of habitats from dry prairie meadows to hillsides and foothills across much of Montana.

Top left: Geyer's onion with asexual bulbs in early July in the Gravelly Range south of Ennis

Top right: Textile onion in mid-June in a forest campground near Landusky

Chives along the wet shore of Crystal Lake in the Big Snowy Mountains near Lewistown

🌿 Mariposa and Sego Lilies *Calochortus* species 🌿

The *Calochortus* genus has seven members in Montana, all beauties, as suggested by the name *mariposa*, which means "butterfly" in Spanish. The three sepals are always narrower than the broad, hairy petals, but flower variations within a species make identification difficult. The sweet, nutritious bulbs of mariposa lilies can be used in salads but are usually boiled, roasted, or steamed.

Pointed Mariposa Lily   *Calochortus apiculatus*

Pointed mariposa lily has distinct dark purple dots (glands) at the base and center of each of the three petals. The erect 6- to 12-inch-tall stem, which grows from a bulb, has a single short, narrow, pointed basal leaf and a few leafy bracts near the top. Each stem may bear one to five flowers with oval, yellowish white petals, pointed at their tips and hairy on the lower half of the inner surface and along the edges. The narrow sepals are shorter than the petals.

Hairy cat's ears (*C. elegans*) resembles pointed mariposa lily but has crescent-shaped glands at the petal bases, sepals that are just slightly shorter than the petals, and a much hairier, greenish white petal surface. The 2- to 6-inch-tall stem has a single narrow basal leaf that is tapered at both ends and is longer than the flowers stalks.

HABITAT/RANGE: Pointed mariposa lily is found in dry open or partly shaded forests from the foothills to montane zones in northwest Montana. Hairy cat's ear grows in meadows, grasslands, or forest margins from the foothills to subalpine zones in western Montana.

Big-pod Mariposa Lily   *Calochortus eurycarpus*

Big-pod mariposa lily has three narrow, long, conspicuous sepals and a bright yellow oval gland within a purple ring at the base of the petal. A brilliant purple arch hovers over a greenish zone above this gland. The grasslike basal leaf is much shorter than the stem, which bears a few short bracts.

HABITAT/RANGE: Found on open slopes, in grasslands, and in forests up to montane zones in west Montana, primarily in the southwest.

Gunnison's Mariposa Lily   *Calochortus gunnisonii*

The unbranched stem of Gunnison's mariposa lily is 10 to 20 inches tall, with several grasslike basal leaves that have parallel veins and are V-shaped in cross section. The stem leaves get shorter toward the top. The flower has three broad, white or cream-colored petals, which may have a greenish tinge, that are separated by shorter, narrow, pointed sepals. The petals have a broad purple band near their base covered with yellowish hairs.

HABITAT/RANGE: Prefers the grassy prairies, foothills, and open forests at lower elevations east of the Rocky Mountains in central Montana.

...inted Mariposa lily in late June on the forest floor along Montana 83 south of Swan Lake

Center left: Hairy cat's ears in early June on the forest floor at the Sam Billings Memorial Campground southwest of Darby

Bottom left: Big-pod mariposa lily in mid-July along Pintler Lake north of Wisdom

Bottom right: Gunnison's mariposa lily in early July near Ackley Lake west of U.S. 191 and north of Harlowton

Sego Lily   *Calochortus nuttallii*

Sego lily, also called *Nuttall's mariposa lily*, most closely resembles big-pod mariposa lily (*C. eurycarpus*), but that species mainly occurs in southwest Montana. The unbranched stems of sego lily are 6 to 18 inches tall, with several grasslike leaves at the base and a few short bractlike leaves on the stem. The white, cream, or lavender flowers have three large, broad, tipped petals separated by shorter, narrow sepals that are greenish to purplish on the outside and pale on the inside. A large dark spot (gland) at the base of each petal is surrounded by yellow hairs and capped by a broad, purplish crescent.

Sego lily is the state flower of Utah, where its sweet, starchy, bulblike roots helped relieve the famine faced by Brigham Young and his followers in 1847.

HABITAT/RANGE: Prefers dry soils among sagebrush and in grassy mountain foothills across Montana.

Camas   *Camassia quamash*

Camas, also called *blue camas*, is a perennial that emerges from an edible bulb. The smooth, slender, unbranched stem is 8 to 24 inches tall, with three or four grasslike leaves at the base. The bright blue to purplish flowers, which may occasionally be light blue or white, are arranged in a loose raceme with those on the bottom opening first. Each flower has three petal-like sepals and three petals arranged in a star. There are six prominent yellow stamens and a single style. A narrow leafy bract is located below each flower.

American Indians ate camas raw, boiled, or roasted, or as flour in bread. Clark described a meadow of Camas flowers like this: "resembles a lake of fine clear water, so complete in this deception that on first sight I could have sworn it was water."

HABITAT/RANGE: Prefers moist or boggy mountain meadows and streambanks on forested hillsides in west Montana.

Queen's Cup   *Clintonia uniflora*

Queen's cup, also called *blue beadlily*, has a short, leafless, 3- to 8-inch-long stem that emerges from a basal rosette of two or three elliptic, shiny, parallel-veined leaves with hairy margins. The leaves are 3 to 8 inches long and one-third as wide. A solitary flower at the end of the stem has three white petals and three similar, white sepals that spread outward in the shape of an open bell, revealing six yellow stamens.

The blue berries of queen's cup, which occur as single fruits, resemble beads and are considered inedible although reportedly are eaten by grouse.

HABITAT/RANGE: Prefers moist soils in shaded coniferous forests or forest clearings from the foothills to subalpine zones in west Montana.

Sego lily in mid-June on dry soils among sagebrush at Bighorn Canyon National Recreation Area in south-central Montana

Camas in early June near Lake Alva along Montana 83 north of Seeley Lake

Queen's cup in late June in a shaded forest near Hungry Horse Reservoir east of Kalispell

Fairy-bells   *Disporum* **species**

Fairy-bells have 1- to 3-foot-tall stems with occasional branching. The alternate, egg- to lance-shaped leaves clasp the stem and have conspicuous parallel veins. Narrow, bell-shaped, creamy white flowers, often in pairs, hang on short stalks that arise from the end of the stems. A pair of terminal leaves tend to hide the flowers. The three petal-like sepals and three petals flare outward, revealing the slightly longer stamens. Two similar species grow in Montana: **Wartberry fairy-bell (***D. trachycarpum***)** has bumps on its red berry. **Hooker's fairy-bell (***D. hookeri***)** has smooth berries and hairier leaves.

HABITAT/RANGE: Found in moist forests, along streambanks, or in subalpine meadows in northwest Montana.

Glacier Lily   *Erythronium grandiflorum*

Glacier lily has 2- to 15-inch-tall stems that hold nodding, bright yellow flowers. Two parallel-veined, 4- to 8-inch-long, broad leaves emerge from the base of the stem. Six brilliant yellow petals and petal-like sepals spread backward, exposing six yellowish to purplish anthers.

American Indians ate the thickened underground stems, which are also a favorite of grizzly bears.

HABITAT/RANGE: Glacier lily follows the receding snow from the foothills to subalpine forests in west and south-central Montana.

Yellow Bell   *Fritillaria pudica*

Although rising just 4 to 10 inches tall, yellow bell is rarely overlooked when it appears in early spring. The long linear leaves, usually a pair or sometimes a whorl of three, are either basal or located midway up the unbranched stem. The single nodding, bell-shaped flower has three petals and three petal-like sepals, which are bright yellow to orange at first but turn red or even purple as they age. The stamens and style are concealed deep inside the bell.

Meriwether Lewis collected a specimen of this flower in Idaho in 1806. The bulblike corm is edible.

HABITAT/RANGE: Found on moist soils in open forests, on grassy prairies, and on sagebrush steppes at montane and subalpine zones in west, central, and southeast Montana.

Sand Lily   *Leucocrinum montanum*

Sand lily, also called *star lily*, reaches no more than 8 inches tall. A clump of grasslike, 8-inch-long leaves, which originate from a root below the ground, cradle the stemless flowers. The star-shaped, white, 1- to $1^{1}/_{4}$-inch-wide flowers have three petals and three petal-like sepals that are fused at their base into a 1- to 3-inch-long tube that is attached underground. Each flower contains six long stamens with yellow anthers.

HABITAT/RANGE: Prefers well-drained soils on sagebrush steppes and in open coniferous forests east of the Continental Divide.

isporum species in early May at Sluice Boxes State Park west of U.S. 89 and south of Great Falls

Left: Glacier lily on May 1 in Bear Creek Canyon in the Gallatin National Forest near Bozeman

Right: Yellow bell in mid-April in the Tobacco Root Mountains west of Pony

Sand lily in mid-May in an open field along Montana 39 south of Colstrip

Wood Lily
Lilium philadelphicum

The unbranched, erect stem of wood lily is 1 to 2 feet tall, bearing long, narrow, alternate leaves near the base and leaves in whorls near the top. Each stem usually has one funnel-shaped flower that has six similar bright orange to brick red, 2- to 3-inch-long petals and sepals with purple spots near the bottom and large anthers. Wood lily is a rare plant, possibly due to frequent removal by humans.

HABITAT/RANGE: Found in meadows, grasslands, and open forests, especially in aspen groves, from the foothills to montane zones in northwest, central, and southeast Montana.

False Solomon's Seal
Smilacina racemosa
Maianthemum racemosum

False Solomon's seal, also called *false lily of the valley*, resembles starry Solomon-plume (*S. stellata*), and they often grow together, but false Solomon's seal differs in having numerous tiny white flowers in a dense panicle. The erect or slightly bent stems are 2 to 3 feet tall. The alternate, long, broad leaves have pointed tips and clasp the stem or are held on a short stalk.

HABITAT/RANGE: Grows in dense patches on moist soils under trees and tall shrubs from the foothills to subalpine zones in west, central, and southeast Montana.

Starry Solomon-plume
Smilacina stellata
Maianthemum stellatum

Starry Solomon-plume, also called *star-flowered false Solomon's seal* and *starry false lily of the valley*, has an unbranched, leafy stem that grows 8 to 24 inches tall. The lance-shaped, stalkless leaves have prominent parallel veins, are up to 6 inches long, and alternate on the stem. About five to ten or more $1/_4$-inch-wide, white starlike flowers are arranged in an unbranched inflorescence at the top of the stem.

HABITAT/RANGE: Prefers moist soils in shaded forests, in meadows, and along streams from montane to subalpine zones in west, central, and east Montana.

Twisted Stalk
Streptopus amplexifolius

Twisted stalk has leafy, $1^1/_2$- to 3-foot-tall stems that appear to twist at each leaf attachment. The broad, lance-shaped leaves clasp the stem. Some branches of the stem arise from leaf axils. A single white to greenish flower hangs under each leaf, supported by a long slender flower stalk that has an unusual twist or kink. The three petals and three sepals flare at their tips.

HABITAT/RANGE: Prefers very moist soils along streambanks and wet areas and in montane forests and thickets in west and central Montana.

ood lily in mid-July near
stal Lake in the Big Snowy
untains near Lewistown

False Solomon's seal in late June along Battle Ridge
in the Bridger Range north of Bozeman

ry Solomon-plume in late May at Missouri
Headwaters State Park near Three Forks

Twisted stalk in early July along Moose Creek
in the Little Belt Mountains west of U.S. 89
and north of White Sulphur Springs

Trillium
Trillium ovatum

Trillium, also called *wake robin*, is a beautiful perennial whose appearance is a welcome sign of spring. Three broad, egg-shaped leaves, arranged in a whorl from a common point on the stem, cradle the single white, showy flower located at the tip of the 4- to 15-inch-tall stem. The flower has three green sepals and three white, egg-shaped petals that turn pinkish or purple with age. Each flower includes six conspicuous stamens and three long styles.

HABITAT/RANGE: Found early in the season when soils in coniferous forests are still very wet from melting snows in west Montana.

Wild Hyacinth
Triteleia grandiflora
Brodiaea douglasii

Wild hyacinth, a perennial that grows from a bulblike root, has an erect, leafless, 1- to 3-foot-tall stem with one or two shorter, grasslike basal leaves. Five to fifteen blue, tubular flowers are arranged in an umbel at the top of the stem. Each flower is about 1 inch long, is attached by a short flower stalk, and consists of fused petals and petal-like sepals, the three outer ones flared outward and the three inner ones ruffled, narrowing the tube mouth. The petals and sepals have prominent dark center stripes. Wild hyacinth might be confused with nodding onion (*Allium cernuum*) and camas (*Camassia quamash*), but can be distinguished by the fused petals and sepals. In addition, camas flowers are arranged in a raceme rather than an umbel.

American Indians and early settlers dug the roots of wild hyacinth in spring and ate them fresh or cooked.

HABITAT/RANGE: Prefers dry to moist but well-drained soils of grasslands, sagebrush steppe, and open pine forests from valleys to foothills in west and south-central Montana.

False Hellebore
Veratrum viride

False hellebore, also called *corn lily*, is a tall cornstalk-like perennial that grows in dense patches of 3- to 6-foot-tall stems. The oblong, basal leaves, sometimes 10 to 14 inches long, have conspicuous parallel veins and clasp the stem. The upper leaves are similar but smaller. The small white or greenish yellow flowers are clustered in a branched panicle. The lower branches of the panicle often droop.

False hellebore contains toxic alkaloids, one of which is called *veratrum*, that often poison domestic animals feeding on the plants in early spring. Drinking the water in which the plant is growing can cause stomach cramps. Native Americans used false hellebore to poison arrows and commit suicide.

HABITAT/RANGE: Grows on moist soils in lowland areas and in mountain meadows and thickets in west and south-central Montana.

...um in late April in Leverich Canyon in the
Gallatin National Forest near Bozeman

False hellebore in late June along the
east side of Hungry Horse Reservoir

Wild hyacinth in early June at Harpers Lake near the junction
of Montana 83 and Montana 200 south of Seeley Lake

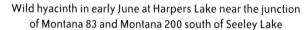

Beargrass   *Xerophyllum tenax*

When in bloom, beargrass is a conspicuous plant, the erect stem reaching 3 to 5 feet tall. Clumps of evergreen, grasslike leaves may represent the only growth of beargrass for several seasons before the flowering stalk arises. The dead stalk may still be visible the following year. The stiff leaves at the base of the plant are 1 to 2 feet long, while those higher on the stem get progressively shorter. The sharp edges of the leaves are lined with stiff, short hairs. The small, white or cream-colored flowers are arranged in a dense, conical raceme.

Meriwether Lewis commented on the use of the leaves of beargrass by American Indians for weaving watertight baskets.

HABITAT/RANGE: Prefers drained soils in open woods and clearings and on mountain slopes from 3,000 to 8,000 feet elevation, primarily west of the Continental Divide, in west and central Montana.

Great Plains Yucca   *Yucca glauca*

Great plains yucca, also called *Spanish bayonet*, is sometimes placed in the agave family rather than the lily family. The 1- to 5-foot-tall, upright stem rises above the basal clump of stiff evergreen leaves, which are 10 to 33 inches long and shaped like narrow daggers. The leaves are covered with a fine powder that rubs off when touched. The 2- to 3-inch-long, creamy or greenish white flowers are arranged in a conspicuous raceme along the top of the stem. Each flower has three broad, thick petals and three similar sepals that surround six stamens and a single green style.

Yucca blossoms open in the evening and are pollinated by small moths that lay their eggs in the plant's ovary, where the insect larvae will later feed on some of the seeds. American Indians used the pods of yucca for food, the leaf fibers for making ropes, and the roots for making soap.

HABITAT/RANGE: Prefers dry well-drained sandy soils of the plains and foothills in southwest, central, and east Montana.

Top left and right: Beargrass in late June in an open forest in the Flint Creek Range near Georgetown Lake

Great Plains yucca in mid-June along a sandy roadside north of Judith Landing on the Missouri River east of Fort Benton

Mountain Death Camas   *Zigadenus elegans*

Mountain death camas, also called *elegant camas*, has a 1- to 2-foot-tall, slender stem with long, narrow leaves that are mostly basal. The flowers are arranged on the stem in a raceme. The six flower parts—three broad, creamy white petals and three similar petal-like sepals—form a striking, starlike blossom and have a distinctive yellowish green, deeply lobed, heart-shaped gland at their base. Each flower has six stamens and three styles, all boldly exposed. The $^1/_2$-inch-wide flower of mountain death camas distinguishes it from **meadow death camas (*Z. venenosus*)**, which has a $^1/_4$-inch-wide flower.

Death camases contain an alkaloid that is extremely toxic and has been responsible for the death of livestock, especially sheep, and humans. American Indians and early settlers were poisoned by mistaking the bulbs of these plants for the edible bulbs of camas (*Camassia quamash*). Meriwether Lewis collected a specimen of mountain death camas in 1806 along the Blackfoot River.

HABITAT/RANGE: Mountain death camas grows in grassy mountain meadows and forests, and along streambanks from montane to subalpine zones in west, central, and east Montana. Meadow death camas grows on plains, sagebrush slopes, and grassy foothills up to montane forests and alpine meadows in west, central, and east Montana.

MADDER FAMILY   **Rubiaceae**

The large madder family includes mostly tropical plants, but two genera are represented in Montana. Members of this family have radially symmetrical flowers that are borne in branched clusters with the terminal flower blooming first. The leaves are simple, usually entire, opposite or whorled, and include stipules. Each white or brightly colored flower has four or five sepals, four or five fused petals, and four or five stamens, all parts attached at the top of the ovary.

Northern Bedstraw   *Galium boreale*

The square stem of northern bedstraw is 8 to 20 inches tall, with four narrow, lance-shaped leaves arranged in whorls at nodes that are sometimes the origin of secondary branches. Numerous rounded masses of white or cream-colored flowers are arranged in panicles. Each tiny starlike flower has four petals, no sepals, four stamens, and two styles. Eight species of bedstraw are found in Montana; some have hooked hairs on the stems or bristles on the fruit.

The square, sweet-smelling stems of bedstraw are hollow and have been used as straw in mattresses.

HABITAT/RANGE: Prefers moist soils in open areas such as grasslands and open forests from low to alpine zones in west, central, and east Montana.

Mountain death camas in late July in the Gravelly Range south of Ennis

Northern bedstraw in late June in an open wet area along Montana 83 south of Swan Lake

Top and bottom right: Meadow death camas in late May along U.S. 191 at the mouth of Gallatin Canyon south of Bozeman

MALLOW FAMILY   Malvaceae

The mallow family, represented by seven genera in Montana, includes several familiar plants, such as ornamental hollyhocks, hibiscus, and cotton. Family members have alternate, simple leaves that are often palmately veined and lobed and have stipules. The often showy flowers are usually bisexual, borne single or in clusters, and have three to five sepals and five broad petals. A key characteristic for recognition is a tassel of stamens fused into a tube at their base where they attach to the petals.

Wild Hollyhock   *Iliamna rivularis*

Wild hollyhock has a 3- to 6-foot-tall, unbranched stem with large, maple-like leaves that are deeply divided into three to seven toothed lobes. The pinkish white to rosy lavender, cup-shaped flowers are arranged in a long, loose raceme near the top of the stem. The 1- to 2-inch-wide flowers have five broad petals, blunt-tipped sepals located above three thin bracts, and numerous stamens fused at the base around a branched style that ends in knobbed stigmas.

The seeds of wild hollyhock germinate best after scouring by water or fire.

HABITAT/RANGE: Prefers rich moist soils along roads and streams in canyons from the foothills to subalpine zones in west and south-central Montana.

Scarlet Globemallow   *Sphaeralcea coccinea*

Scarlet globemallow, a low, spreading perennial, often forms patches of flowers. The stems are usually less than 8 inches long. The small leaves, yellowish green above and gray below, are alternate and deeply divided into three to five segments. The gray appearance is due to star-shaped hairs, the star shape visible only with a hand lens. The saucer-shaped, short-stalked flowers, arranged in racemes, vary from orange to brick red. Each flower has five broad petals that have shallow notches at their tips, five reddish hairy sepals, and stamens fused at their base.

Meriwether Lewis collected a specimen of scarlet globemallow from the plains along the Marias River in 1806. Dakota Indians chewed this plant, which contains a sticky sap, and used it to treat wounds and promote healing of inflamed sores.

HABITAT/RANGE: Prefers dry soils in open areas, growing from prairies to montane zones, primarily east of the Continental Divide in west, central, and east Montana.

Wild hollyhock in mid-July along North Fork Lost Creek in the Swan Valley north of Seeley Lake

Scarlet globemallow in late May at Tongue River Reservoir State Park in south-central Montana

MILKWEED FAMILY   Asclepiadaceae

The large milkweed family, represented by a single genus in Montana, is characterized by a milky juice in the stems. The leaves are simple, usually opposite and arranged in whorls on the stem. The flowers are mostly small with parts in fives—five sepals and a corolla composed of five united petals, all arranged in umbel-like clusters.

Showy Milkweed   *Asclepias speciosa*

Showy milkweed, a stout perennial, has 2- to 4-foot-tall, unbranched stems that bear long, egg-shaped, opposite leaves with conspicuous veins and held on short petioles. Short grayish hairs cover the stem and leaves, which if broken exude a milky juice. Flowers arranged in umbels arise from the axils of upper leaves. Each small, star-shaped flower has five reddish sepals concealed by five pinkish or purplish, lance-shaped petals that are bent sharply backward. A unique structure in the flower center has five pinkish, pouch-shaped hoods. Once you examine this flower closely, you will never forget it.

  Showy milkweed is edible and has medicinal qualities, although some other milkweeds are poisonous. The silky down on the seedpods of showy milkweed was collected during World War II by school children (including the author) to provide buoyancy in life jackets and military flight suits.

> HABITAT/RANGE: Prefers dry to moist soils along streams and rivers or disturbed soils along roadsides, in ditches, and in cultivated fields in west, central, and east Montana.

Whorled Milkweed   *Asclepias verticillata*

Whorled milkweed has an unbranched stem less than 2 feet tall. Many soft, threadlike leaves are attached in whorls of three to six along the stem. Twenty or fewer greenish white flowers occur in each cluster, located at the top of the plant. Each small, stalked flower has five greenish petals and five erect white hoods.

> HABITAT/RANGE: Grows on dry prairies, pastures, and disturbed soils in northeast and south-central Montana.

Showy milkweed in mid-June in the
Charles M. Russell National Wildlife Refuge
on the north side of the Missouri River

Whorled milkweed in late July in a thinned, burned
forest in the Custer National Forest east of Ashland

MINT FAMILY   Lamiaceae

Members of the mint family, represented by twenty-one genera in Montana, are easily distinguished by three characteristics: the flowers have bilateral symmetry, the stems are square, and the leaves are opposite or whorled on the stem. Flowers are arranged on the stem in long clusters or in separated whorls. Each flower has five fused sepals and five fused petals, forming the corolla, often with upper and lower lips. The leaves are pinnately veined and often dotted with small glands that contain volatile oils. Mints have many medicinal uses, and many species are edible, especially the wild mints (*Mentha* species).

Giant Hyssop   *Agastache urticifolia*

Giant hyssop, also called *nettle-leaved horsemint*, has square, 1- to 5-foot-tall stems with a coarse surface. The opposite, arrow-shaped, toothed leaves are either smooth or lightly covered with long hairs on the lower surface. The white to purplish flowers are arranged in a dense spike above spiny-margined bracts at the end of the stem. The corolla is slightly longer than the calyx, which has spine-tipped lobes. Each flower contains four stamens, the two upper ones longer than the two lower ones. Both the style and stamens protrude beyond the petal tube.

> HABITAT/RANGE: Grows on moist soils in riparian areas and on open hillsides from the valleys to lower subalpine zones in west and central Montana.

Dragonhead   *Dracocephalum parviflorum*
                                        Moldavica parviflora

Dragonhead is an erect, 8- to 24-inch-tall, short-lived perennial with many sharp-toothed leaves along one or several clustered stems. The light purple, bluish, or pinkish flowers form a dense spike and are interspersed with large-veined, sharp-toothed bracts that have a stiff bristle at the tip. The light blue corolla is slightly longer than the calyx and holds stamens that are shorter than the petals.

> HABITAT/RANGE: Germinates only on disturbed soils, especially on burned-over areas, from the foothills to montane zones in west and central Montana.

Field Mint   *Mentha arvensis*

The square stems of field mint are 1 to 3 feet tall. Lance-shaped, opposite leaves with sharp-toothed margins are held on short petioles and extend laterally from stem nodes. Small lavender, pink, or occasionally white cup-shaped flowers are arranged in clusters in the axils of upper and middle leaves. Flower petals differ from most members of the mint family by being nearly equal in size and shape.

Field mint is a flavorful mint to use in cooking.

> HABITAT/RANGE: Prefers moist soils along streambanks and on open meadows from the valleys to subalpine zones in west, central, and east Montana.

Giant hyssop in mid-July in an open meadow along Stemple Pass Road northwest of Helena

Dragonhead in mid-July in a meadow in the Swan Valley south of Swan Lake

Field mint in mid-July along Stemple Pass Road northwest of Helena

Wild Bergamot   *Monarda fistulosa*

Wild bergamot, also called *mintleaf bee balm*, usually grows in large patches and gives off a pleasant mint aroma. The hairy, unbranched stems, usually found in bunches, are 1 to 3 feet tall. The lance-shaped, toothed, hairy leaves are opposite on the stem. The flower head is 1 to 3 inches wide and surrounded by leaflike bracts. Each pink to purplish flower is about 1 inch long, composed of a narrow upper lip that hangs over a broad, lobed, and drooping lower lip. Two stamens and the single style extend beyond the upper lip.

The leaves and flowers of wild bergamot have been used to prepare tea and for food flavoring. The plant has antiseptic and anesthetic properties; the leaf is used to deaden toothaches. Cattle and wild game animals eat this wildflower.

HABITAT/RANGE: Found on moist or semidry soils in open meadows, valleys, foothills, and montane forests in west, central, and east Montana.

Selfheal   *Prunella vulgaris*

Selfheal, also called *healall*, is a small, 4- to 8-inch-tall mint that is easily overlooked, especially when growing among grasses. A few oval leaves are located opposite on a square stem. The purple to pink flowers are arranged in a dense, short, terminal spike with green bracts. The purplish calyx is usually hairy. Each flower has an upper lip or hood and a three-lobed lower lip, the middle lobe with a fringed edge.

Selfheal has numerous medicinal properties; a tea made from the roots and leaves has been used to treat sore throat, fever, and intestinal disorders.

HABITAT/RANGE: Prefers moist soils of meadows and shaded forests, and disturbed soils on roadsides, up to montane zones in west and central Montana.

Hedge Nettle   *Stachys palustris*

The square, hairy stems of hedge nettle, usually unbranched and sticky, are 8 to 28 inches tall. The egg-shaped to oblong, toothed, hairy leaves are opposite on the stem and stalkless or with short petioles. The leaves have a broad, rounded base and taper to pointed tips. The pink or lavender flowers, splotched with white, are arranged in several whorls, usually with two to six flowers per whorl. The hairy, green calyx has five teeth, and the tube-shaped corolla has two lips, the upper hooded with two lobes and the lower broader with three lobes. Four colorful stamens are visible under the upper lip. The air surrounding this plant may be filled with a pleasant mint aroma.

HABITAT/RANGE: Found on wet soils in prairies and meadows or along streams from the foothills to montane zones in central and northeast Montana.

d bergamot in early August at Crystal Lake the Big Snowy Mountains near Lewistown

Hedge nettle in mid-July along a stream adjacent to the Charles M. Russell Trail southwest of Utica

Selfheal in early August at Crystal Lake in the Big Snowy Mountains near Lewistown

MORNING-GLORY FAMILY   Convolvulaceae

Plants in the morning-glory family, represented by five genera in Montana, are often trailing vines with large, attractive, funnel-shaped flowers. Leaves are alternate with small stipules.

Bindweed   *Convolvulus arvensis*

Bindweed, also called *field morning-glory*, is a noxious weed from Europe. The vine crawls over lawns and fields or uses coiled stems and tendrils to climb other plants, which may eventually die when deprived of sunlight. The slender underground stems penetrate deep into the soil and make eradication difficult. The leaves along the stem are hairless, shaped like an arrowhead, and have pointed lobes. One or two showy flowers with white to rosy purple petals arise from each leaf axil. Two narrow bracts are located on the flower stalk well below the sepals. The flower folds along ridges between the petals and may go unnoticed in early morning before it opens.

> HABITAT/RANGE: Covers fields, roadsides, lawns, and other disturbed moist areas from low to middle elevations in west, central, and east Montana.

MUSTARD FAMILY   Brassicaceae

A typical characteristic of members of the mustard family, represented by thirty-nine genera in Montana, is four petals in the form of a cross. Leaves are usually alternate and sometimes pinnately lobed. Flowers are small but often showy, and usually have six stamens, two shorter than the other four. The calyx usually has four sepals in two rows that fall off early. The family includes some plants that have spread so widely that they are considered noxious weeds.

Yellow Alyssum   *Alyssum alyssoides*

Yellow alyssum, also called *pale alyssum*, has 3- to 10-inch-tall, spreading stems that normally branch at the base. The narrow leaves are $^1/_4$ to 1 inch long and lack petioles. Both the leaves and stems are covered with small hairs. The small yellow to white flowers are arranged in compact racemes along the upper part of the stems. The petals just exceed the length of the sepals.

> HABITAT/RANGE: Yellow alyssum was introduced from Europe and is now a common weed on grasslands and croplands, along roadsides, and in waste areas in west, central, and southeast Montana.

Bindweed in early June at the Otter Creek Fishing Access
along the north side of the Yellowstone River near Big Timber

Yellow alyssum in late June northwest of Big Timber

Mouse-ear Cress　　　　　　　*Arabidopsis thaliana*

Mouse-ear cress, also called *thale cress*, has simple or branched stems that are 4 to 12 inches tall and are hairy below but less so above. The hairy basal leaves are lance-shaped or spoon-shaped with shallow teeth near the tip, while the stalkless stem leaves are entire. Small white to pinkish flowers are borne on slender, upward-projecting stalks. Each flower has four deeply cleaved petals and no bracts.

> HABITAT/RANGE: A weed, introduced from Europe, on disturbed soils from valleys to subalpine zones in west Montana.

Nuttall's rockcress　　　　　　*Arabis nuttallii*

Nuttall's rockcress is somewhat shorter than many rockcresses, with small stem leaves and a rosette of basal leaves covered sparsely with long stiff hairs. Five to twenty white, four-petaled flowers are arranged in a somewhat open inflorescence.

> HABITAT/RANGE: Prefers moist flat areas often sheltered by taller plants in valleys and on alpine ridges in west and central Montana.

Shepherd's Purse　　　　*Capsella bursa-pastoris*

The smooth or somewhat hairy stems of shepherd's purse are 4 to 16 inches tall and have several branches. The variable basal leaves sometimes have wavy margins and sometimes are deeply lobed. Clasping stem leaves are smaller and have smooth or irregularly toothed margins. The first small white flowers that appear cluster densely along the stem but spread out with age. Each flower has four green sepals, four petals, six stamens, and one pistil. The mature fruits are flattened and triangular or heart-shaped.

A single plant of shepherd's purse may produce up to 40,000 seeds, rapidly spreading across fields. This weed is an alternate host for several viral and fungal diseases of important vegetable plants.

> HABITAT/RANGE: A widespread weed, introduced from southern Europe, in cultivated fields and gardens across Montana.

Hoary Cress　　　　　　　　*Cardaria draba*

Hoary cress, also called *whitetop*, is a noxious, perennial weed introduced from Europe. It spreads by underground stems and is difficult to eradicate. It resembles two other introduced *Cardaria* species found in Montana, **lens-podded whitetop (C. chalapensis)** and **hairy whitetop (C. pubescens)**, and the three can only be distinguished by differences in seed capsules and fruits. Hoary cress, by far the most common, is about 2 feet tall with bluish green, lance-shaped leaves. Numerous white, four-petaled flowers are arranged in a flat-topped inflorescence.

> HABITAT/RANGE: Common noxious weed on disturbed soils, such as roadsides, where it often drives out other plants and covers large areas in west and central Montana.

...se-ear cress in ...June along the ...dison River east ...orris

Center: Nuttall's rockcress in late April in Leverich Canyon in the Gallatin National Forest east of Bozeman

Bottom left: Shepherd's purse, bearing both flowers and mature fruits, in late June along the Madison River east of Norris

Bottom right: Hoary cress in late May along Montana 55 south of Whitehall

Blue Mustard   *Chorispora tenella*

Blue mustard is a weedy annual that was introduced from Eurasia. The sticky stem is 4 to 18 inches tall and branches from its base. The elliptical or lance-shaped, toothed leaves are 1 to 3 inches long at the base of the stem and smaller above. Gland-tipped hairs cover the plant. The sepals of the purple to rose-colored flowers form a tubular base. The four-petaled flowers are borne on short stems and arranged in crowded racemes.

HABITAT/RANGE: Common weed on dry sites along roadsides, in pastures, and on other disturbed soils in west, central, and east Montana.

Whitlow Grass   *Draba* species

Draba is a large genus with twenty-three species reported in Montana. Identification of individual *Draba* species requires knowledge of the types of hairs on the leaves and the characteristics of the fruit. Some species of *Draba* grow close to the ground in mats of branching, leafy stems, while others have leafless stems that rise above a clump of basal leaves. The flowers are held on short stalks and arranged in a raceme. Each flower has four white or yellow petals in the shape of a cross and four sepals.

Six species of yellow-flowered cushion drabas grow in alpine sites in Montana. These species have numerous bright yellow flowers growing in a loose to tight, matted cushion on rocky and windswept sites.

Draba comes from Latin, meaning "acrid," a reference to the sharp and caustic sap of these plants.

HABITAT/RANGE: Grows in a variety of habitats from valleys to alpine zones in west and central Montana.

Wallflower   *Erysimum asperum*

Wallflower, also called *prairie rocket*, is an 8- to 30-inch-tall biennial, with bright yellow or orangish yellow, four-petaled flowers arranged in a tight raceme. The stem is occasionally branched and has a cluster of spreading, linear to elliptical leaves at the base and numerous alternate, linear stem leaves. The margins of the leaves are entire or may be toothed, and the surface is covered with fine hairs.

HABITAT/RANGE: Separated patches in meadows and open forests and on hills and slopes at all elevations in west, central, and east Montana.

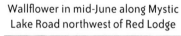

mustard in early May in a dry field along the road into the Pryor Mountains south of Billings

Inset: Dense patches of blue mustard in early spring along
Road 314 near Tongue River Reservoir in southeast Montana

ellow-flowered cushion draba in early July along the
rtooth Highway between Red Lodge and Cooke City

Wallflower in mid-June along Mystic
Lake Road northwest of Red Lodge

Dame's Rocket   *Hesperis matronalis*

Dame's rocket has one to several stems that may exceed 40 inches tall. The lance-shaped, 2- to 8-inch-long leaves are shallowly toothed and alternate on the stem. Lower leaves are held on petioles, while the upper leaves are smaller and stalkless. Long hairs cover the stem and both sides of the leaves. The showy, pinkish purple, stalked flowers are arranged in elongated racemes on stems that arise from axils of the upper leaves. Each fragrant, four-petaled flower has four sepals. Six stamens and one style are mostly hidden within the flower tube.

> HABITAT/RANGE: Common weed, introduced from Europe, on moist disturbed soils in ditches and along fencelines in west, central, and northeast Montana.

Yellow Pepperweed   *Lepidium perfoliatum*

Yellow pepperweed, a weedy annual, was introduced from Europe. The 16-inch-tall stems are sparsely hairy below and hairless above. The lower parsleylike leaves are divided into linear segments, but the upper stem leaves are spade-shaped with entire margins and completely clasp the stem, giving the impression that the stem has grown through the leaves. The flowers are very small with yellowish petals.

> HABITAT/RANGE: Common weed on roadsides and disturbed grasslands in valleys across Montana.

Alpine bladderpod   *Lesquerella alpina*

Alpine bladderpod, a low, dense, tufted perennial, is covered with star-shaped hairs. The many stems are 1 to 5 inches long and bear narrow, silver basal leaves. The small, four-petaled, yellow flowers arise from the center of the leafy mat. At high elevations, alpine bladderpod differs from other bladderpods by having narrow leaves and more erect stems.

> HABITAT/RANGE: Found on dry open slopes from the plains to subalpine zones in west, central, and east Montana.

Twinpod   *Physaria* species

The flowers and foliage of twinpods are difficult to distinguish from bladderpods (*Lesquerella* species), but the inflated fruits of twinpods are divided by a notch into two balloonlike lobes, whereas the fruits of bladderpods are nearly round with a slender style at the tip. Distinguishing the four *Physaria* species in Montana also requires detailed examination of the fruits. Twinpods have weak spreading stems with numerous spoon-shaped to linear leaves that occur mostly in a basal rosette. Star-shaped hairs densely cover the stems, leaves, and sepals. Bright yellow flowers, rarely purplish, are arranged on the stem tip in a tight raceme.

> HABITAT/RANGE: Prefers sandy or gravelly soils on the plains, slopes, and sagebrush steppes over much of Montana, depending on species.

ame's rocket in late June in a large patch bout 5 miles from Crystal Lake in the Big Snowy Mountains near Lewistown

Yellow pepperweed in early May around Freezeout Lake near Choteau

Alpine bladderpod on June 1 in the Gravelly Range south of Ennis

Twinpod in late April along the Cooney Reservoir Road south of Columbus

Tumble Mustard   *Sisymbrium altissimum*

Tumble mustard, also called *Jim Hill mustard*, has an unbranched lower stem but an extensively branched upper stem, forming a bushy, 2- to 5-foot-tall plant. The lower alternate leaves are divided into broad leaflets and toothed, whereas the upper leaves are much smaller with fine narrow lobes. The numerous small pale yellow flowers have four petals and are arranged in racemes. The long, slender fruits spread at an angle to the stem.

The mature plant breaks loose from the soil and tumbles in the wind, spreading its seeds as it goes.

HABITAT/RANGE: Common introduced weed on waste areas, prairies, roadsides, and small grain fields throughout Montana.

Alpine Smelowskia   *Smelowskia calycina*

Alpine smelowskia, a low cushion plant, has 2- to 8-inch-long stems bearing mostly hairy, pinnately lobed basal leaves with stiff hairs on the petioles. The stem leaves are smaller. The flowers are arranged in a crowded, elongated raceme at the top of the stem. Each small flower has four white petals that may be tinged with pink or purple.

HABITAT/RANGE: Grows on loose gravel and rocky slopes at subalpine or alpine zones in west and south-central Montana.

Pennycress   *Thlaspi arvense*

Pennycress is an erect, weedy annual that is 6 to 18 inches tall with many upper branches, although smaller plants may have only a single stem. The alternate leaves are 3 to 4 inches long. The entire to lobed, lance-shaped basal leaves are deeply notched and stalked, whereas the slightly toothed stem leaves, shaped like elongated arrowheads, are stalkless or clasping. The small, white, rather inconspicuous flowers occur in clusters at the top of the stems. Each flower has four sepals and four petals. The common name arises from the pennylike, round, thin fruits.

The milk from cows that eat pennycress has a strong odor and bitter flavor, characteristics that can be removed by special processing at the dairy plant. Young leaves are edible but have a bitter taste that is reduced by cooking. Before the twentieth century, pennycress was used as a poison antidote. In more recent times the leaves have been eaten for general health, and the seeds for treating conditions like eye inflammation and lumbago. The plants contain antimicrobial properties, but their use is discouraged because they irritate the treated tissues.

HABITAT/RANGE: A common weed, introduced from Europe, in grain fields, along roadsides, and on disturbed soils across Montana.

Tumble mustard in mid-June near Judith Landing on the Missouri River east of Fort Benton

Alpine smelowskia in late June along the Beartooth Highway between Red Lodge and Cooke City

Pennycress in mid-June along Sheep Creek Road north of White Sulphur Springs

NIGHTSHADE FAMILY   Solanaceae

The nightshade family, often called the *potato family* because it includes potatoes, is represented by six genera in Montana. Members of the family are highly variable. The often showy flowers are radially symmetrical with five petals, which are fused but sometimes only at the base, five fused sepals, and usually five stamens, equal in number to and alternating with corolla lobes.

Henbane   *Hyoscyamus niger*

Henbane, a biennial weed introduced from Europe, has a 1- to 3-foot-tall stem with stalkless, hairy, lance- or oval-shaped leaves that are sharply toothed and pinnately lobed. The funnel-shaped flowers are arranged in a spike on one side of the stem, arising from leaf axils or located at the tip. The flowers are a unique greenish or brownish yellow with dark purple veins and a deep purple throat. The sepals are arranged in an inverted bell with five teeth on its rim. Glandular hairs on the plant emit a tobacco-like odor.

Henbane is highly poisonous and should not be handled. It contains some hypnotic and sedative compounds, and was long used in the past as a painkiller and for treatment of nervous system and cardiac disorders.

HABITAT/RANGE: Common introduced weed along roadsides and dry waste areas from valleys to montane forests in west, central, and northeast Montana.

Climbing Nightshade   *Solanum dulcamara*

Climbing nightshade, also called *bittersweet nightshade*, is an introduced, 1- to 9-foot-long vine that climbs over other vegetation or fences. The leaves vary from entire to egg- or heart-shaped, and often have two prominent pointed lobes at their base. The flowers are supported by short stalks on the end of branches extending from the stem. The starlike flowers have five blue to violet petals that bend backward toward the stem as the flower matures. Five yellow stamens form a prominent yellow cone that hangs downward.

Many species in the genus *Solanum*, which includes the common potato, contain poisonous alkaloids. The green and red mature berries and leaves of climbing nightshade can cause vomiting, liver damage, paralysis, and death. Both cattle and sheep have been poisoned by eating these plants. Stem extracts have been used for medicinal purposes, such as treatment of skin and respiratory diseases.

HABITAT/RANGE: Native to Eurasia, it grows on disturbed moist soils along rivers and streams, and in thickets, open woods, and clearings, from valleys to montane zones in west, central, and northeast Montana.

Henbane
in late May
in Keating
Gulch near
Radersburg

Climbing nightshade in early July near the author's residence northwest of Bozeman

Buffalo Bur   *Solanum rostratum*

Buffalo bur is a highly branched, low, sprawling annual, forming an 8- to 24-inch-tall, rounded mound. Tiny star-shaped hairs cover the stems and leaves, and thin, sharp, yellow spines are present on the stems and leaf veins. The alternate, oval leaves are 2 to 5 inches long and deeply segmented into irregular lobes. Bright yellow flowers, about 1 inch in diameter, have five partially fused petals that form five spreading lobes at the opening. Five erect, yellow anthers occur in the throat of the flower, one of which is longer and larger than the others. The flowers develop into spiny burs containing many small seeds.

> HABITAT/RANGE: Common on sandy soils in disturbed areas and on dry prairies, plains, and hills across Montana.

ORCHID FAMILY   **Orchidaceae**

Members of the large orchid family, represented by nine genera in Montana, are monocots and include some of the most attractive wildflowers you will encounter in nature. The ornate, bilaterally symmetrical flowers have characteristics designed for specialized modes of pollination. Orchid flowers have three sepals and three petals. The two lateral petals often resemble the sepals, but the lower petal, called the *lip*, differs in size, shape, and color, and often bears a backward-projecting spur. The style, stigma, and stamen(s) are fused to form a structure called a *column*, which resembles a petal, and the ovary is inferior.

Fairy Slipper   *Calypso bulbosa*

Fairy slipper, also called *calypso*, has a spectacular, slipper-shaped flower. The pinkish brown, sheathed stem is 2 to 6 inches tall, with a single small, oval basal leaf that emerges after the flower has appeared. The stem has two or three clasping bracts. Each flower has three sharp-pointed sepals and two similar petals with purple stripes. The third petal or cuplike lip forms an apron with dark purple stripes inside and below and three short rows of white or yellow hairs on the upper surface.

Picking this lovely flower can pull up the shallow bulb and destroy it. The destruction of forests also threatens the existence of this wildflower.

> HABITAT/RANGE: Blooms after the snow has melted in moist cool forests with decaying duff on the floor from montane to subalpine zones in west and central Montana.

Buffalo bur in late July in a barren dry area east of Miles City

Fairy slipper in late June at Crystal Lake in the Big Snowy Mountains

❀ Coralroots *Corallorhiza* species ❀

The coralroots are saprophytes—plants that obtain their nutrients from soil fungi and do not photosynthesize. They lack leaves and chlorophyll.

Spotted Coralroot   *Corallorhiza maculata*

Spotted coralroot grows in clumps of yellowish or reddish stems that are 8 to 18 inches tall. The plant has no leaves, and the stems are lined instead with several membranous clasping bracts. The orchidlike flowers are arranged near the top in an open raceme. The two upper petals and the three sepals are pinkish red, while the lip petal, which has two small basal lobes, is white with purple spots.

A similar species, **western coralroot (*C. mertensiana*)** has reddish, 6- to 18-inch-tall stems that usually grow in a clump and bear membranous, sheathing bracts and a raceme of ten to thirty flowers near the tip. Each funnel-shaped flower, formed by the fusion of the sepals and petals, has two lateral, narrow, pinkish lobes, an upper drooping cap, and a lower downward-turning pink lip that usually has white patches and dark pink veins.

HABITAT/RANGE: Spotted coralroot grows on rich soils in moist to dry shaded woods from montane to lower subalpine zones in west and central Montana. Western coralroot grows in moist, humus-rich coniferous forests in spaces where it finds a bit of sunlight at middle to high elevations in west and south-central Montana.

Striped Coralroot   *Corallorhiza striata*

Striped coralroot usually grows singly or with just a few others. The leafless, erect, purplish stem is 6 to 16 inches tall and the upper part holds seven to twenty-five flowers arranged in a spikelike raceme. Small membranous bracts line and wrap the stem. The yellowish pink sepals and upper petals have conspicuous reddish brown to purple stripes. The lower petal forms a broad unlobed lip. No spurs are present.

HABITAT/RANGE: Grows on rich soils in deep, shaded, montane and subalpine forests in west and north-central Montana.

Yellow Coralroot   *Corallorhiza trifida*

Yellow coralroot is a 2- to 10-inch-tall plant with a leafless stem. Two or three sheathing bracts on the stem are yellowish green. Three to twelve pale greenish yellow flowers are held in an elongated raceme. Each flower has two linear petals and a white lip, sometimes with red or purple spots, which has a small tooth on each side. Both the sepals and petals are longer than the lip of the flower.

HABITAT/RANGE: Grows on shaded rich soils on the floor of montane and subalpine forests in west and central Montana.

Spotted coralroot in mid-July near Lake Alva north of Seeley Lake

Western coralroot in late June in the forest at Stemple Pass south of Lincoln

Striped coralroot in late June near Crystal Lake in the Big Snowy Mountains near Lewistown

Yellow coralroot in late June in a wet area along the Boulder River south of Big Timber

Mountain Lady's Slipper   *Cypripedium montanum*

The white lip petal that forms a slipper differentiates mountain lady's slipper from **yellow lady's slipper (*C. calceolus*)**, which has a yellow lip petal. The stem of mountain lady's slipper is 1 to 2 feet tall, bearing numerous lance-shaped, parallel-veined, clasping leaves. A large, green, leafy bract partially encloses each of the one to three blossoms per stem. The sepals and lateral petals are brownish with purple stripes and are twisted or wavy. The stamens and pistils are fused into a brilliant yellow column, often with red or purple spots, located in the opening of the slipper.

Meriwether Lewis observed mountain lady's slipper near Lolo Creek in west Montana. It is a rare plant and should never be removed from its wild habitat.

HABITAT/RANGE: Prefers moist soils under trees and shrubs in montane forests in west and central Montana.

White Bog Orchid   *Habenaria dilatata*
Platanthera dilatata

White bog orchid, also called *tall white rein-orchid*, has a 1- to 3-foot-tall, unbranched stem with several lance-shaped leaves that clasp the stem and get progressively smaller toward the top. A dense spike of white, fragrant flowers adorns the top of the stem. The upper sepal and two petals of each flower join at their tip to form a hood, while the two lower sepals spread wide to the sides. The white, drooping, broad-based lip of the flower has a prominent spur that varies from half to twice the length of the lip petal.

HABITAT/RANGE: Found only in lush wet areas, seepages, streambanks, and meadows from lowlands to subalpine zones throughout west and central Montana.

Long-bracted Orchis   *Habenaria viridis*
Coeloglossum viride

The leafy stems of long-bracted orchis are 6 to 20 inches tall. The lower, smooth, shiny leaves are broad and blunt-tipped and clasp the stem. Pale yellowish green flowers, sometimes purple tinged, are arranged in a long inflorescence, each flower partially covered by a long, green, leafy bract that is two to six times longer than the flower. The sepals and petals form an upper hood. The drooping lip petal has two to three lobes at the tip, giving the appearance of a frog's tongue and inspiring another common name, *frog orchis*. A tiny spur is mostly hidden by the petals.

HABITAT/RANGE: Grows in open forests, on grassy meadows, and on mountain slopes up to subalpine zones in west and central Montana.

ntain lady's slipper on June 30 in
cier National Park east of Essex

Long-bracted orchis in late June
near Crystal Lake in the Big Snowy
Mountains near Lewistown

White bog orchid in late June along Sixmile Road
east of Swan Lake in northwest Montana

Ladies-tresses   *Spiranthes romanzoffiana*

The stem of ladies-tresses is 4 to 24 inches tall, with numerous bright green, narrow, lance-shaped basal leaves and smaller leaflike bracts on the upper part. A dense spike of sixty or more fragrant flowers overlap in three vertical spirals like a barber pole. Each flower arises from the axil of a leafy bract. The creamy white to greenish flowers, which are better appreciated under a hand lens, have three sepals and three petals forming a funnel with a hood. The lip petal, which is narrow at the base and wider at the front, has fine teeth and curls along the edges. Ladies-tresses lacks a spur, differentiating it from the spurred white bog orchid (*Habenaria dilatata*).

> HABITAT/RANGE: Prefers wet areas, streambanks, and moist meadows in open areas from foothills to montane zones in west and central Montana.

PARSLEY FAMILY   Umbelliferae

The large parsley family, also called the *carrot family* and represented by eighteen genera in Montana, includes species that are mostly native to North America, with many in the West. The family includes common edible plants, such as carrots, celery, and dill, but it also includes some extremely poisonous plants, such as water hemlock (*Cicuta douglasii*). Determining whether a plant is in the family is fairly easy, but identifying individual species is difficult. All members of the parsley family have an umbrella-shaped flower cluster called an *umbel* that is sometimes divided further into a compound umbel. Flower parts are in groups of five—five petals, five or no sepals, and five free stamens alternating with petals, all parts attached to the top of the ovary. The sepals are small and scalelike. Most family members have parsleylike, alternate leaves that are often wrapped around the stem at their base.

Lyall's Angelica   *Angelica arguta*

Lyall's angelica, also called *sharptooth angelica*, is a 2- to 6-foot-tall perennial with a thick, hollow, unbranched stem with two or three twice-divided compound leaves. The rather large, lance-shaped, sharp-tipped leaflets have irregular sharp teeth along the margins. The lateral leaf veins run to the end of the tooth on the leaf margin. The basal leaves clasp the stem and are supported by petioles that have broad leaflike wings. Numerous small white or pinkish flowers are arranged in one or more flat-topped compound umbels.

Lyall's angelica has many reputed medicinal properties. However, collection for personal use carries the risk of misidentification with similar-appearing water hemlock (*Cicuta douglasii*), a violently poisonous plant. The veins of the leaflets on water hemlock end at the notches between the teeth on the margins.

> HABITAT/RANGE: Found along streams and lakes and in wet meadows from montane to subalpine zones throughout Montana.

Ladies-tresses
in late July in
the Pioneer
Mountains south
of Wise River

Lyall's angelica in mid-July
on the bank of the Judith
River southwest of Utica

Water Hemlock

Cicuta douglasii
C. maculata

The thick, hollow stems of water hemlock are 2 to 7 feet tall and support pinnately compound, alternate leaves that hold oblong to lance-shaped, veined leaflets with saw-toothed margins. The swollen base of the stem is divided by cross-walls into many chambers. Greenish to white flowers are arranged in compound umbels. The plant contains an oily, foul-smelling sap. Water hemlock may be confused with Lyall's angelica (*Angelica arguta*) and with water parsnip (*Sium suave*) but can be distinguished by having veins in the leaflets that terminate at the notches between the teeth.

Water hemlock contains a highly toxic component that attacks the central nervous system and may cause death within fifteen minutes of ingestion.

HABITAT/RANGE: Grows in low wet places, often with the roots immersed in water, from the plains to subalpine zones in west, central, and east Montana.

Cow Parsnip

Heracleum lanatum

Cow parsnip, a 3- to 8-foot-tall perennial, has hollow, hairy, thick stems that tower above neighboring plants. The maplelike leaves are 12 to 16 inches across. The large, flat-topped umbel sits on the main stalk with smaller umbels arising from leaf axils. The only thing small about this plant is the individual flower, with white petals less than $1/4$ inch wide.

Animals often graze on this nutritious plant, and American Indians peeled and roasted the large stalks.

HABITAT/RANGE: Prefers moist soils in wet meadows, in open woods, and along streams from valleys to subalpine zones in west, central, and southeast Montana.

Fern-leaved Lovage

Ligusticum filicinum

Fern-leaved lovage grows 2 to 4 feet tall and has finely dissected leaves, most located at the base with some smaller stem leaves. Small white flowers are arranged in a flat-topped compound umbel. The plant has a celery-like odor.

HABITAT/RANGE: Grows in shady areas on moist soils on streambanks, in meadows, and in open woods from montane to subalpine zones in west Montana.

Water hemlock in early July along a small stream near Park Lake southwest of Helena

w parsnip in late June on Battle Ridge in the
Gallatin National Forest north of Bozeman

Bottom right and inset: Fern-leaved
ovage in mid-July on the bank of the
Judith River southwest of Utica

Cous

**Lomatium cous
L. montanum**

Cous, also called *biscuitroot*, has 4- to 10-inch-tall, usually hairless stems that may or may not bear leaves. The basal leaves are finely dissected, three to five times, into short, slender, crowded segments. The yellow, sometimes purplish, flowers are arranged in dense compound umbels. Below each flower is a whorl of rather large, egg- or spatula-shaped, green to purplish bracts.

Meriwether Lewis collected a specimen of cous in 1806 and mentioned the use of its roots for pounding into a flour. Cous can be confused with inedible plants, so harvest with extreme caution.

HABITAT/RANGE: Common on rocky, dry soils on open slopes, grasslands, and sagebrush steppes from valleys to alpine zones in west, central, and northeast Montana.

Fern-leaved Desert Parsley

Lomatium dissectum

Fern-leaved desert parsley has 1- to 5-foot-tall, smooth, hairless stems. The highly dissected, lacy, mostly basal leaves appear fernlike. The small, yellow to deep purple or near black flowers are arranged in a twice-divided, flat-topped umbel on a long leafless stalk. Tiny narrow bracts are located at the base of the flowers.

HABITAT/RANGE: Grows on open, dry, rocky soils on slopes and in meadows from the valleys to subalpine forests in west, central, and northeast Montana.

Fennel-leaved Lomatium

Lomatium foeniculaceum

Fennel-leaved lomatium varies in height from 4 to 12 inches and lacks stems. The entire plant is covered with fine whitish hairs. The alternate, lacy leaves are divided three to four times into numerous short linear segments less than $1/2$ inch long. The sheath of the leaf stalk is purplish. The small yellow to yellowish green flowers are arranged in a flat or slightly convex, compound umbel about 4 inches wide.

HABITAT/RANGE: Prefers dry rocky soils on the plains and hills in open woods throughout Montana but is most common east of the Rockies.

Large-fruit Lomatium

Lomatium macrocarpum

Large-fruit lomatium, also called *large-fruited biscuitroot*, has 4- to 10-inch-long stems that are unbranched, spreading, and smooth. The grayish leaves, covered with short hairs, are held on winged petioles and are clumped at the base of the plant. Each oblong or triangular-shaped leaf is pinnately dissected about three times into many small lance-shaped segments. White or purplish tinged flowers are arranged in compound, ball-like umbels. Conspicuous linear bracts are located below one side of the uppermost umbel.

The roots of this species are edible and have been used to prepare flour.

HABITAT/RANGE: Grows on rocky soils of open prairies, sagebrush steppe, and the foothills in west and central Montana.

Cous in early April along Road 295 south of Interstate 90 and east of Livingston

Fern-leaved desert parsley in early May north of Belgrade

Fennel-leaved lomatium on the last day of April just west of Cooney Reservoir southeast of Columbus

Large-fruit lomatium in early May in the Pryor Mountains east of Bridger

PEA FAMILY — Fabaceae (Leguminosae)

The large pea family, also called the *bean family* or *legume family*, is represented by twenty-two genera in Montana. The family members share a distinctive flower that usually has an upper enlarged petal called a *banner*, two side petals called *wings*, and two partially fused lower petals called a *keel* because it resembles the keel of a boat. Ten stamens and the style are enclosed inside the keel, which, when depressed by an insect, spring forward to deposit pollen on the unknowing transporter. The leaves are usually compound, and

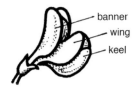

Flower of the Pea Family

the fruit is a pod that splits open, releasing the seeds. Some legumes, such as alfalfa (*Medicago sativa*) and clovers (*Trifolium* species), fix nitrogen by harboring symbiotic bacteria that convert atmospheric nitrogen to a soluble form available to other plants. The family also includes the poisonous locoweeds (*Astralagus* species) and crazyweeds (*Oxytropis* species).

Locoweeds and Milkvetches — *Astragalus* species

Astragalus is the largest genus of wildflowers in the western United States and includes forty-seven species reported in Montana. The name *locoweed* is often applied to a different genus, the crazyweeds (*Oxytropis*), which resemble *Astragalus* species. Two features that distinguish locoweeds from crazyweeds are the presence of stem leaves and a rounded or blunt keel petal. Locoweeds also resemble vetches (*Vicia* species) but lack the characteristic tendrils of vetches. The leaves of locoweeds are usually pinnately divided into several leaflets with stipules where the leaf attaches to the stem. The pealike flowers are supported on short stalks that originate in the axils of the upper leaves. Distinguishing individual species is difficult, often requiring microscopic examination.

Alpine Milkvetch — *Astragalus alpinus*

For a locoweed, alpine milkvetch is fairly easy to identify. The low, highly branched, matted stems of alpine milkvetch are 4 to 12 inches long. The leaves are pinnately compound with two to eleven pairs of elliptical leaflets that are sometimes shallowly notched at the tip. The upper surface of the leaflets is usually smooth, but the lower surface has short, white, bristly hairs. Ten or more flowers on short stalks are crowded in a loose raceme on a leafless stem. The pealike flowers are bicolored, the banner and keel tip lavender, and the wings and keel base white. The wing petals are slightly shorter than the keel petal, which is more like sweetvetches (*Hedysarum* species) than milkvetches.

HABITAT/RANGE: Grows from valleys to subalpine zones, especially on moist meadows, on riverbanks, and in shaded woods, in west and central Montana.

Alpine milkvetch in late June in an open woods in the
Little Belt Mountains north of White Sulphur Springs

Buffalo plum locoweed   *Astragalus crassicarpus*

The sprawling stems of buffalo plum locoweed vary from 4 to 18 inches long, lying prostrate in a cluster of fifteen or more. Numerous faded, alternate and compound, short-stalked, green leaves contain thirteen to twenty-seven short

leaflets with round tips and short stiff hairs on the lower surface. The leaflets are arranged featherlike along the leaf axis with one at the tip. The flowers are pale violet to white with a keel petal that is conspicuously tinged with purple. The upper petal of the flower is the largest and flares at its tip. Each flower has a small, pale green, five-toothed calyx.

American Indians and pioneers ate the young, juicy green pods of this plant, which taste like raw peas.

HABITAT/RANGE: Prefers dry prairies, grasslands, and fields in the foothills in west, central, and east Montana.

Buffalo plum locoweed in early May
at Tongue River Reservoir State Park
in south-central Montana

Pea Family   177

Drummond's Milkvetch — *Astragalus drummondii*

Drummond's milkvetch resembles at least three other milkvetches found in Montana that have whitish or cream-colored flowers: **loose-flowered milkvetch (*A. tenellus*)**, **Canada milkvetch (*A. canadensis*)**, and **American milkvetch (*A. americanus*)**. Drummond's milkvetch has several thick, hairy, bunched stems that are 16 to 36 inches tall. The pinnately compound leaves have at least twenty-one oblong, smooth-margined leaflets that have fine hairs on the underside. The creamy white, drooping flowers, sometimes purplish-tipped, are arranged in a dense, 2- to 6-inch-long, spikelike raceme that extends above the leaves. Each flower has a calyx with dark hairs.

HABITAT/RANGE: Grows on dry plains and fields from the foothills to lower montane zones across Montana.

Plains Milkvetch — *Astragalus gilviflorus*

Plains milkvetch forms a dense, low mat without stems and with silvery gray leaves, each with three leaflets. At the base of the leaf is a pair of thin, translucent, sharp-pointed stipules. The flowers have either a short stalk or are stalkless and arise from the leaf axils. The flowers are whitish to yellow, but the short keel petal often has a purple, blue, or lilac tip. Plains milkvetch resembles **Barr's matted pea (*A. barrii*)**, found only in southeast Montana, which has blue or purple banner petals and white wing petals.

HABITAT/RANGE: Found on the plains and foothills across Montana.

Thistle Milkvetch — *Astragalus kentrophyta* / *A. tegetarius*

Thistle milkvetch, one of the easier *Astragalus* species to identify, grows in a 2- to 3-inch-tall cushion or mat of slender, branched, 4- to 16-inch-long stems. The alternate, linear, silvery leaflets, five to eleven on each pinnately divided leaf, are spine-tipped. The yellowish white flowers, often with a purplish tinge, are held on short stems and arranged in clusters that are often hidden by the leaves.

HABITAT/RANGE: Grows on dry open deserts and plains to open alpine ridges and slopes in west, south-central, and southeast Montana.

Bent-flowered Milkvetch — *Astragalus vexilliflexus*

Bent-flowered milkvetch, a prostrate mat-forming milkvetch, is widely branched. The small, pinnately compound, slightly hairy, alternate leaves have seven to thirteen leaflets with pointed tips. Five to ten deep lavender purple flowers are loosely clustered along the stem on short stalks. The wings and keel of each flower are much shorter than the erect banner. Bent-flowered milkvetch may be confused with thistle milkvetch (*A. kentrophyta*), which has lance- rather than awl-shaped leaflets.

HABITAT/RANGE: Grows on rocky slopes and knolls from the foothills to subalpine zones in west and central Montana.

Drummond's milkvetch in early June north of Winifred

Plains milkvetch in early May in the dry, open sagebrush habitat surrounding Tongue River Reservoir in south-central Montana

Thistle milkvetch in mid-July on an open high plateau in the Gravelly Range south of Ennis

Bent-flowered milkvetch in mid-July in the Little Snowy Mountains southeast of Lewistown

Crown Vetch
Coronilla varia

Crown vetch, a garden plant introduced from Europe, has been used to stabilize roadbanks. The hairless, sprawling stems of crown vetch grow up to 20 inches long. The leaves are pinnately compound with eleven to fifteen small leaflets. Fourteen to twenty stalkless, pink and white flowers arise from leaf axils to form a cloverlike cluster.

HABITAT/RANGE: Not widespread but potentially increasing in Montana.

White Prairie Clover
Dalea candida
Petalostemon candidus

The several slender stems of white prairie clover reach 30 inches tall, with dull green, alternate compound leaves on the lower stem that are divided into five to nine narrow, linear leaflets. The white flowers are arranged in fluffy cylinders along a terminal spike, with the bottom flowers blooming first, producing a wreath that migrates up the column. Each flower has one large and four smaller petals, a small green calyx, a bract longer than the calyx, and five extended stamens.

White prairie clover is less common than purple prairie clover (*Dalea purpurea*). Meriwether Lewis collected a specimen of white prairie clover in Nebraska in 1804. In his journal, Lewis described the similarity with but different color from purple prairie clover.

HABITAT/RANGE: Prefers dry to moist but well-drained hillsides, rocky soils, and roadsides in the prairies, plains, and hills across Montana except the far west.

Purple Prairie Clover
Dalea purpurea
Petalostemon purpureus

Purple prairie clover has erect, slender, ½- to 3-foot-tall stems that are much branched and semiprostrate. The alternate compound leaves are divided into three to nine shiny, narrow leaflets less than 1 inch long and ⅛ inch wide. The numerous tiny, bright purple flowers, each with one large and four smaller petals, plus five protruding orange stamens, are arranged in compact rings along a spike. The bottom flowers bloom first and the ring migrates up the spike over the blooming season.

Meriwether Lewis collected a specimen of purple prairie clover in Nebraska in 1804, noting in his journal: "it is a stranger to me."

HABITAT/RANGE: Prefers dry to moist but well-drained soils on hillsides in the prairies and plains of northwest, central, and east Montana.

Crown vetch in late June on a roadside east of
Hungry Horse Reservoir in northwest Montana

White prairie clover in late July near
U.S. 12 east of Harlowton

Purple prairie clover in late July in the
Red Shale Campground in the Custer
National Forest east of Ashland

Wild Licorice   *Glycyrrhiza lepidota*

The erect, branching, sticky, reddish stems of wild licorice reach 12 to 36 inches in height, with alternate, pinnately compound leaves that have seven to fifteen lance-shaped to oval leaflets. The yellowish white, pealike flowers, sometimes with a purple tinge, form tight clusters that rise from leaf axils. The flowers mature into rusty brown burs armed with hooked prickles that cling to passersby.

American Indians ate the roots of wild licorice and used the plant to treat of a variety of ailments. Meriwether Lewis wrote in his journal in 1806 that the roasted root had an "agreeable flavour not unlike the sweet pittaitoe."

HABITAT/RANGE: On waste soils or other moist low ground along the banks of streams or ponds from the plains to lower montane zones throughout Montana.

🌿 Sweetvetches *Hedysarum* species 🌿

Sweetvetches, represented by four species in Montana, can resemble some locoweeds (*Astragalus* species), but sweetvetches have wing petals on the flower that are shorter than or equal to the keel petal, and the pod is constricted between the seeds. American Indians, trappers, and settlers ate the licorice-flavored roots.

Northern sweetvetch   *Hedysarum boreale*

Northern sweetvetch is a bushy, highly branched perennial with numerous reclining or erect, 2- to 3-foot-tall stems. The leaves are pinnately compound with seven to fifteen elliptic or oblong, entire leaflets. They are hairy, especially on the lower surface, inconspicuously veined, and dotted on the upper surface with small brown glands. Thin brownish stipules are attached at the base of each leaf. Pink or magenta pealike flowers are arranged in elongated racemes. The keel petal of the flower extends farther out than the wings.

Alpine sweetvetch (*H. alpinum*) resembles northern sweetvetch but it has conspicuous veins on the lower surface of the leaflets. **Western sweetvetch (*H. occidentale*)** also resembles northern sweetvetch, but it is found only in west Montana and has much wider fruits.

HABITAT/RANGE: Northern sweetvetch prefers fine dry clay soils in open or lightly shaded areas on prairies, and among sagebrush or aspen groves, in west, central, and northeast Montana.

Yellow sweetvetch   *Hedysarum sulphurescens*

Yellow sweetvetch has 8- to 24-inch-tall stems, although they may be shorter at high elevations. The stem leaves are pinnately compound with numerous pairs of oval leaflets. Twenty or more (depending upon elevation) pale yellow, pealike flowers droop from the flower stalk. The keel petal is much larger than the wing petals.

HABITAT/RANGE: Yellow sweetvetch grows in forest openings and on rocky slopes from montane to subalpine zones in west and central Montana.

Wild licorice in mid-July in a roadside ditch along Road 297 north of Shawmut

Yellow sweetvetch in early July in the Pryor Mountains east of Bridger

Northern sweetvetch in early July along the road to Delmoe Lake east of Butte

Cream-flowered Peavine — *Lathyrus ochroleucus*

Cream-flowered peavine, a trailing or climbing vine, has angled, hairless, 12- to 32-inch-long stems. Each leaf usually has six (with a range of four to eight) egg-shaped or elliptical leaflets, a pair of large, heart-shaped stipules on one side at the base of the stalk, and branching tendrils at the tip. Six to fourteen yellowish white, pealike flowers arise from leaf axils. *Lathyrus* species differ from vetches (*Vicia*) by their larger flowers, fewer leaflets, and the presence of hairs along one side of the style instead of at the tip.

HABITAT/RANGE: Grows on moist soils in open or wooded sites on the plains or foothills in northwest, north-central, and southeast Montana.

Bird's Foot Trefoil — *Lotus corniculatus*

Bird's foot trefoil, an introduced plant from Europe, trails on the ground and has compound leaves that resemble a bird's foot. Each leaf has five leaflets, three near the tip of the stem and two at the junction of the leaf stalk with the stem. From the axils of the leaves arise bright yellow, red-tinged, pealike flowers, clustered in a head on a long, leafless stalk. The flowers resemble clover (*Trifolium* species), but trefoil has five rather than three leaflets.

HABITAT/RANGE: Common weed on disturbed soils along roadsides and ditches and also invading meadows in west Montana.

Lupine — *Lupinus* species

Ten *Lupinus* species grow in Montana and are easily identified to the genus level by their more or less hairy, palmately divided leaves, each leaf having five to nine long narrow leaflets at the tip of the petiole. Identifying individual species, however, is much more difficult. Lupine flowers are arranged in narrow elongate racemes and are usually blue or purple, sometimes two-toned, but may be white, rose, or cream. The corolla of the pealike flower has a strongly upturned banner, the upper lip is two-lobed, the keel is crescent-shaped, and the calyx is two-lipped.

Silvery Lupine — *Lupinus argenteus*

Silvery lupine varies in height from 7 to 34 inches, with stems and leaf petioles covered with short hairs. The leaves are palmately divided into leaflets that are upturned at the tip and slightly hairy below. Fifteen to ninety-two bluish purple flowers are arranged in a long spike. The banner petal is usually hairless on the back surface and has a central yellow or white spot. Several varieties of this species, varying in leaf size and shape, have been described.

HABITAT/RANGE: Silvery lupine prefers pine forests, grasslands, and open subalpine slopes and ridges in west, central, and east Montana.

Cream-flowered peavine in late June
an open wet woods along Montana 83
south of Swan Lake

Bird's foot trefoil in late summer
along a road in Bozeman

Silvery lupine in mid-June along the
Pryor Mountain road east of Bridger

Spurred Lupine

Lupinus laxiflorus
L. arbustus

Spurred lupine has a unique spur or sac, about 0.1 inch long, on the calyx. The erect to spreading, leafy stems are slightly branched and 12 to 20 inches tall. The upper leaves are held on long petioles, and the leaflets are inversely lance-shaped and have sharp or round tips. The upper surface of the leaflets may be hairless or have stiff hairs, whereas the lower surface is silky or also covered with stiff hairs. The banner of the flower is slightly bent backward and usually hairy on the back above the center. The wings are usually hairy at the tips, and the keel is fringed with hairs on the margin.

HABITAT/RANGE: Found most often in open forests at low elevations in west Montana.

Dwarf Lupine

Lupinus pusillus

Dwarf lupine is usually less than 8 inches tall, with hairy stems that branch from the base. The alternate, palmately compound leaves have 1¼-inch-long leaflets that are smooth above and covered with long hairs on the underside. Each leaf is supported on a hairy, 1½- to 3-inch-long petiole. The bright blue, pealike flowers are supported by short stalks and enclosed in a hairy calyx. The short raceme contains five to ten flowers on a hairy stalk that is less than 1 inch long. Each flower is about ½ inch long and has a white or yellowish spot at the center.

It is believed that Meriwether Lewis collected his specimen of this wildflower on his return trip in 1806 along the Missouri River near Great Falls.

HABITAT/RANGE: Prefers sandy soils and dunes on the plains and foothills in southwest, central, and east Montana.

Silky Lupine

Lupinus sericeus

The stems of silky lupine grow in clumps and are 1 to 2 feet tall. The alternate leaves are pinnately divided with seven to nine narrow leaflets that are densely covered with silky hairs on both the upper and lower surfaces. The flowers are usually purplish or light blue but sometimes yellowish white. The banner of the pealike flower is conspicuously hairy and is angled to form a wide V-shaped opening. Don't be surprised if you occasionally see a white mutant form of this flower.

HABITAT/RANGE: Found on dry open or shaded soils in sagebrush or forests from the plains to subalpine zones in west and central Montana.

rred lupine in mid-June in
in Canyon south of Bozeman

Dwarf lupine in mid-June north of Judith
Landing on the Missouri River east of Fort Benton

Silky lupine in mid-July along Park Lake Road southwest of Helena

Inset: A white form of silky lupine among many plants with
purplish blue flowers in mid-July along Park Lake Road south of Helena

Alfalfa   *Medicago sativa*

The branched stems of alfalfa, hairless or sometimes with fine, stiff, short hairs, are 12 to 40 inches tall. The numerous dark green, alternate leaves are divided into three elliptic to oblong leaflets that are sharply toothed on the upper half and are about ⅜ to 1¼ inches long. The terminal leaflet is held on a short stalk. Narrow, lance-shaped stipules have entire margins. The deep purple to bluish, pealike flowers, rarely pink or all white, are arranged in a tight raceme, originating from leaf axils. Each flower is ⅜ to 1¼ inches long.

HABITAT/RANGE: Alfalfa, an introduced plant from Europe, has escaped cultivation and become common along roadsides, in ditches, and on abandoned farmlands in west, central, and northeast Montana.

❧ Crazyweed *Oxytropis* species ❧

Crazyweeds differ from locoweeds (*Astragalus*) in having leafless stems and a keel petal that is sharply pointed like a beak. The basal leaves, which originate from the root crown, are pinnately divided. Stipules, pointed leaflike appendages at the base of petioles, are fused. Livestock that feed on crazyweeds can suffer from loco poisoning, a potentially fatal condition.

Bessey's Crazyweed   *Oxytropis besseyi*

Bessey's crazyweed appears silvery gray due to a covering of silky hairs. The pinnately compound leaves are 1 to 4 inches long with five to twenty-one leaflets that are hairy on both sides. Stipules at the base of the leaf are united with the petiole for more than one-half its length. Three to twenty pealike, deep purplish magenta flowers are on long stalks and arranged in a raceme. The keel, shorter than the banner, has a straight or curved point.

HABITAT/RANGE: Grows on the plains and grassy slopes of the foothills in west, central, and east Montana.

Cusick's Crazyweed   *Oxytropis campestris*
                                        O. cusickii

Cusick's crazyweed, also called *field crazyweed*, is highly variable, and several varieties have been described. The short, clumped, erect, grayish-hairy, leafless stems are 4 to 8 inches tall with pinnately compound basal leaves with eleven to thirty-three leaflets, depending on the variety. Five to fifteen off-white to pale yellow flowers grow in a spikelike cluster. The banner petals of the pealike flower bend sharply backward.

HABITAT/RANGE: Grows on rocky soils in high montane to alpine zones in west and south-central Montana.

Alfalfa in mid-June along Road 240 south of Chinook

Bessey's crazyweed in mid-June east of Bridger

Cusick's crazyweed in mid-July on an open rocky plateau in the Gravelly Range south of Ennis

Rabbitfoot Crazyweed *Oxytropis lagopus*

Rabbitfoot crazyweed is a low, tufted plant with leafless, hairy stems and basal leaves that are also densely covered with fine silky hairs. The pinnately compound leaves are shorter than the flowers and have seven to fifteen oval leaflets. The pealike flowers are blue to lavender purple and are arranged in crowded racemes at the top of a leafless stalk. The plant takes its common name from the fuzzy sepals that resemble a rabbit's foot.

HABITAT/RANGE: Found on dry gravelly soils in sagebrush steppe at lower elevations in west and central Montana.

Silky Crazyweed *Oxytropis sericea*

The leafless stems of silky crazyweed are 3 to 16 inches tall, and like the leaves and calyx, are covered with dense silky hairs. Tufts of basal leaves reach 12 inches long and are pinnately compound with five to ten pairs of leaflets along the axis. Ten to thirty cream, pink, or yellow to white flowers are arranged in a raceme at the top of the stem. The pointed tip of the keel is often purple.

HABITAT/RANGE: Prefers dry grasslands and open prairies from foothills to alpine zones in west, central, and east Montana.

Showy Crazyweed *Oxytropis splendens*

The leafless, erect, hairy stem of showy crazyweed is 4 to 14 inches tall, surrounded by 4- to 10-inch-long, pinnately compound basal leaves. The numerous hairy leaflets are usually arranged in whorls of three to six. The pealike flowers are pinkish purple to blue, with ten to thirty-five arranged in woolly, spikelike clusters.

HABITAT/RANGE: Prefers dry, rocky, or gravelly soils in meadows or aspen groves from valleys to low mountains in west and central Montana.

Rabbitfoot crazyweed in late April at Bear Trap Canyon along the Madison River west of Norris

Silky crazyweed in late May at Tongue River Reservoir in south-central Montana

Showy crazyweed in mid-July along the Charles M. Russell Trail bordering the Judith River south of Utica

Silvery Scurf Pea

Pediomelum argophyllum
Psoralea argophyllum

Silvery scurf pea, an open bushy and widely branched wildflower, has 10- to 40-inch-long stems. The alternate, stalked, palmately compound leaves are smooth and covered with white hairs on both sides, giving a silvery gray appearance. Each leaf has three to five narrow to oval, pointed leaflets that have a common attachment point. The small deep blue to purple, pealike flowers are arranged in whorls along a spike and have a spreading upper petal, two side or banner petals, and an extended lower lip.

American Indians used silvery scurf pea to treat wounds and fevers, and early settlers thought it was effective for treating snakebite. Meriwether Lewis collected specimens of the plant in North Dakota in 1804 and described in his journal a preparation from the leaves that was "good for inflamed eyes."

HABITAT/RANGE: Frequent inhabitant of dry, rocky prairies, plains, and hills in central and east Montana.

Slimflower Scurf Pea

Psoralidium tenuiflorum
Psoralea tenuiflora

Slimflower scurf pea, an open bushy perennial, has wide-spreading stems about 3 feet tall. The alternate, stalked leaves are segmented in three to five narrow, round leaflets that emerge from a common point. The blue to purple or reddish flowers are arranged in elongated clusters on stalks that arise from leaf axils.

Meriwether Lewis collected two specimens of slimflower scurf pea in South Dakota in 1804.

HABITAT/RANGE: Grows on moist but well-drained plains, prairies, and hills in southwest, central, and southeast Montana, although it is most common in the south-central part of the state.

Golden Pea

Thermopsis montana

Golden pea, also called *false lupine*, has a 1- to 3-foot-tall stem that is sometimes hairy. The compound leaves have three leaflets that are lance-shaped and pointed or rounded at the tip. Two leaflike bracts or stipules are located at the base of each leaf stalk. Two to twenty-three brilliant yellow, pealike flowers are arranged in a dense raceme. Ten stamens in each flower are separated and distinct, which, along with three instead of five or more leaflets, distinguishes this flower from true lupines (*Lupinus* species).

Golden pea is distasteful to wild animals and livestock and can crowd out desirable forage plants, especially if the land has been overgrazed.

HABITAT/RANGE: Prefers the moist soils of plains and hills and grows in dense patches in open fields and meadows and along roadsides at elevations up to 8,000 feet in west and central Montana. A similar species, **prairie golden banner (*Thermopsis rhombifolia*)** is more common in eastern Montana.

Silvery scurf pea in late July on a dry
prairie northwest of Broadus

Slimflower scurf pea in late July near
U.S. 12 east of Harlowton

Golden pea in early May adjacent to U.S. 89 north of Dupuyer

Dwarf Clover   *Trifolium nanum*

Dwarf clover forms dense mats less than 1 inch above the ground. The compound leaves have three leaflets. Each stem bears one to four strikingly beautiful flowers with rose or purplish, parallel stripes on a lighter colored base. This clover is distinguished from others in the Rocky Mountains by its short height and four or fewer flowers in each head.

Dwarf clover is a popular food of mountain goats, bighorn sheep, and pikas.

HABITAT/RANGE: Grows on open and rocky slopes at subalpine and alpine zones in west-central and southwest Montana.

Red Clover   *Trifolium pratense*

The 1- to 3-foot-tall stems of red clover bear compound leaves, with three broad oval leaflets, that emerge just below the flower head. The upper surface of each leaflet often shows an inverted V pattern. Fifty to two hundred small, pealike, pink to purple flowers are arranged in globe-shaped heads.

Bees and other insects are attracted to the red, fragrant flowers; red clover is an important forage plant for commercial beehives.

HABITAT/RANGE: Red clover was introduced from Europe as a forage crop but has escaped into fields and pastures and is very common along roadsides in west and south-central Montana.

American Vetch   *Vicia americana*

The 6- to 30-inch-long stems of American vetch are weak and often recline along the ground or on other vegetation. The leaves are pinnately compound with eight to twelve leaflets that may or may not be hairy depending upon the variety of this wildflower. A tendril at the end of each leaf permits the plant to cling to other vegetation. Four to ten reddish lavender, purple, or violet, pealike flowers grow in racemes on stalks that arise from leaf axils.

HABITAT/RANGE: Prefers open fields, prairies, or woods and is often found along roadsides and on fences in west, central, and east Montana.

Hairy Vetch   *Vicia villosa*

The stem of hairy vetch is 20 to 80 inches long and covered with soft wavy hairs, which also cover the leaves and sepals. There are ten to twenty linear or lance-shaped leaflets in each pinnately compound leaf, which terminates with a long branched tendril. A stipule is located at the base of the petiole. Twenty to sixty reddish purple flowers crowd one side of the stalk. Hairy vetch resembles **bird vetch (*V. cracca*)** but has longer hairs.

HABITAT/RANGE: Hairy vetch was introduced from Europe to stabilize road banks and now grows along roadsides, fencerows, and disturbed soils in the mountains of western Montana.

Dwarf clover in late June along the Beartooth Highway between Red Lodge and Cooke City

American vetch in early June at the Suce Creek Trailhead in Paradise Valley southeast of Livingston

Red cloves in late June along the road next to Hungry Horse Reservoir west of Kalispell

Hairy vetch among dense growth in mid-June near Interstate 90 west of Missoula

PHLOX FAMILY   Polemoniaceae

Members of the phlox family, represented by nine genera in Montana, have five sepals and five petals that are fused into a trumpet-shaped, showy flower. Another distinguishing characteristic is the presence of three styles on the stigma. *Phlox* comes from Greek, meaning "flame," a reference to the colored flowers.

Narrow-leaved Collomia   *Collomia linearis*

The 4- to 6-inch-tall, usually unbranched stem of narrow-leaved collomia has long sticky hairs on the upper part and short hairs on the lower part. The narrow, lance-shaped, alternate leaves are stalkless and sometimes clasp the stem. The pink, lavender, blue, or white, mostly stemless flowers are arranged in a dense cluster arising from axils of leafy bracts. The small tubular flower has five oval, spreading lobes.

    Collomia comes from Greek, meaning "glue," a reference to a mucus coating that occurs on wetted seeds.

> HABITAT/RANGE: One of the first plants to appear in spring on disturbed soils in coniferous forests or along roads from the plains to montane zones in west, central, and east Montana.

Scarlet Gilia   *Ipomopsis aggregata*
                                         Gilia aggregata

The trumpet-shaped, brilliant red flowers of scarlet gilia, which may sometimes be pale pink or yellowish with red speckles, attract hummingbirds. The five pointed lobes of the corolla bend backward, and the throat of the flower may have yellow or white spots. The 1½-inch-long flowers hang mostly from one side of the unbranched, 1- to 3-foot-tall stem. This biennial grows a clump of deeply dissected basal leaves the first year and a stem with flowers the second year. The stem and leaves are sticky and crushed upper leaves give off a skunklike odor.

> HABITAT/RANGE: Prefers dry soils on grassy hills and slopes, among sagebrush, and in woodlands from valleys to montane zones in west Montana.

Ballhead Gilia   *Ipomopsis congesta*
                                         Gilia congesta

Ballhead gilia has an erect or spreading stem that is branched and woody near the base and is 8 to 12 inches tall. The long leaves are divided into three to five narrow lobes that may be further segmented. The small, stalkless white flowers are arranged in a ball-like cluster containing long and tangled hairs. The filaments of the stamens are longer than the bluish anthers.

> HABITAT/RANGE: Found on dry or rocky soils in open areas of valleys or foothills in only a few counties in west, south-central, and east Montana.

Narrow-leaved collomia in late June at the Suce Creek Trailhead southeast of Livingston

Scarlet gilia in mid-July near Painted Rocks Lake west of Sula

Ballhead gilia in late May on dry soil bordering the Ruby Reservoir south of Alder

Pink Microsteris   *Microsteris gracilis*

Pink microsteris may reach 10 inches tall. The hairy stems branch above the middle and support tiny flowers that have white, pink, or lavender petals with slightly notched lobes. The hairy, stalkless, elliptical leaves are located opposite on the lower part of the stem and alternate on the upper part, where they are more narrow and pointed. The calyx is narrow and sticky, with the hairy, green sepals separated by transparent areas.

HABITAT/RANGE: Found in meadows, on rock outcrops, and on roadsides in west, central, and southeast Montana.

Phlox *Phlox* species

Identification of individual *Phlox* species requires observation of microscopic features. Most phlox are relatively small plants, growing close to the ground, and are woody at their base. The narrow leaves are stalkless and arranged opposite on the stem. The corolla is a slender tube that abruptly opens into a spreading ring of five petals that varies from white to pink, purple, or blue. The filaments are short, and the anthers may sometimes extend beyond the tube opening.

Spreading Phlox   *Phlox diffusa*

Spreading phlox forms dense, wide mats rarely more than 4 inches above the ground. The linear, opposite, green leaves are less than 1 inch long and sharply pointed and hairless. The leaves overlap and have a hairy tuft at their base. Solitary flowers at the end of short stems cover the mat with blue- or pink-tinged white petals.

HABITAT/RANGE: Found in moist areas from montane to subalpine zones in west and south Montana.

Hood's Phlox   *Phlox hoodii*

Hood's phlox, also called *carpet phlox*, has stems that spread along the ground and give rise to branches that may reach 6 inches tall at low elevations but barely extend beyond a compact mat at higher elevations. Tiny, narrow, spine-tipped, woolly leaves cover the stems. Single white flowers fade to pink or lilac later in the season. Woolly hairs also cover the calyx.

HABITAT/RANGE: Blooms in early spring on dry soils in open forests, sagebrush foothills, valleys, and the plains in west, central, and east Montana.

Missoula Phlox   *Phlox kelseyi* var. *missoulensis*

Missoula phlox is a low, mat-forming perennial with erect or somewhat prostrate stems up to 4 inches long. The succulent leaves, much longer than wide, have thick margins and vary from smooth to glandular or hairy. Missoula phlox has white to light blue flowers.

HABITAT/RANGE: Missoula phlox grows on dry and rocky soils in west and central Montana.

Pink microsteris in mid-June in a partially shaded area near Miner Lakes west of Jackson

Spreading phlox in mid-May along the Madison River south of Ennis

Hood's phlox in late April on a dry, rocky area at Missouri Headwaters State Park near Three Forks

Missoula phlox in late May on Waterworks Hill, n open, well-rained slope ear Missoula

Long-leaf Phlox
Phlox longifolia

The solitary or clumped stems of long-leaf phlox may reach 16 inches tall and are woody at their base. They can be somewhat prostrate but are more erect than many other common phloxes. The narrow, soft leaves, which occur in pairs at nodes along the stems, reach 3 inches in length. Flowers are borne at the ends of the stems in clusters, with the central or terminal flower blooming first. The long corolla tube varies from white to pink or lavender.

HABITAT/RANGE: Common on dry rocky soils, the plains, and grasslands, often among sagebrush, in west and south Montana.

Cushion Phlox
Phlox pulvinata

Cushion phlox forms a compact mat with short tufted stems crowded with short, linear, rigid, spine-tipped leaves. A single, rather large, white or bluish, short-stemmed flower occurs on each stem. The entire cushion, including the calyx, is lightly to densely glandular and hairy.

HABITAT/RANGE: Cushion phlox prefers dry rocky soils in alpine meadows in west and central Montana.

Showy Jacob's Ladder
Polemonium pulcherrimum

The weak but mostly erect, hairy stem of showy Jacob's ladder is rarely more than 12 inches long and grows in clusters. The pinnately compound leaves have many pairs of leaflets along the main axis, resembling a ladder. Flowers grow in clusters at the tip of the stem. The pale blue to lavender petals form a bell-shaped tube with a white or yellowish orange ring at the bottom. Five white stamens usually extend beyond the petals.

HABITAT/RANGE: Prefers moist soils in grassy areas along streams and in meadows and open forests from montane to alpine zones in west and central Montana.

Sky Pilot
Polemonium viscosum

Sky pilot, also called *skunkweed* and *sticky Jacob's ladder*, has 4- to 16-inch-tall stems that grow in dense clumps. The long leaves are pinnately compound with a whorl of thirty to forty small leaflets. Both the leaves and stems are covered with sticky glandular hairs that smell like a skunk. The funnel-shaped, blueish violet flowers have five lobes and five conspicuous orange or yellow stamens.

The skunklike odor may be a defense against grazing animals. The blue portion of the flower reflects ultraviolet light while other parts absorb it, a feature that attracts insects past the stamens and stigmas and to the plant's nectar.

HABITAT/RANGE: Prefers open rocky disturbed soils in alpine zones in west and central Montana.

Long-leaf phlox along Rye Creek
Road south of Darby

Cushion phlox in mid-July on a barren rocky
plateau in the Gravelly Range south of Ennis

Showy Jacob's ladder in
early May at Sluice Boxes
State Park west of U.S. 89
and northwest of Monarch

Sky pilot in late June
along the Beartooth
Highway between Red
Lodge and Cooke City

PINK FAMILY
Caryophyllaceae

Members of the large pink family, represented by sixteen genera in Montana, generally have opposite, entire leaves and swollen stem nodes. The radially symmetrical flowers usually have four or five separate petals that are notched at the tip and five separate or united sepals. Each flower includes five or ten stamens. The pistil has two to five styles that are rarely united.

Sandwort *Arenaria* species

Although not a comparatively large genus, the sandworts are very similar in appearance and difficult to identify. Many sandworts are cushion plants with narrow, sometimes spiny, opposite leaves that lack petioles and stipules. The plants have several cup-shaped flowers with blunt-tipped, white petals with entire margins and five sepals either separated or united at the base. Each flower usually includes ten stamens and three styles.

Ballhead Sandwort
Arenaria congesta

The erect, thin, hairless stems of ballhead sandwort are 6 to 20 inches tall and bear two to four pairs of small opposite leaves plus a clump of narrow, sharp-pointed, grasslike basal leaves. A ball-shaped cluster of small white flowers forms at the terminal end of the stem, each flower consisting of five petals and five shorter, lance-shaped sepals with papery margins and pointed tips.

HABITAT/RANGE: Grows in sandy slightly dry soils among sagebrush and grasses in pine forests to alpine slopes in west and central Montana.

Hooker Sandwort
Arenaria hookeri
Eremogone hookeri

Hooker sandwort forms dense cushions several inches wide and usually less than 4 inches tall, although the stems are up to 6 inches long. The narrow, more or less rigid leaves are linear or awl-shaped. The stalkless flowers have petals that are often twice as long as the sepals.

HABITAT/RANGE: Grows on dry hills, plains, and slopes east of the Continental Divide in southwest, central, and southeast Montana.

Nuttall's Sandwort
Arenaria nuttallii

The slightly woody stems of Nuttall's sandwort crawl along the ground and are seldom more than 5 inches tall. The flowers congregate at the top of the stem and are composed of five white petals and five sharp-pointed sepals of the same length as the petals. The small, lance-shaped leaves have a sharp smell. Glandular hairs cover the foliage.

HABITAT/RANGE: Found infrequently on open sites among sagebrush and up to alpine zones in west and central Montana.

head sandwort
te June
theast
ivingston

ker sandwort
id-June among
ebrush in
horn Canyon
ional Recreation
a in south-
tral Montana

tall's sandwort
ate May in
horn Canyon
ional Recreation
a in south-
tral Montana

Field Chickweed   *Cerastium arvense*

The branched stems of field chickweed may grow up to 20 inches tall but often form mats on the ground. Slender leaves are arranged opposite on the stems, often with clusters of secondary leaves crowded in the axils of the larger, primary leaves. The white flowers, about ½ inch across, have five deeply notched petals, about three times as long as the sepals, ten stamens, and five styles. The bracts below the flowers are lance-shaped with a thin membranous margin.

HABITAT/RANGE: Found from valleys to alpine meadows in west, central, and east Montana.

Grass Pink   *Dianthus armeria*

Grass pink, an introduced garden plant from Europe, is also called *Deptford pink* after a location in London. This biennial has one or several stiff stems that are swollen at the point where the leaves attach. The very narrow, opposite leaves are 1½ to 4 inches long. The flowers are arranged in a tightly forked, hairy cluster. The calyx of the flower is a narrow tube about ½ inch wide. The five long petals have long, slender bases and broad upper ends that are toothed on the outer edges.

HABITAT/RANGE: Grows on roadsides, in empty lots, and on old fields in northwest Montana.

White Campion   *Lychnis alba*

The several 1- to 3-foot-tall, branched stems of white campion have glandular hairs and bear opposite, lance-shaped to elliptic leaves, the lower ones with petioles and the smaller upper ones without. The calyx forms a long, striped tube with glandular hairs. Five white petals on each flower are deeply notched at the tip and narrow at the base. Small appendages form a prominent circle where the corolla emerges from the calyx. Male and female flowers occur on separate plants.

HABITAT/RANGE: White campion was introduced from Europe and is commonly found along roadsides and on other disturbed soils in west and central Montana.

Moss Campion   *Silene acaulis*

Moss campion forms low mats, 1 foot or more wide, with 2- to 6-inch-tall stems. Narrow, opposite, bright green leaves are congested at the base of the flowering stems. A single pink to deep rose, and occasionally white, flower has five petals that are notched at the tip and have two small appendages near the tube opening. The sepals are united into a bell-shaped tube that hides the base of the petals. Moss campion may be confused with Rocky Mountain douglasia (*Douglasia montana*) but differs in having exposed rather than hidden stamens and styles.

HABITAT/RANGE: Common on rocky ridges, crevices, and scree slopes in alpine zones in west and south-central Montana.

Field chickweed in mid-May along
the Madison River south of Ennis

Grass pink in mid-July
east of St. Regis

White campion in late June at
Natural Bridge State Park on the
Boulder River south of Big Timber

Moss campion in mid-June along the Beartooth
Highway between Red Lodge and Cooke City

Bladder Campion

Silene vulgaris
S. cucubalus

Bladder campion has a distinctive calyx, composed of five sepals, that looks like an inflated globe. The calyx is hairless, pale green to purplish, and has pinkish brown veinlets, similar to a paper lantern. The flowers, with a three-styled pistil and stamens, have five white petals that are deeply split into two lobes and are grouped in flat-top clusters. The leaves are opposite and lance-shaped.

> HABITAT/RANGE: Bladder campion, introduced from Europe, is found in disturbed places like roadsides, cultivated areas, and waste ground in west, central, and northeast Montana.

Long-stalked Starwort

Stellaria longipes

The small ¼-inch-long flowers of long-stalked starwort occur alone or with a few others at the tip of the stem. The five white petals are split into lobes nearly to their base. Five sepals are shorter than the petals. The 2- to 8-inch-high stems are slender and hairless and bear opposite, stalkless, bluish green leaves that are lance-shaped to linear, ⅜ to 1¼ inches long, stiff, and sharp-tipped. **Northern starwort (S. calycantha)** is similar but has sepals that are longer than the petals.

All starworts are edible as salad greens or as a cooked vegetable, providing a good source of vitamin C and minerals.

> HABITAT/RANGE: Found in dry to wet, open to wooded habitats from low to high elevations in west and central Montana.

PRIMROSE FAMILY

Primulaceae

Members of the primrose family, represented by eight genera in Montana, have showy flowers that usually have five sepals fused at their base, five petals fused into a tube with lobes, and five stamens. The pistil is superior with a single style and stigma. Leaves are usually simple and basal.

Few-flowered Shooting Star

Dodecatheon pulchellum

The leafless stem of few-flowered shooting star is 6 to 12 inches tall, with a basal rosette of long, elliptical, usually hairless leaves. Pink or magenta petals bend backward from a yellow base to reveal the downward-pointing style that is clasped tightly by yellow to purplish stamens. Four species of shooting star have been reported in Montana, all similar in general appearance and differing in details such as degree of hairiness, filament length, and stigma shape.

> HABITAT/RANGE: Prefers moist soils in meadows and along streambanks from valleys to alpine zones in west, central, and east Montana.

ladder campion in early August along the
mas entrance road to Glacier National Park

Long-stalked starwort in mid-July at
Pintler Lake north of Wisdom

-flowered shooting star on May 1 near East
Rosebud Lake west of Red Lodge

Dodecatheon species covering a meadow
in late June around Crystal Lake in the
Big Snowy Mountains near Lewistown

Rocky Mountain Douglasia   *Douglasia montana*

Rocky Mountain douglasia is a low, spreading cushion plant with small, lance-shaped leaves that are tightly grouped into mats. Each 1- to 3-inch-long stem that arises from the mat supports a single bright pink to violet, wheel-shaped flower, consisting of a funnel-shaped tube with five flaring lobes. The stamens never project beyond the yellow-rimmed tube opening, distinguishing Rocky Mountain douglasia from moss campion (*Silene acaulis*), which has a similar flower but with stamens and style that extend beyond the petals. The lack of conspicuous stamens and pistils also distinguishes Rocky Mountain douglasia from members of the phlox family.

> HABITAT/RANGE: Blooms in spring at low elevations and in early summer in alpine zones in west and central Montana.

PURSLANE FAMILY   *Portulacaceae*

Members of the purslane family, with six genera listed in Montana, have succulent leaves, usually with a smooth margin and sometimes in basal rosettes. The stems are often prostrate and sometimes contain a bitter sap. The small, showy flowers, partially enclosed by two unequal-sized bracts, commonly have two sepals, which is an unusual number in wildflowers. There are usually five or more petals that often have distinctive pink stripes.

Springbeauty   *Claytonia lanceolata*

Springbeauty has one to several basal leaves with long petioles, and two opposite, stalkless, lance-shaped leaves located near the middle of the 2- to 8-inch-long stem. The saucer-shaped flowers have five ½- to 1-inch-wide petals that have shallow notches at their tips and are white to pink, usually with dark pink or red to purple veins on the upper surface. The flower has two green sepals, five stamens, and three styles.

All parts of springbeauty are edible either fresh or cooked. Meriwether Lewis collected a specimen of springbeauty in Idaho in June 1806 and noted in his journal that the root was eaten by Shoshones, and that it had "a good deel in flavor an consistency like the Jerusalem Artichoke."

> HABITAT/RANGE: Appears in cool moist soil where the snow has recently melted in west and central Montana.

A mat of Rocky Mountain douglasia in late April on the foothills west of Townsend

Springbeauty on May 1 near East Rosebud Lake west of Red Lodge

Pygmy Bitterroot
Lewisia pygmaea

Though pygmy bitterroot has a spectacular blossom, it is easy to overlook when it is growing among other vegetation. One or several short stems emerge from a rosette of linear, fleshy leaves that, unlike bitterroot (*L. rediviva*), remain present throughout the short blooming season. The narrow leaves, up to 6 inches long, are longer than the flowering stems and tend to cradle the flowers. Each stem, with opposite, leaflike bracts halfway up, supports a single white to pink or purple flower. The flowers have about seven petals, a two-cleft style, and two sepals that have tiny toothed margins.

HABITAT/RANGE: Blooms for a short period in midsummer on gravelly slopes of moist to dry ridges at subalpine to alpine zones in west and central Montana.

Bitterroot
Lewisia rediviva

Bitterroot, the state flower of Montana, will not be confused with any other wildflower in Montana when it's in full bloom. Each large flower has twelve to sixteen rose or pink, and occasionally white, rounded or pointed petals. The short, narrow, fleshy leaves first appear in fall in a basal rosette, renew growth in early spring, and then wither when the flowers bloom. The flowers unfold from a tubular structure held close to the ground on a short stem.

The genus name *Lewisia* honors Meriwether Lewis, leader of the Lewis and Clark Expedition, who collected a specimen of bitterroot near Lolo. American Indians harvested the roots and boiled them for food.

HABITAT/RANGE: Grows on open, dry or rocky, shallow soils, which may occur among sagebrush, from the prairies and foothills to montane forests in west and central Montana. Observing the flower requires being in the right location during the short blooming season, which may vary from mid-May to late June.

Miner's lettuce
Montia perfoliata
Claytonia perfoliata

The feature of miner's lettuce that easily distinguishes it from other members of this genus is the distinctive, wide, green disk below the flower cluster, a structure formed by the fusion of two stem leaves. The slender stems appear to grow through the middle of this succulent, circular leaf. Tiny white or pinkish, five-petaled flowers are clustered above the leaf. Long-stemmed basal leaves vary in shape and color.

The leaves of miner's lettuce make tasty salad greens.

HABITAT/RANGE: Miner's lettuce grows in moist areas along brooks and springs up to 6,000 feet in west and south-central Montana.

my bitterroot
arly July in the
velly Range
th of Ennis

itterroot in late June just
outside the entrance to
Yellowstone National
Park at Gardiner

nset: White bitterroot in
nid-June on Waterworks
Hill on the outskirts of
Missoula

Miner's lettuce in early June on a
forest floor southeast of Darby that was
destroyed by wildfire the year before

ROSE FAMILY   Rosaceae

Members of the rose family, which includes trees, shrubs, and herbs, have five petals, five sepals, multiple pistils, and numerous stamens, all supported on a cup-, saucer-, or tube-shaped hypanthium. The stamens are commonly inserted in several whorls of five on a disk just inside the petals. See **Shrubs** for descriptions of serviceberry, chokecherry, wood's rose, wild plum, mountain-mahogany, mountain spray, ninebark, thimbleberry, steeplebush, and Cascade mountain ash.

Wild Strawberry   *Fragaria virginiana*

Wild strawberry spreads by slender, reddish stolons that lie on the ground and root at leaf nodes. The basal leaves are divided into three sharply toothed leaflets that are hairless on top and often have a bluish white cast. White flowers grow in clusters on slender stalks that are 2 to 6 inches long. Each flower has five broad, egg-shaped petals, five green sepals, twenty yellow stamens, and many pistils, all supported on a saucer-shaped hypanthium. **Woods strawberry (*F. vesca*)**, the only other *Fragaria* species in Montana, can be identified by the leaf surface, which bulges up between the veins.

Most cultivated strawberry plants were developed from *F. virginiana*.

HABITAT/RANGE: Prefers moist soils in meadows, along streams, and in woods in west, central, and southeast Montana.

Alpine Avens   *Geum rossii*

Alpine avens, also called *Ross's avens*, has stems that are usually less than 1 foot tall and bear one to four bright yellow, five-petaled flowers that resemble cinquefoil (*Potentilla* species) but are somewhat depressed in the center instead of flat. The pinnately compound basal leaves have many narrow segments. Stem leaves are much smaller. The flowers have many stamens and from few to many pistils. The style arises from the top of the ovary rather than the base, a feature that distinguishes *Geum* species from other similar plants in the rose family. The broad petals fall off early, leaving triangular sepals.

HABITAT/RANGE: Grows on moist soils from subalpine to alpine zones in west and south-central Montana.

Prairie Smoke   *Geum triflorum*

Prairie smoke, also called *old man's whiskers*, has a 6- to 24-inch-tall stem with hairy, fernlike, mostly basal leaves. There are usually three bell-shaped flowers per stem, each with light yellow or rosy petals that are nearly hidden by the pink or reddish sepals. Five bracts curve outward after fertilization and display feathery styles that assist in seed dispersal by wind.

American Indians used the roots of prairie smoke to make a beverage and eyewash.

HABITAT/RANGE: Prefers moist open meadows from prairies to alpine zones in central and east Montana.

Wild strawberry
mid-June at
Miner Lakes
west of Jackson

Alpine avens in
early July along
the Beartooth
Highway between
Red Lodge and
Cooke City

Prairie smoke in
late May along U.S.
191 at the mouth
of Gallatin Canyon
south of Bozeman

Ivesia   *Ivesia gordonii*

The tufted, mostly leafless stems of ivesia are 2 to 6 inches long with pinnately compound, hairy leaves consisting of many tiny, lobed leaflets. The small yellow flowers, later turning reddish brown, are arranged in a dense, compact head. The structure of the individual flower, difficult to discern without magnification, includes five pointed sepals that alternate with five short, rounded petals and five yellow stamens.

> HABITAT/RANGE: Occurs on barren gravelly soils, meadows, and talus slopes at high montane to alpine zones in west and south-central Montana.

🌿 Cinquefoil *Potentilla* species 🌿

Cinquefoils, twenty-six of which inhabit Montana, are difficult to identify, with the exception of shrubby cinquefoil (*P. fruticosa*), which is a highly branched shrub (see **Shrubs**), and marsh cinquefoil (*P. palustris*), which has purple or deep red petals. The leaves of cinquefoils are either palmately or pinnately divided into leaflets that have toothed or lobed margins. Stipules occur at the base of the leaf petiole. All cinquefoils have saucer-shaped, stalked flowers with five petals that vary from creamy white to pale or bright yellow. Each flower has numerous stamens and styles.

Silverweed   *Potentilla anserina*

Silverweed spreads by long reddish runners, forming a low mat. The pinnately compound basal leaves have eleven to twenty-five coarsely toothed leaflets that are green on the upper surface and covered with white, silky hairs beneath. The flowers are borne singly on long, leafless stalks that originate in leaf axils. Each flower, about 1 inch in diameter, has five bright yellow petals.

Lewis and Clark collected a specimen of silverweed in Oregon prior to their return trip in 1806. The leaves are rich in tannin, an astringent.

> HABITAT/RANGE: Found on moist soils along rivers and streams and on disturbed soils from the plains to montane zones across Montana.

Tall Cinquefoil   *Potentilla arguta*

Tall cinquefoil has stiff, erect, 16- to 32-inch-tall stems that are unbranched below the inflorescence. The pinnately compound, long-stalked basal leaves have five to eleven lobed, toothed leaflets. The fewer stem leaves are smaller. Both the stem and leaves are covered with glandular, sticky hairs. The pale yellow, cream, or white, five-petaled flowers are arranged in a crowded inflorescence in which the terminal flower blooms first. Five pointed, hairy, green sepals are nearly as long as the petals. Numerous yellow stamens are crowded in the cone-shaped flower center. Tall cinquefoil resembles **sticky cinquefoil (*P. glandulosa*)**, which is a smaller plant with a more open inflorescence.

> HABITAT/RANGE: Common on rich moist meadows and open hillsides and woods from the valleys to subalpine forests in west, central, and northeast Montana.

Potentilla species with white flowers in late May on Waterworks Hill near Missoula

Ivesia in mid-July on a barren plateau in the Gravelly Range south of Ennis

Tall cinquefoil in early July in the Gravelly Range south of Ennis

Silverweed in mid-May along the Musselshell River west of Roundup

Varileaf Cinquefoil   *Potentilla diversifolia*

Varileaf cinquefoil has many other common names, most referring to its distinctive bluish green leaves. The spreading stems are less than 12 inches long. The mostly basal leaves are palmately compound with five to seven deeply toothed leaflets that have silky hairs on their underside. Petioles of the leaves are longer than the leaf blade. Bright yellow flowers are arranged along the branched stems.

HABITAT/RANGE: Common on dry to moist soils of subalpine meadows and grasslands, and on rocky slopes up to treeline, in west and central Montana.

Fan-leaf Cinquefoil   *Potentilla flabellifolia*

Fan-leaf cinquefoil tends to grow in clumps with stems reaching 12 inches tall. The mostly basal leaves are held on long petioles, with three round, deeply toothed leaflets. The two to five bright yellow flowers at the top of the stem have five petals held on a saucer-shaped hypanthium surrounded by five sepal-like bracts.

HABITAT/RANGE: Often found in subalpine meadows and along streambanks in west Montana.

Snow Cinquefoil   *Potentilla nivea*

Snow cinquefoil is only 1½ to 6 inches tall, growing in mats. The long-stalked, mostly basal leaves are greenish above with silvery, feltlike hairs below and are palmately three-lobed and toothed on the margins. One to five flowers occur in flat-topped clusters. The broad petals of the flower, slightly lobed on the end, are yellow, sometimes with orange streaks, and are slightly longer than the silky or woolly sepals. The petals surround numerous stamens and pistils.

HABITAT/RANGE: Found on drained rocky soils or in meadows at subalpine to alpine zones in west and central Montana.

Marsh Cinquefoil   *Potentilla palustris*

The red or purplish stems of marsh cinquefoil crawl along the ground and root at the nodes. The pinnately compound leaves with five to seven toothed leaflets are smooth above and finely haired below. The basal leaves have long clasping petioles, while the reduced stem leaves are essentially stalkless. The reddish flowers have five pointed petals and five purplish, spreading sepals, the latter alternating with linear bracts and both longer than the petals. Each flower includes ten to thirty reddish stamens and a smooth style.

HABITAT/RANGE: Prefers wet meadows and marshes or the banks of streams and lakes from low to high elevations in northwest Montana.

Varileaf cinquefoil along the road to astle Town, a ghost town near Lennep

Fan-leaf cinquefoil in early June at the base of the Beartooth Highway south of Red Lodge

w cinquefoil in mid-June at the Gardiner e Trailhead along the Beartooth Highway between Red Lodge and Cooke City

Marsh cinquefoil in mid-July in a swampy area adjoining a lake north of Noxon

ST. JOHN'S-WORT FAMILY   Hypericaceae

The small St. John's-wort family, with a single genus in Montana, includes herbs and shrubs that have opposite leaves, often with black dots. The plants contain a clear or colored, resinous sap. The flowers are arranged in branched clusters and are usually yellow or orange. Each flower has five petals, five sepals, and many stamens that are joined at the base of the ovary into several bunches.

Common St. John's-Wort   *Hypericum perforatum*

Common St. John's-wort was introduced from Europe and has become a noxious weed. Its creeping, horizontal stems spread over and under ground and reach a height of 1 to 3 feet. The rust-colored, two-ridged stems have many branches and are woody at the base. The opposite, stalkless, short leaves are longer than wide, tapered at the base, and covered with translucent dots. The showy, yellow, starlike flowers have five petals, sometimes edged with black dots. Each flower has numerous stamens, which are longer than the petals. Common St. John's-wort resembles the native **western St. John's-wort (*H. formosum*)**, but its leaves are lance-shaped rather than broadly elliptic, and the sepals have pointed rather than rounded tips.

Herbalists recommend common St. John's-wort for treating depression and several other ailments. Livestock who have eaten this plant may develop severe skin lesions with exposure to sunlight.

HABITAT/RANGE: Grows on dry pastures and sandy or gravelly disturbed soils, often present on roadsides, in west and north-central Montana.

SANDALWOOD FAMILY   Santalaceae

Members of the sandalwood family, with two genera listed in Montana, have alternate leaves and small flowers with no petals but five greenish purple sepals. The mature flower produces a berry that is juicy and usually red.

Bastard Toadflax   *Comandra umbellata*

Bastard toadflax is 4 to 13 inches tall, with ⅜- to 1¼-inch-long, alternate leaves that are linear, lance-shaped, or narrowly elliptical. The thick leaves are grayish green due to a whitish substance that covers their surface. The flowers lack petals. The calyx, fused at the base, has five flaring, fleshy, white to purple lobes. The stamens are located opposite the calyx lobes, with a tuft of hair emerging from the base of each lobe and behind each stamen.

Bastard toadflax spreads by underground stems that attach to and parasitize over two hundred other plant species. The fruits are edible but may be toxic if the plant is growing on soils high in selenium.

HABITAT/RANGE: Found in large numbers in many dry habitats in west, central, and east Montana.

Common St. John's-wort in mid-August in the
National Bison Range west of St. Ignatius

: Common St. John's-wort in mid-July east of St. Regis

Bastard toadflax in late May along U.S. 191 at the
mouth of Gallatin Canyon south of Bozeman

SAXIFRAGE FAMILY   Saxifragaceae

Members of the saxifrage family, represented by fourteen genera in Montana, have white but sometimes yellowish or reddish flowers that are arranged at the tip of the stems and commonly have five sepals, five petals, and either five or ten stamens. The sepals, petals, and stamens form a saucer- or cup-shaped structure. Each flower usually has more than one pistil.

Roundleaf Alumroot   *Heuchera cylindrica*

The 6- to 18-inch-tall stem of roundleaf alumroot is leafless but has one to three membranous, brown to green bracts. It is densely covered with glandular hairs near the top. Leaves held on hairy, white petioles are clustered at the base and are egg- to heart-shaped with five to seven rounded and toothed lobes. The cuplike flower has five large, cream or yellowish green, blunt-tipped sepals and five stamens that are opposite the sepals. The petals are usually absent. The short-stalked flowers are arranged in a narrow, spike-like inflorescence.

Roundleaf alumroot has many medicinal uses because of its alumlike properties—tannin found in the root is an astringent and can shrink tissue and blood vessels.

HABITAT/RANGE: Grows on gravel or rocky soils from valleys to subalpine zones in west and central Montana.

Bulbiferous Prairie Star   *Lithophragma glabrum*
                                                        L. bulbifera

Bulbiferous prairie star, also called *rockstar*, may have small red bulbs in the axils of some of the stem leaves. These bulbs provide a vegetative means of reproduction. The reddish purple stems are 2 to 10 inches tall and covered with fine glandular hairs. Short, palmately compound basal leaves have three to five leaflets, while the stem leaves have three lobes that in turn are divided into three. The flowers have five white or pinkish petals that are usually divided into five narrow, pointed lobes with the middle lobes longer and wider. Each flower contains ten stamens and three styles.

HABITAT/RANGE: Grows on grasslands and in open woods in west and central Montana.

Roundleaf alumroot in early July at the Moose Creek Campground in the Little Belt Mountains north of White Sulphur Springs

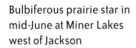

Bulbiferous prairie star in mid-June at Miner Lakes west of Jackson

Small-flowered Fringecup   *Lithophragma parviflora*

Small-flowered fringecup is distinguished from the other two *Lithophragma* species in Montana by its long, cone-shaped calyx that tapers to the base and petals that are mostly three-lobed. The leafy, 3- to 15-inch-tall stems have glandular hairs. The basal leaves, sparsely covered with white hairs, have petioles and are divided to the base into three to five segments, each with two to three lobes. Several white, star-shaped flowers with five lobed petals occur at the end of the stem in a raceme.

HABITAT/RANGE: Grows on moist to well-drained soils among sagebrush, on grasslands, in meadows, and in open forests from the foothills to lower montane zones in west and south-central Montana.

Fringed Grass-of-Parnassus   *Parnassia fimbriata*

Fringed grass-of-Parnassus has a striking white flower with a prominent fringe at the base of each of the five petals. The stem grows to about 14 inches tall and bears kidney-shaped basal leaves on short petioles. A single bractlike leaf clasps the stem at about its midpoint. Five sepals below the petals have fine teeth near the tip. Surrounding the greenish yellow pistil are pawlike sterile stamens, separated by five infertile stamens with long filaments that separate the petals.

HABITAT/RANGE: Common on wet shaded streambanks or meadows from montane to alpine zones in west, central, and northeast Montana.

Small-flowered Grass-of-Parnassus   *Parnassia parviflora*

The white petals of small-flowered grass-of-parnassus have mostly five veins and no fringe. The sterile stamens have gland-tipped lobes. The flower stalks have a single leaf or bract, located above the base, that is not clasping and tapers at the base.

HABITAT/RANGE: Prefers wet sites, such as grassy streambanks, in west and south-central Montana.

Brook Saxifrage   *Saxifraga arguta*
S. odontoloma

Brook saxifrage has shiny basal leaves that are mostly round with teeth on the margins. The single, leafless stem varies from 8 to 24 inches tall. Ten or more flowers are arranged in an open panicle. The tiny white or pinkish flowers have five green to purple sepals, five white round petals, and ten conspicuous red stamens. **Red-stemmed saxifrage (*S. lyallii*)** resembles brook saxifrage but is usually less than 8 inches tall and has a smaller, closed inflorescence.

HABITAT/RANGE: Found along the mossy sides of small streams and brooks from montane to subalpine zones in west and central Montana.

Top left and inset: Small-flowered fringecup in early June north of Marion

Top right: Fringed grass-of-Parnassus in late August at Lower Seymour Lake in the Anaconda-Pintler Range north of Wisdom

ll-flowered grass-of-Parnassus in late July along Rock Creek at the base of the Beartooth Highway south of Red Lodge

Brook saxifrage in late July at the base of the Beartooth Highway south of Red Lodge

Bog Saxifrage
Saxifraga oregana

The leafless, sometimes purple stem of bog saxifrage is 1 to 2 feet tall and covered with fine glandular hairs. The 2- to 7-inch-long basal leaves are wider above the middle and tapered to the base, where they are attached by broad, winged petioles. The leaves have smooth to serrated margins. The small, delicate, white to greenish flowers are crowded in an open panicle. Each flower has five broad petals and ten stamens with pink to orange anthers. The flower stalks are covered with red sticky hairs, visible only with a magnifying lens.

HABITAT/RANGE: Prefers wet meadows and streambanks from subalpine forests to alpine tundra in west and central Montana.

Snowball Saxifrage
Saxifraga rhomboidea

Snowball saxifrage has a 3- to 12-inch-tall stem coated with sticky hairs. Egg- or diamond-shaped leaves, up to 3 inches long, are arranged in a basal rosette. They are smooth with round-toothed edges, have silky hairs on their lower surface, and are held on broad, flat stalks. The small, white, short-stalked flowers form a dense, round cluster at the top of the stem. Each short-stalked flower has five egg-shaped petals, five sepals, and ten stamens. This flower might be confused with American bistort (*Polygonum bistortoides*), but that species has long, narrow basal leaves.

HABITAT/RANGE: Prefers moist, open slopes from sagebrush steppe to alpine zones in west and central Montana.

Fringecup
Tellima grandiflora

The stems of fringecup reach 3 feet in height and bear round to heart-shaped, mostly basal leaves, which are 1 to 4 inches long but smaller above, have shallow lobes and many irregular teeth along the margins, and are supported by long, hairy petioles. The striking flowers have five white to reddish petals that are fringed on the edge and held on a green, cup-shaped calyx. The flowers occur at intervals along one side of the stem.

HABITAT/RANGE: Prefers moist soils in woods, along streambanks, and in meadows from valleys to subalpine zones in northwest Montana.

Foamflower
Tiarella trifoliata

The solitary or more often clustered stems of foamflower are 6 to 15 inches tall, bearing maplelike, mostly basal leaves on long petioles and a few smaller stem leaves on short stalks. The tiny, delicate, white flowers are arranged in an open elongated inflorescence and attached by wiry stalks to the upper part of the stem. The calyx forms a short cuplike base holding five white, linear petals and ten white, protruding, pendulous stamens.

HABITAT/RANGE: Grows on moist soils in shady coniferous forests and along streambanks at low to high montane zones in west Montana.

Bog saxifrage in late July in a small stream in the Pioneer Mountains south of Wise River

Snowball saxifrage in late May at the base of the Beartooth Highway south of Red Lodge

Fringecup on the last day of June just inside the southern border of Glacier National Park east of Essex

Foamflower in mid-July along North Fork Lost Creek in the Swan Valley north of Seeley Lake

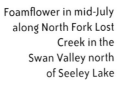

SPURGE FAMILY   Euphorbiaceae

Most of the members of the large spurge family, with just two genera listed in Montana, occur in warm regions of the world. The stems of the herbs in the family contain a milky sap, sometimes poisonous and irritating to the eyes. The flowers are unisexual—male (staminate) and female (pistillate) flowers are separate.

Leafy Spurge   *Euphorbia esula*

The erect, smooth stems of leafy spurge are 1 to 3 feet tall, and if broken will exude a milky sap, which is also present in the leaves. The 1- to 3-inch-long, narrow leaves alternate on the stem and often droop. The flowers are arranged in an umbel with the branches originating from a leaf bract. The yellowish green "flower" is a pair of heart-shaped bracts that cradle the small, greenish, cuplike flowers that lack petals and sepals.

Leafy spurge is a noxious weed that was introduced into North America sometime during the 1800s and became established in Canada and the northern part of the United States. Its ability to produce numerous seeds and spread by rhizomes makes it difficult to control. Cattle and horses avoid this toxic plant, but sheep will eat it without any adverse effects.

HABITAT/RANGE: Found in valleys, mountain foothills, and montane forests, and on disturbed soils on roadsides and in pastures, in west, central, and east Montana.

Snow-on-the-Mountain   *Euphorbia marginata*

The finely hairy or smooth, mostly erect stems of snow-on-the-mountain reach 3 feet in height. The 4-inch-long, entire, stalkless leaves have pointed tips and alternate on the stem. A whorl of leaves occurs near the upper part of the stem just below leafy branches. The upper leaves are opposite, densely clustered, and have broad white bands, which are occasionally light pink, around their margins. The small flower heads, less conspicuous than the leaves, have five white petals that surround one female and several small male flowers.

The milky juice in the stems of this plant may irritate the skin of some people. The plant is not favored by cattle, and it may increase on grazed pastures.

HABITAT/RANGE: Having escaped cultivation, it grows on dry plains, in valleys, and on roadsides in east and south-central Montana.

Leafy spurge in late May along Canyon Ferry Reservoir north of Townsend

Snow-on-the-mountain in
late July along a country road
northwest of Miles City

STONECROP FAMILY   Crassulaceae

The stonecrop family represents a variety of flowers, including house and garden plants, but only the genus *Sedum* occurs in the wild in Montana. Most members of the family grow in dry areas and have succulent, simple leaves. The flowers are usually small and star-shaped with four or five sepals, and four or five or no petals.

Seven stonecrops (*Sedum* species) grow in Montana and are difficult to distinguish from one another. Stonecrops conserve water by closing small pores, called *stomata*, on the leaf surface during the day. Leaves and shoots of stonecrop are eaten raw in salads or cooked in soups and stews, but older plants become bitter. Stonecrops are rich in vitamins A and C, and have been used to treat skin wounds, burns, and bites.

Lanceleaf Stonecrop   *Sedum lanceolatum*

The green, yellow, or red stems of lanceleaf stonecrop, which tends to grow in clumps, are less than 12 inches tall. The narrow, fleshy, linear leaves are mostly basal and vary from green to reddish brown. They have a sharp ridge and taper to a slender point. Short stem leaves are alternate, fleshy, and lance-shaped, and usually drop off shortly after flowering. The bright yellow, star-shaped flowers, sometimes with a purple tinge, have five sepals, five sharply pointed petals, and eight to ten stamens.

HABITAT/RANGE: Prefers rocky and gravelly dry soils exposed to the sun in west and south-central Montana.

Rose Crown   *Sedum rhodanthum*

Rose crown has an erect, unbranched, 4- to 15-inch-tall stem that usually grows in clusters and bears many fleshy, short, smooth, flattened leaves. The pale pink and white flowers, with conspicuous dark red or purple stamens, are crowded in racemes in the axils of leaves at the top of the stem. Rose crown resembles king's crown, but the latter is shorter and has purple to dark red flowers and grows on well-drained rather than wet soils.

HABITAT/RANGE: Found along streams or in marshes and wet meadows at montane, subalpine, and alpine zones in west and south-central Montana.

King's Crown   *Sedum roseum*
                                                    S. integrifolium

King's crown, also called *roseroot*, is a striking wildflower with clustered, 2- to 6-inch-tall stems. The alternate, egg-shaped, succulent leaves are smallest near the base and have smooth to scalloped margins that are often reddish. The tiny, dark red to maroon flowers are tightly concentrated in heads at the top of the stem.

HABITAT/RANGE: Found on rocky moist soils on cliffs and open ridges from subalpine to alpine zones in west and central Montana.

Lanceleaf stonecrop in early July at the Moose Creek Fishing Access in the Little Belt Mountains north of White Sulphur Springs

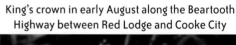
crown in a wet area along the Beartooth way between Red Lodge and Cooke City

King's crown in early August along the Beartooth Highway between Red Lodge and Cooke City

Wormleaf Stonecrop   *Sedum stenopetalum*

Wormleaf stonecrop has prostrate, nonflowering stems and erect, clustered, fleshy, flowering stems that are 4 to 8 inches tall. Basal leaves are narrow and arranged in a tight rosette. The linear or lance-shaped, alternate stem leaves are narrowed at the tip and twist into a wormlike shape with age. The star-shaped, yellow flowers have four to five spreading, pointed petals, four to five sepals, and eight to ten stamens. Wormleaf stonecrop resembles lanceleaf stonecrop (*S. lanceolatum*), but differs in having flattened leaves with a raised midvein that taper to fine points, and usually having bulblike plantlets in upper stem leaf axils. In addition, the starlike capsules of wormleaf stonecrop are wide-spreading rather than erect.

HABITAT/RANGE: Common on dry and well-drained rocky soils in open sunlit spaces from the foothills to alpine zones in west and south-central Montana.

SUNFLOWER FAMILY   Compositae/Asteraceae

The sunflower family, also called the *composite*, *aster*, or *daisy family*, is one of the largest of the plant families, with more than 2,600 species in the United States and Canada. Members of the family are characterized by a radially symmetrical flower head composed of two different types of flowers: (1) ray flowers, which have a single petal resembling a strap and are arranged around the outside margin of the head, and (2) disk flowers, which have petals fused into a tube with five lobes, and are located in the center of the head. A flower may have both ray and disk flowers, or just one type. At the base of each flower, and attached to the top of the ovary, is the pappus, which consists of hairs, bristles, or scales.

Included in this large family are many yellow-flowered species that resemble sunflowers and are fondly referred to as the DYCs (damn yellow composites). Individual species within this group are difficult to identify.

Yarrow   *Achillea millefolium*

The single or clumped stems of yarrow are 8 to 40 inches tall, branched near the top, and covered with soft, woolly hairs. The distinctive fernlike, aromatic leaves are up to 12 inches long near the bottom of the stem but much smaller near the top. Ten to twenty white or occasionally pink or yellow flower heads form a flat-topped cluster at the top of the stem. Each flower head is composed of five ray flowers and ten to thirty slightly darker disk flowers. About twenty bracts with pale to dark margins are arranged in three to four overlapping rows.

Yarrow has many medicinal properties, in part due to the alkaloid achilleine.

HABITAT/RANGE: Common, often in large patches, along roadsides, in pastures, and in open woods from the plains to alpine zones across Montana.

Wormleaf stonecrop in mid-July east of St. Regis

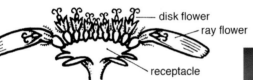

disk flower
ray flower
receptacle

Flower of the Sunflower Family

Yarrow in late May along
U.S. 191 at the mouth
of Gallatin Canyon
south of Bozeman

Orange Agoseris *Agoseris aurantiaca*

Orange agoseris, also called *orange mountain dandelion*, has one or several 4- to 24-inch-tall stems that yield a milky sap when broken. The stems emerge from a clump of narrow, shallowly toothed basal leaves that are about one-half as long as the stem. Each stem bears a single bright orangish red flower head composed of ray flowers only. The bracts of all species of *Agoseris* are similar in size and extend forward. The flower resembles that of orange hawkweed (*Hieracium aurantiacum*) but is larger and there is only a single head rather than multiple heads per stem.

HABITAT/RANGE: Grows on meadows or in grassy forest openings from montane to alpine zones in west and central Montana.

False Dandelion *Agoseris glauca*

False dandelion, also called *pale mountain dandelion*, resembles the common dandelion (*Taraxacum officinale*) but is a duller yellow. False dandelion may also be confused with hawksbeard (*Crepis* species); seed characteristics distinguish these plants. The leafless, unbranched stem of false dandelion is 4 to 20 inches tall, emerging from a basal cluster of deeply divided, toothed leaves that vary from grasslike to lance-shaped. The stem and leaves exude a milky juice when broken. The ½- to 1¼-inch-wide, yellow flower head contains only ray flowers with the middle ones being much shorter.

Agoseris species are edible and can be eaten in salads or as cooked greens. American Indians used dried plant juice or leaves as gum, a practice that gave the plant the name *Indian bubble gum*.

HABITAT/RANGE: Prefers dry to wet soils in meadows and open areas among sagebrush and in coniferous forests in west, central, and east Montana.

Pearly Everlasting *Anaphalis margaritacea*

Pearly everlasting may sometimes be confused with pussytoes (*Antennaria* species), but those species have basal leaves. Pearly everlasting has lance-shaped leaves, with soft hairs on their bottom, that are opposite and distributed uniformly along the stem with none being basal. The stems vary greatly in height from 8 to 36 inches. The flower heads, arranged in clusters, contain inconspicuous disk flowers surrounded by white "pearly" bracts. Sometimes the bracts have a black dot at their base.

Pearly everlasting is reported to have anti-inflammatory and mild antihistamine properties. American Indians smoked dried plants for their medical benefits and used boiled plants for treating sores, arthritis, and burns.

HABITAT/RANGE: Found in large patches on disturbed soils in forest openings and on slopes at montane and subalpine zones in west and central Montana.

Top left and right:
Orange agoseris
in late June in
the Swan Valley
northeast of
Seeley Lake

False dandelion
in late May along the
Charles M. Russell
Trail south of Utica

Pearly everlasting
in early August at
Holland Lake east of
Montana 83 and
north of Seeley Lake

🌿 Pussytoes *Antennaria* species 🌿

Thirteen *Antennaria* species have been described in Montana. Pussytoes often grow from mat-forming stolons with stems that vary in height from 2 to more than 8 inches. Basal leaves are held on petioles, whereas the alternate stem leaves are stalkless. The leaves are covered to varying degrees with white woolly hairs. Male and female flowers occur on separate plants. Flower heads, consisting of small white disk flowers with a tubular corolla, occur alone or in terminal clusters. Several layers of papery, white, pink, brown, or black bracts partially enclose the flower.

Tall Pussytoes   *Antennaria anaphaloides*

The 8- to 20-inch-tall stem of tall pussytoes is taller than most other pussytoes. This wildflower might be confused with pearly everlasting (*Anaphalis margaritacea*), but that species doesn't have basal leaves. Tall pussytoes has large, lance-shaped basal leaves and progressively smaller, stalkless stem leaves. The leaves have a woolly hair on both surfaces. The several to many flower heads, arranged in congested clusters, contain whitish disk flowers only. The bracts around the heads are whitish and translucent, and often are blackish at their base.

> HABITAT/RANGE: Prefers moist soils in meadows and open forests from the foothills to montane zones in west and north-central Montana.

Rosy Pussytoes   *Antennaria microphylla*
                                                          A. rosea

Rosy pussytoes can sometimes be identified by the rosy bracts, but the bracts can also be white. In addition, a few other *Antennaria* species can have pinkish bracts. The stems are 2 to 12 inches long, arising from creeping surface stems. The spoon-shaped basal leaves are woolly on both surfaces. The stem has very few leaves. Three to twenty flower heads, consisting of disk flowers only, are arranged in a small tight cluster.

> HABITAT/RANGE: Prefers dry to slightly moist soils on grassy slopes, hillsides, and meadows or in clearings and open forests from low to subalpine zones in west, central, and northeast Montana.

Field Pussytoes   *Antennaria neglecta*

Field pussytoes has 8- to 16-inch-tall stems with hair on the upper part. Basal leaves up to 2 inches long form a mat. The stalkless, narrow, alternate leaves are dull green and slightly woolly on the upper surface and have curved edges, pointed tips, and a conspicuous midvein on the lower surface, which is densely covered with white hairs. Numerous flower heads crowd the terminal end of the stem and are partially enclosed by white, narrow, pointed bracts.

> HABITAT/RANGE: Found in open forests from valleys to lower subalpine zones in northwest, north-central, and southeast Montana.

ll pussytoes in
e June along
ttle Ridge in
e Bridger Range
rth of Bozeman

sy pussytoes
late June near
orgetown
ke west of
aconda

ld pussytoes
mid-June
ong Mystic
ke Road
uthwest
Roscoe

🌿 Arnica *Arnica* species 🌿

Twelve *Arnica* species have been described in Montana. Most arnicas have yellow to orange flower heads that look like small sunflowers. The single or branched stem bears simple, opposite leaves. Green bracts are arranged in one to two series and are equal in length. The pappus is composed of fine, white to brown bristles. Identifying individual species is difficult, in part because many species hybridize and some species have several varieties.

Arnicas have long been used in liniments and salves for treating bruises and sprains. Arnicas are toxic, however, and should not be applied to broken skin where toxins can enter the bloodstream.

Heartleaf Arnica   *Arnica cordifolia*

The stem of heartleaf arnica is 6 to 20 inches tall, bearing two to four pairs of opposite, heart-shaped basal leaves and lower stem leaves with irregular teeth on their margins. The flower head contains nine to fifteen yellow ray flowers with shallow teeth on their ends and numerous deep yellow disk flowers.

HABITAT/RANGE: Grows in patches on moist soils in open but shaded coniferous forests, especially abundant in lodgepole pine forests, from low to subalpine zones in west and central Montana.

Mountain Arnica   *Arnica latifolia*

The solitary or clustered, slightly hairy stems of mountain arnica are 4 to 24 inches tall. The basal leaves are round to lance-shaped and usually are withered by the time flowers develop. The two to four pairs of opposite stem leaves are egg- or lance-shaped and stalkless, and those in the middle of the stem are often as large as those lower down. The leaves have fine hairs and usually have coarse teeth on the margins. The flower head has 8 to 12 yellow ray flowers, which are toothed along the tips, and many yellow disk flowers. Mountain arnica resembles heartleaf arnica (*A. cordifolia*), but the broad basal leaves are rarely heart-shaped.

HABITAT/RANGE: Prefers moist soils in open forests, along streambanks, and in subalpine and alpine meadows in west and central Montana.

Twin Arnica   *Arnica sororia*

The stems of twin arnica are 8 to 24 inches tall with a cluster of basal leaves with petioles. The smaller, narrow, lance-shaped stem leaves may have white hairs at their base. Two or three relatively flat, pale to deep yellow flower heads occur on each stem. The ray flowers are about 1 inch long.

HABITAT/RANGE: Grows on dry soils on hillsides, among sagebrush, and in open forests at lower elevations in west, central, and east Montana.

Top left: Heartleaf arnica in mid-June in the Highwood Mountains east of Great Falls

Top right: Mountain arnica on June 30 along Tally Lake Road north of Kalispell

Bottom: Twin arnica in late June at Natural Bridge State Park along the Boulder River south of Big Timber

Meadow Aster   *Aster campestris*

The stems of meadow aster are 4 to 20 inches tall and bear narrowly oblong, rather firm, usually stalkless leaves with entire margins. The stems are glandular near the top and have short hairs near the bottom. The stem splits into a few branches that support a small number of flower heads. Each head has fifteen to twenty light violet or purplish ray flowers. The glandular bracts have long, green, pointed tips.

HABITAT/RANGE: Found in valleys and on montane grasslands in west, central, and east Montana, but appears to be more common in the west.

Hoary Balsamroot   *Balsamorhiza incana*

Hoary balsamroot differs from arrowleaf balsamroot (*B. sagittata*) by having deeply toothed, pinnately divided leaves. Both the stems and leaves are covered with woolly, tangled hairs. The flower heads, containing many yellow ray flowers, are about 4 inches in diameter.

HABITAT/RANGE: Grows on rocky soils on the plains and meadows from the foothills to subalpine zones in west, south-central, and east Montana.

Arrowleaf Balsamroot   *Balsamorhiza sagittata*

Arrowleaf balsamroot is 8 to 36 inches tall and has numerous arrowhead-shaped, hairy basal leaves that are 2 to 6 inches wide and 10 to 12 inches long. The single 4- to 5-inch-wide flower head on each stem has numerous disk flowers and eight to twenty-five ray flowers that are 1 to 1½ inches long.

American Indians used the roots of arrowleaf balsamroot for medicinal purposes, and also ground the roasted seeds into flour. Meriwether Lewis collected a specimen in 1806 near Lewis and Clark Pass.

HABITAT/RANGE: Blooms in early spring and often covers open, sunny areas on mountain foothills, grasslands, meadows, open pine forests, and roadsides in west, central, and southeast Montana.

Musk Thistle   *Carduus nutans*

Musk thistle, also called *nodding thistle*, is a tall, branching biennial that reaches 6 feet tall. The dark green, alternate leaves are deeply lobed and jagged and have a light green midrib. The lobes have three to five spines with a yellow or white one at the tip. The stems are winged and the wings have spines. Upper and lower surfaces of the leaves are covered with fine woolly hairs. Solitary, deep rose to violet or purple flower heads, containing disk flowers only, are 1½ to 3 inches wide and usually nodding. Each flower is partially enclosed by broad, stiff bracts with purplish spiny tips, the lower bracts bending backward.

HABITAT/RANGE: Common noxious weed, introduced into North America in the early 1900s, on disturbed soils on roadsides, in pastures, and in grain fields in west, central, and northeast Montana.

Top left: Meadow
Aster in late July
along Montana 43
west of Wisdom

Top right: Hoary
Balsamroot in late
April along the
road to Cooney
Reservoir south
Columbus

Arrowleaf
Balsamroot in
late May on a
rocky hillside
near Springhill

Musk thistle in
mid-July along
Cottonwood
Reservoir north
Wilsall

Spotted Knapweed   *Centaurea maculosa*

The leafy, often green and purple-striped stem of spotted knapweed, which grows during the second year from a rosette of long, pinnately divided leaves, is 1 to 3 feet tall. Numerous branches, with a sandpaper-like surface, bear alternate, somewhat hairy leaves with translucent dots, the lower leaves divided and the upper ones undivided. A single pinkish purple flower head, which appears at the end of each branch, contains only ray flowers, the outer ones enlarged. The stiff bracts have comblike, hairy margins and dark tips that look like spots.

Introduced from Europe, spotted knapweed produces a chemical that inhibits other nearby plants.

HABITAT/RANGE: Common noxious weed on dry sandy or gravelly, disturbed, but not regularly cultivated, soils along roadsides, and on overgrazed pastures in west and central Montana.

Russian Knapweed   *Centaurea repens*

Russian knapweed is a bushy, highly branched perennial about 16 to 32 inches tall. The upper leaves are small and narrow, while the lower leaves are larger, about 5 inches long, and toothed or lobed. Numerous flower heads, each about ½ inch in diameter, contain purple ray flowers, with the marginal ones not enlarged. The greenish, straw-colored calyx has broad middle and outer bracts. The bracts have smooth margins and papery tips.

Russian knapweed, another noxious knapweed, was introduced into North America about 1900 from Turkestan. It spreads by seed and rhizome.

HABITAT/RANGE: Grows in hayfields but tolerates drought and is found throughout Montana, although it appears to be more common in the western part of the state.

Dusty Maiden   *Chaenactis douglasii*

The stiff stems of dusty maiden are 12 to 20 inches tall, with grayish woolly hairs that appear dusty. The basal rosette of leaves and the alternate stem leaves, which are smaller, are deeply divided and fernlike. The flowers are arranged in a flat-topped cluster. The white or sometimes pinkish flower heads contain fifty to seventy tubular disk flowers and no ray flowers.

HABITAT/RANGE: Prefers dry to slightly moist, sandy or gravelly soils found on open or shaded prairies, sagebrush steppe, and rocky areas from the foothills to alpine zones in west, central, and southeast Montana.

Spotted
knapweed in
mid-July along
Montana 37
south of
Libby Dam

Russian
knapweed in
early July in
a dry gully
south of
Bridger

Dusty maiden
in mid-June
in Bighorn
Canyon National
Recreation Area
in south-central
Montana

Oxeye Daisy   *Chrysanthemum leucanthemum*

The slender stem of oxeye daisy is 1 to 2 feet tall, usually branching at the top with two solitary flower heads. The basal leaves have long stalks and are spoon-shaped with rounded teeth and lobes, whereas the alternate stem leaves are smooth, smaller, and stalkless. Each flower head is 1 to 2 inches wide, containing fifteen to thirty-five white ray flowers and many yellow female disk flowers. The narrow bracts have brown, papery edges.

HABITAT/RANGE: Oxeye daisy was introduced into the United States as a garden flower and soon became a very common roadside weed, often occurring over long strips along highways and secondary roads. Found in west and south-central Montana.

Golden Aster   *Chrysopsis villosa*
Heterotheca villosa

The clumped stems of golden aster are 6 to 20 inches tall with numerous alternate, lance-shaped leaves, held on petioles at the base of the stem and covered with slightly stiff hairs. The stem is branched at the top where it holds yellow flower heads, each about ½ inch wide and containing disk flowers and ten to twenty-five ray flowers.

HABITAT/RANGE: Found on open dry soils along roadsides and foothills from the plains to montane zones in west, central, and east Montana.

Canada Thistle   *Cirsium arvense*

The leafy, thin, hollow stems of Canada thistle are 2 to 5 feet tall, branch at the top, and usually grow in patches, spreading by deep rhizomes. The margins of the leaves are sharply toothed or lobed and wavy. The leaves are usually stalkless and sometimes whitish on the underside. Many terminal, pinkish purple flower heads on smooth stalks are arranged in a cluster. The flower heads contain disk flowers only and are either male or female, each plant usually confined to a single sex. The single-seeded fruits are produced by the female flower heads.

The stems and leaves of thistles are often sweet and juicy, but flavor varies with the species, age, and habitat. Early roots can be eaten raw but may cause gas and are better roasted or boiled. Dried and ground roots have been used to make flour. Thistles have been used to make medicinal teas for eliminating intestinal worms, treat skin sores, and to relieve melancholy.

HABITAT/RANGE: Common noxious non-native weed found in fields, pastures, and meadows and along many roadsides across Montana.

Above: A large patch
of oxeye daisies on
June 30 in a field
along U.S. 93 north
of Kalispell. Inset:
Oxeye daisy in mid-
July around Painted
Rocks Lake near
the Idaho border
west of Sula

Center: Golden
aster in early July
around Clark
Canyon Reservoir
south of Dillon

Canada thistle in early
August along the road near
Crystal Lake in the Big Snowy
Mountains near Lewistown

Elk Thistle   *Cirsium scariosum*

Elk thistle, a native short-lived perennial, has an 8- to 40-inch-tall stem, though it may be nearly stemless, especially during its early years of growth or at higher elevations. In this latter case, the large flower head is located in the center of a basal rosette of long, white, hairy leaves. The stems of tall plants are thick and fleshy and vary little in size from bottom to top. The large grayish green leaves, with spine-tipped lobes on their margins and smooth upper surfaces, clasp the stem at their base. One to eight creamy white to pink and purplish flower heads, containing only disk flowers, are located at the top of each stem. Both the stems and leaves are covered with long white hairs that extend into the flower heads. Wide, overlapping bracts occur below the flowers, the outer ones having a short spine at their tip. **White thistle (*C. hookerianum*)**, another common native species, differs from elk thistle by having a less succulent stem with smaller, less crowded leaves and usually a white flower head.

The peeled stems and roots of elk thistle are edible, and some American Indians ate the buds. In Yellowstone National Park, this plant may be called *Everts' thistle* in memory of Truman Everts, an explorer who lost his way in the park in 1870 and subsisted on mostly thistle roots until his rescue.

HABITAT/RANGE: Grows on moist soils in meadows, in open forests, on hillsides, and along streams at montane and subalpine zones in west and central Montana.

Purple Coneflower   *Echinacea angustifolia*

The solitary, rarely branched stems of purple coneflower are 1 to 3 feet tall, often grow in clumps, and have stalked basal leaves and smaller, stalkless stem leaves. The leaves are 3 to 8 inches long, have entire margins and three to five conspicuous parallel veins, and are covered, like the stems, with stiff hairs. Each stem supports a single flower containing ten to fifteen pale purple, drooping, sterile ray flowers, which may be as long as $3\frac{1}{2}$ inches, surrounding a cluster of fertile, reddish purple or purplish brown disk flowers in a broad dome that may be $1\frac{1}{4}$ inches high.

Echinacea species stimulate the immune system to fight viral infections. Extracts from the plant have also been promoted for treating vaginal yeast infections, headaches, and burns. Overharvesting of wild plants has threatened its existence; however, plants are now cultivated for commercial use. Meriwether Lewis collected a specimen of purple coneflower in 1805 and noted its medicinal use by American Indians.

HABITAT/RANGE: Locally common on dry to moist but well-drained soils in west, south-central, and, more commonly, east Montana.

Elk thistle in late June
near Ashley Lake
west of Kalispell

Purple coneflower in
late July near U.S. 12
east of Miles City

🌿 Daisies and Fleabanes *Erigeron* species 🌿

Erigeron, the largest genus in the sunflower family in Montana, with thirty-six species, includes many similar species. Daisies and fleabanes have alternate or basal leaves that are entire or dissected. The showy flower heads consist of yellow disk flowers and narrow, white, pinkish, bluish, purple, or even yellow ray flowers. Most species have a single flower head on each stem. The bracts are narrow and mostly equal in length. The receptacle is naked and the pappus consists of numerous white, rather brittle bristles, occasionally circled by a ring of short bristles or scales. Some species resemble asters (*Aster* species), but asters usually have leafy, erect stems with several to many flower heads per stem and normally flower in mid- to late summer rather than spring. Some daisies and fleabanes resemble *Townsendia* species, but townsendias usually have larger flower heads, shorter flower stalks, and a scalelike pappus.

Cutleaf Daisy   *Erigeron compositus*

Cutleaf daisy has several stems, usually less than 8 inches tall, that rise from a clump of basal leaves, each supporting a single flower. The distinctive leaves are divided two or three times into threes, ending in narrow, fingerlike segments. The flower heads are ½ to 1 inch in diameter and contain numerous yellow disk flowers surrounded by many ray flowers that are usually white but sometimes pink or lavender.

HABITAT/RANGE: Grows on dry, gravelly, or rocky soils in open forests and meadows from the foothills to alpine zones in west and central Montana.

Buff Fleabane   *Erigeron ochroleucus*

The 4- to 8-inch-tall stem of buff fleabane has narrow, linear basal leaves that are 1 to 3 inches long with sharp, stiff, bristly hairs on the lower surface and a pointed tip. Narrow stem leaves are present. The blue, purple, or white flower heads usually occur singly on each stem. Green bracts are densely covered with long white hairs.

HABITAT/RANGE: Buff fleabane is more common east of the Rockies in west and central Montana.

Shaggy Daisy   *Erigeron pumilus*

The stems of shaggy daisy grow to 20 inches and are more erect than many daisies. The basal leaves are linear or inversely lance-shaped, and the stem leaves are smaller or absent. Coarse stiff hairs cover the foliage. The bracts are sometimes covered with softer, long hairs. Each flower head has fifty to one hundred white or sometimes pale pink or blue ray flowers that surround a cluster of yellow disk flowers.

HABITAT/RANGE: Found on the sandy soils of prairies and open areas among sagebrush or in the foothills across Montana.

Cutleaf daisy in mid-May in the
Gravelly Range south of Ennis

Buff fleabane in mid-June on dry
and sandy soil on the road to the
Pryor Mountains east of Bridger
in south-central Montana

Shaggy daisy in mid-June along the road leading to the Pryor Mountains east of Bridger

Showy Fleabane   *Erigeron speciosus*

Showy fleabane has 6- to 30-inch-tall stems that grow in clusters and bear alternate, lance-shaped leaves with conspicuous hairs along their edges. Basal leaves are 3 to 6 inches long and slightly larger than the stem leaves. Branches of the stem bear the showy 1- to 2-inch-wide flower heads, each head held on a short stalk arising from a leaf axil. Each stem has from one to eleven flower heads. Each flower head consists of yellowish orange, tubular disk flowers and numerous narrow ray flowers that vary from lavender, to light pink, blue, or occasionally white.

HABITAT/RANGE: Prefers dry to moist soils in open meadows and woods, especially on burned sites in coniferous forests from foothills to subalpine zones in west and central Montana.

Gaillardia   *Gaillardia aristata*

Gaillardia, also called *blanketflower*, has a purple to purplish brown bull's-eye of disk flowers surrounded by bright yellow ray flowers, which are sometimes reddish at the base. The tips of the ray flowers are divided into three lobes. Spiny hairs cover the convex receptacle of the flower head. The hairy, 6- to 24-inch-tall stem bears long, lance-shaped, alternate, mostly basal leaves. However, the leaves are variable and are sometimes toothed and divided into lobes.

Meriwether Lewis collected a specimen in 1806 along the upper Blackfoot River in Montana. American Indians used gaillardia for a variety of medicinal purposes.

HABITAT/RANGE: Grows in clumps on sunny and open meadows and prairies from valleys to montane forests in west, central, and east Montana.

Little Sunflower   *Helianthella uniflora*

Little sunflower has leafy stems that are 1 to 2 feet tall, with oblong to lance-shaped leaves that are usually opposite but sometimes alternate. The leaves have fine stiff hairs and three prominent parallel veins. Each stem bears a single yellow flower head. The pappus has a pair of bristle-shaped structures. Little sunflower resembles showy goldeneye (*Viguiera multiflora*) but that flower's center of disk flowers is rounded not flat. Little sunflower also resembles true sunflowers (*Helianthus* species), but true sunflowers usually have toothed leaves and larger flower heads.

HABITAT/RANGE: Grows on hillsides and in open woods from the foothills to montane zones in west and central Montana.

Showy fleabane in late July at
Pintler Lake north of Wisdom

Showy fleabane in mid-July along the Charles M.
Russell Trail south of Utica

Gaillardia in mid-June along Road 236 near Judith
Landing on the Missouri River south of Great Falls

Little sunflower in late June in the
Gravelly Range south of Ennis

Common Sunflower   *Helianthus annuus*

Common sunflower, a relative of the garden sunflower, is often just a few feet tall in the wild but may grow up to 6 feet. The rough stem and leaves are covered with stiff hairs. The heart-shaped leaves have irregularly toothed margins and are mostly alternate on the stem. The central bracts of the receptacle are hairy but not always obviously so. The secondary bracts just below the flower head are egg-shaped and tapered at the tip. The usually solitary, large flower heads are 3 to 5 inches wide and contain yellow ray flowers and dark brownish or reddish disk flowers.

> HABITAT/RANGE: Found on open mostly dry soils on prairies and foothills and along roadsides in west, central, and east Montana.

Hawkweed *Hieracium* species

The hawkweeds are glandular and somewhat hairy and have alternate leaves or all basal leaves. The stems exude a milky sap when broken. The flower heads, which contain ray flowers only, occur singly or in a branching cluster. The bracts occur in two or three unequal overlapping rows, and the pappus bears many fine, usually brownish bristles. Hawkweeds are easily confused with hawksbeards (*Crepis* species), which also contain a milky juice, but their bracts and pappus are white rather than yellowish, brownish, dark green, or black. *Hieracium* species with yellow flowers are difficult to distinguish from one another.

White Hawkweed   *Hieracium albiflorum*

White hawkweed has 1- to 3-foot-tall, erect stems that exude a milky sap when broken. The 2- to 7-inch-long, oblong to lance-shaped, stalked basal leaves are smooth or shallowly toothed with bristly hairs on the upper surface. Stem leaves are alternate, hairy, and much smaller. The fifteen to thirty flower heads per stem have white or creamy ray flowers and no disk flowers. The linear or lance-shaped, greenish or blackish bracts are nearly equal in length.

> HABITAT/RANGE: Prefers dry to moderately moist soils in open forests and on roadsides from the foothills to montane zones in west and central Montana.

Orange Hawkweed   *Hieracium aurantiacum*

The reddish orange flower heads of orange hawkweed occur in tight clusters and contains only ray flowers, which are notched at their tips. The leafless stems are 10 to 20 inches tall, with elliptic leaves in a basal rosette. Margins of the leaves are smooth, and both the upper and lower surfaces are covered with stiff hairs. Orange hawkweed resembles orange agoseris (*Agoseris aurantiaca*), but that species has only a single flower head per stem.

> HABITAT/RANGE: Orange hawkweed, a native of Europe, occurs on mountains, fields, and open woods, especially on disturbed soils, in northwest and west-central Montana.

Hieracium species with yellow flowers in mid-June along Hungry Horse Reservoir east of Kalispell

Common sunflower in mid-August along a dirt road near Pony

Bottom right: Orange hawkweed covering a field in late June along U.S. 93 north of Kalispell

Inset: Orange hawkweed in late June along the road bordering Hungry Horse Reservoir east of Kalispell

ttom left: White hawkweed on ine 30 along Tally Lake Road northwest of Kalispell

Hyalineherb   *Hymenopappus filifolius*

The clustered erect stems of hyalineherb, with tufts of cottony hairs, are 6 to 24 inches tall. The mostly basal leaves are alternate and pinnately divided twice into short threadlike segments. The creamy white to light yellow, conical or bell-shaped flower heads are about ½ inch wide and contain ten to fifty-nine disk flowers. The lance-shaped bracts are nearly equal in length and have papery margins.

HABITAT/RANGE: Grows on dry plains and hills across Montana.

Colorado Rubberweed   *Hymenoxys richardsonii*

The slightly hairy, tufted stems of Colorado rubberweed arise from a crown full of dead and living leaves and reach a height of 12 to 24 inches. The alternate, dark green leaves are mostly basal and segmented into linear lobes about 1½ inches long. The solitary bright yellow flower heads occur on long stems, forming a flat-topped cluster. The few drooping ray flowers are about ½ inch long and lack stamens. The disk flowers include both stamens and pistil.

HABITAT/RANGE: Grows on dry soils of prairies and overgrazed pastures and in roadside ditches from the plains to subalpine zones in west, central, and northeast Montana.

Blue Lettuce   *Lactuca pulchella*
                                      L. oblongifolia

The prickly, erect stem of blue lettuce, which contains a milky juice, is 15 to 36 inches tall and usually branched. The higher leaves are alternate, thick, and lance-shaped with lobes that point backward, whereas the lower leaves are reduced to a narrow lobed wing. Flower heads in each flat-topped cluster contain ray flowers only.

HABITAT/RANGE: Grows on roadsides, in pastures, along streams, and on disturbed soils from the plains to the foothills across Montana. Though native, it is considered a noxious weed in agricultural areas, where it spreads by rhizomes.

Gayfeather   *Liatris punctata*

The clustered, unbranched stems of gayfeather are 1 to 2 feet tall, with numerous stiff, entire leaves that nearly cover the lower part. The leaves have tiny dots on their lower surface that are visible with background lighting. A spike of brilliant purple flower heads covers the tip of the stem. Each flower head contains four to six disk flowers, each with five tiny petals, surrounded by overlapping bracts. The pistil has two long, purple appendages that give the flower a feather appearance.

The stems of gayfeather arise from an enlarged base resembling a bulb, with a taproot that may extend to 15 feet below the ground surface.

HABITAT/RANGE: Found on the plains and foothills and in montane forests east of the Continental Divide in west, central, and east Montana.

...alineherb in
...d-June east
...Bridger

...lorado
...bberweed in
...d-June north
...Winifred

...om left: Blue
...uce in early July
...st of the Pryor
...untains and
...th of Warren

...om right:
...feather in early
...gust along the
...d to Crystal
...e in the Big
...wy Mountains
...r Lewistown

Skeletonweed

Lygodesmia juncea

Skeletonweed is 4 to 18 inches tall, with a tangled mass of nearly bare, rigid, finely grooved, branched stems that yield a milky or yellowish sap when broken. Small, narrow, scalelike, alternate leaves line the stems. A single pinkish, pale lavender, or sometimes white flower head sits at the top of each stem branch and consists of five small ray flowers that have a five-lobed tip.

American Indians chewed the sap of skeletonweed, which apparently turns blue when mixed with saliva.

HABITAT/RANGE: Common undesirable weed along roadsides and on disturbed soils in pastures and croplands in west, central, and east Montana.

Pineapple Weed

Matricaria matricarioides

Pineapple weed has 2- to 12-inch-tall, branched stems, with alternate leaves that are divided several times into narrow segments. Both the shiny stems and leaves lack hairs. If the delicate fernlike leaves are crushed, they emit a pineapple aroma. The cone-shaped flower heads contain tiny yellowish green disk flowers. Small egg-shaped bracts with thin translucent margins surround the base of the flower.

Flathead Indians used pineapple weed for treating colds, intestinal upset, and menstrual cramps. The flower heads were used to make a necklace.

HABITAT/RANGE: Though pineapple weed is native to North America, it can be weedy and is common on disturbed soils of roadsides and fields in west, central, and northeast Montana.

White lettuce

Prenanthes sagittata

White lettuce, also called *rattlesnake root*, has 2-foot-tall stems that contain milky juice and bear alternate leaves that do not clasp the stem and are toothed on the margins. The long basal leaves are shaped like arrowheads with the basal lobes pointing downward or outward. The heads contain white ray flowers only and are arranged in a narrow inflorescence. The pappus consists of many brown bristles.

HABITAT/RANGE: Grows in moist places in west and south-central Montana.

Prairie Coneflower

Ratibida columnifera

The stem of prairie coneflower is 1 to 3 feet tall, with narrow, smooth-edged, alternate, hairy leaves that are deeply divided into five to thirteen narrow segments. The upper part of the stem is leafless and holds a single flower head, the center of which is a grayish green, 1- to 2-inch-tall, fingerlike column that has many fertile, dark reddish brown disk flowers. These disk flowers open first at the base of the column, changing from grayish green to brown with yellow-tipped stamens. Three to seven infertile, yellow to reddish brown ray flowers droop from the base of the column.

HABITAT/RANGE: Found on dry to moist soils on open plains, valleys, and foothills in west, central, and east Montana.

Skeletonweed in late July along
Montana 48 near Anaconda

Pineapple weed in late June along
the Madison River east of Norris

Prairie coneflower along the
roadside near Judith Landing on the
Missouri River east of Fort Benton

White lettuce in mid-July on
the wooded bank of a stream near
Tally Lake northwest of Kalispell

🌿 Groundsel *Senecio* species 🌿

The genus *Senecio*, with several similar species and some that are quite different from one another, has twenty-six species in Montana. The leaves of groundsels are often all basal or alternate on the stem. Flower heads, mostly of medium or small size, usually have both ray and disk flowers, but a few species have only disk flowers. Tips of the bracts are often black. Groundsels are smooth or slightly hairy but lack the rough, stiff hairs of true sunflowers (*Helianthus* species) and the sticky hairs of the arnicas (*Arnica* species).

Silvery Groundsel   *Senecio canus*

The clumped stems of silvery groundsel grow 4 to 12 inches tall. The foliage appears silvery gray due to thin entangled hairs; however, the top surface of the leaves become hairless at flowering time. The narrow, lance- to egg-shaped leaves occur mostly in a basal cluster. The leaves have smooth margins or are lobed at the base, and are usually widest above their middle. The basal and lower leaves have short or long petioles. The middle and upper stem leaves are much smaller. Several flower heads are arranged in a convex or flat-topped cluster. Each deep yellow head has 8 to 12 ray flowers that surround a yellow circle of disk flowers. The bracts are arranged in one row.

HABITAT/RANGE: Prefers dry open and rocky soils on the plains and in open woods from valleys to alpine zones in west, central, and east Montana.

Arrowleaf Groundsel   *Senecio triangularis*

Arrowleaf groundsel is a tall plant, the clustered stems reaching 2 to 4 feet tall. The basal leaves are alternate, twice as long as wide, wedge- or arrow-shaped, and sharply toothed on the margins. The lower leaves are stalked and the upper ones are stalkless. The stem is crowned by a few or several flower heads in a flattened cluster. The flower head has six to twelve yellow ray flowers surrounding yellow disk flowers. The bracts are greenish with tufts of black hair on their tips. This plant may be confused with **butterweed groundsel (*S. serra*)**, which has egg-shaped or lance-shaped leaves.

HABITAT/RANGE: Found on moist to wet soils along streambanks and in open forests from valleys to subalpine zones in west and south-central Montana.

Silvery groundsel in late May on the open slopes
of Waterworks Hill near Missoula

Arrowleaf groundsel in early July in a moist meadow
along Lindbergh Lake Road in the Swan Valley

Canada Goldenrod   *Solidago canadensis*

The hairy, usually unbranched stems of Canada goldenrod, which may reach more than 60 inches tall, bear many narrow, alternate leaves, which are up to 6 inches long, are hairy on the underside, and have a short petiole or none at all. The largest leaves occur in the middle of the stem but those above are nearly the same size. The leaves have three prominent veins and a few sharp teeth near their tips. The yellow flower heads contain ten to seventeen narrow, petal–like ray flowers and more disk flowers. Many heads are crowded in a showy pyramidal cluster. The styles have a spear–pointed yellow stigma.

Goldenrods get unfairly blamed for many summer allergies; their pollen is too heavy to be carried by wind.

HABITAT/RANGE: Prefers moist soils in open areas, especially where disturbed, from the prairies to the mountains in west, central, and east Montana.

Perennial Sowthistle   *Sonchus arvensis*

Perennial sowthistle, an introduced perennial weed from Europe, has smooth, often waxy stems that are 1 to 6 feet tall and exude a milky juice when broken. The leaves vary from 4 to 10 inches long and 1 to 1½ inches wide, with prickly margins. The lobes of the pinnately divided basal leaves, held on winged petioles, are pointed toward the leaf base. The upper leaves tend to clasp the stem and the highest on the stem are bractlike. Numerous yellow flower heads, each 1 to 1½ inches wide, are arranged in a terminal flat cluster. Depending on the subspecies (*arvensis* or *uliginosus*), the bracts and flower stalks may or may not have numerous gland-tipped hairs. *S. arvensis* ssp. *uliginosus* is sometimes considered a separate species (*S. uliginosus*) and called *marsh sowthistle*.

HABITAT/RANGE: An unwelcome weed on croplands in west, south-central, and northeast Montana.

Prickly Sowthistle   *Sonchus asper*

Prickly sowthistle, an introduced annual weed from Europe, is 1 to 5 feet tall, with leafy, smooth stems that have a powdery surface and exude a milky juice when broken. The stiff leaves usually lack lobes but have prickly, toothed margins and rounded flanges at their base that clasp the stem. Several flower heads are arranged in a flat-topped inflorescence at the tip of the stem. Each head contains only yellow ray flowers. **Common sowthistle (*S. oleraceus*)** resembles prickly sowthistle, but it has pointed leaf flanges.

HABITAT/RANGE: Common weed on cultivated fields and disturbed soils in west, south-central, and northeast Montana.

Canada goldenrod in late July at
ed Rock Lakes National Wildlife Refuge
west of West Yellowstone

Prickly sowthistle in early September along
a fenceline just west of Bozeman

Perennial sowthistle in late July in Red Rock Lakes
National Wildlife Refuge west of West Yellowstone

Common Tansy

Tanacetum vulgare

Common tansy, an introduced garden plant from Europe, is an aromatic perennial that spreads by rhizomes and has become weedy in moist areas. The 1½- to 6-foot-tall stems have alternate, fernlike leaves that are pinnately divided into numerous sharply toothed segments. Glandular dots on the leaves produce the strong unique odor. The button-shaped yellow flower heads contain disk flowers only and are arranged at the stem top in a flat-topped cluster in which the outer flowers bloom first. The bracts are arranged in two to three unequal series and have papery margins.

Herbalists use common tansy for expelling worms, treating scabies, and stimulating digestion and menstruation.

HABITAT/RANGE: Weedy on moist disturbed soils in meadows, along streams, and on roadsides from the valleys to montane forests in west, central, and northeast Montana.

Stemless Sunflower

Tetraneuris acaulis
Hymenoxys acaulis

Stemless sunflower, also called *Butte marigold* and *stemless hymenoxys*, has no true stem; a 12-inch-long, leafless flower stalk supports each solitary flower. The bright yellow flower head includes ray flowers, with three-toothed tips, and numerous yellow disk flowers. The linear basal leaves, forming a snarled cluster, are covered with woolly, silky, gray hairs. This species is highly variable, with at least seven recognized varieties.

American Indians used the leaves of this plant for preparing a tea and also applied them as a local anesthetic.

HABITAT/RANGE: Grows on dry rocky or gravelly soils on open hillsides and open plains from low to near-subalpine zones in west, central, and east Montana.

Old Man of the Mountain

Tetraneuris grandiflora
Hymenoxys grandiflora

Old man of the mountain, also called *alpine sunflower*, has many 1- to 12-inch-tall stems. The leaves are divided into fingerlike segments and covered with woolly hair. At 2 to 4 inches wide, the yellow flower heads are probably the largest yellow flowers of the sunflower family that you'll find in an alpine environment. Each flower head contains twenty or more ray flowers, each with a three-lobed tip, surrounding a wide disk.

HABITAT/RANGE: Grows on tundra and windy ridges and rocky soils from subalpine to alpine zones in west and south-central Montana.

Common tansy
in mid-July
along Montana
85 east of
St. Regis

Stemless
sunflower in
early May at
Bighorn Canyon
National
Recreation Area
in south-central
Montana

Old man of
the mountain
in early July at
about 9,000 feet
elevation in the
Gravelly Range
south of Ennis

Hooker's Townsendia   *Townsendia hookeri*

Hooker's townsendia is a cushionlike plant that one may easily overlook. The basal leaves are sharply pointed, succulent, linear, and about 1 to 2 millimeters wide. The flowers are essentially stemless, one or a few nestled in a clump of leaves. About fifteen to thirty white ray flowers with a pinkish tinge surround a yellow center of disk flowers. This wildflower resembles the rare *Townsendia exscapa*, which has been reported only in Gallatin County. *T. exscapa* has slightly larger disk and ray flowers and lacks a tuft of hair at the tip of the involucral bracts.

HABITAT/RANGE: Prefers dry, open, rocky areas from the foothills to montane zones east of the Continental Divide.

Silvery Townsendia   *Townsendia incana*

Silvery townsendia reaches a maximum height of 4 inches. The stems and lance-shaped leaves are covered with white hairs. The flower heads are about 1 inch in diameter, with twelve to thirty-four white ray flowers that are pinkish or lavender on the underside. The bracts are egg-shaped or elliptical with blunt or pointed tips.

HABITAT/RANGE: Grows on dry open sites in the steppe and foothills in south-central Montana.

Parry's Townsendia   *Townsendia parryi*

One to several leafy, erect stems of Parry's townsendia reach 1 foot in height, bearing lance- or spatula-shaped basal leaves and a few small stem leaves. The single flower head on each stem is 1½ to 3 inches wide, large compared to the rest of the plant. The showy, bluish lavender to purplish ray flowers surround a button of yellow disk flowers. Parry's townsendia might be confused with alpine daisy (*Erigeron simplex*), but the latter flower is more restricted to alpine sites and is much smaller.

HABITAT/RANGE: Grows on open gravelly soils with sparse vegetation on prairies and in valleys up to timberline in west and central Montana.

Yellow Salsify   *Tragopogon dubius*

Yellow salsify, an introduced biennial weed from Europe, has hairless, hollow stems that contain a milky juice and may reach 3 feet in height. The narrow, stalkless leaves are 5 to 6 inches long and clasp the stem. Each stem has one flower head surrounded by a single row of ten to fourteen bracts that are longer than the flowers, which are composed of yellow ray flowers only. The flowers are closed on cloudy days, and on sunny days they follow the sun from morning until they close again in midafternoon. The mature flower forms a conspicuous globe of whitish pappus hairs attached to seeds that blow away in the wind like dandelion seeds.

HABITAT/RANGE: Common weed of roadsides, fields, and waste areas across Montana.

Hooker's townsendia in late April on a dry sagebrush-cedar area along Indian Creek Road west of Townsend

Silvery townsendia in mid-June in Bighorn Canyon National Recreation Area in south-central Montana

Parry's townsendia in late May on an open roadside bank of U.S. 12 east of Townsend

Yellow salsify in early June in Corbley Gulch near Springhill north of Belgrade

Showy Goldeneye

Viguiera multiflora
Heliomeris multiflora

Showy goldeneye, one of the many yellow-flowered species in the sunflower family, can be distinguished by its domelike center of dark golden disk flowers that looks like a golden eye. The flower heads are 1 to 1½ inches wide and include ten to fourteen yellow ray flowers. The highly branched, finely hairy stems are 1 to 4 feet tall and bear opposite leaves near the bottom and alternate leaves near the top. The leaves are lance-shaped and slightly toothed. Leafy, lance-shaped, overlapping bracts surround the base of the flower.

HABITAT/RANGE: Prefers dry disturbed soils on open slopes, hillsides, and roadsides from valleys to foothills and subalpine zones in southwest Montana.

White Mule's Ears

Wyethia helianthoides

The stems of white mule's ears reach 2 feet long and are not always upright. Large leaves arise from the root crown on short petioles and reach 2 feet in length, whereas alternate stem leaves are stalkless and smaller. The leaves are covered with long silky hairs. The flower heads are about 4 inches wide and consist of white or creamy ray flowers surrounding a button of yellow disk flowers. White mule's ears resembles **mule's ears (*W. amplexicaulis*)**, but that species has yellow ray flowers, is not hairy, and grows on dry rather than moist soils. These two species may hybridize and produce a plant with pale yellowish flowers and little hair.

HABITAT/RANGE: Prefers moist meadows in woods and along streambanks from medium elevations to subalpine zones in southwest Montana.

Rough Mule's Ears

Wyethia scabra

Rough mule's ears, also called *badlands mule's ears* and *whitestem sunflower*, has coarse, stiff stems that are 1 to 3 feet tall and grow in equally wide, or wider, clumps. The linear to elliptical, 1- to 7-inch-long, alternate leaves are, like the stems, covered with rough, stiff hairs. The leaves feel like sandpaper and the species name *scabra* means "rough." If basal leaves are present, they are reduced or similar in size to stem leaves. The 1- to 3-inch-wide, yellow flower heads are usually solitary at the stem tip and smell of vanilla. Each flower has ten to twenty-three ray flowers and numerous disk flowers.

HABITAT/RANGE: Grows on dry, sandy plains in Big Horn and Carbon Counties.

owy goldeneye
early August
ong a roadside
the Gravelly
nge south
Ennis

hite mule's ears
early
ne in a wet
assy and
ushy area in
idger Canyon
ortheast of
ozeman

ough mule's
rs in mid-
ne in Bighorn
nyon National
creation Area

VALERIAN FAMILY   Valerianaceae

Members of the small valerian family, with just two genera reported in Montana, have opposite or basal leaves that are often pinnately divided. The small but showy, white, pink, or red flowers are usually arranged in a flat- or round-topped, terminal cluster. The petals are fused into a narrow tube with five lobes. There are usually three stamens fused to the petal tube, which extend beyond it. The ovary is inferior.

Mountain Valerian   *Valeriana dioica*

Mountain valerian, also called *marsh valerian*, has 10- to 18-inch-tall, slender, clustered stems with elliptic, usually undivided basal leaves that have entire margins and are held on long petioles. The two to four pairs of opposite, divided, nearly stalkless stem leaves have nine to fifteen leaflets. The small white or occasionally pink flowers are arranged in compact hemispheric clusters at the ends of stem branches. Some flowers are bisexual, while others are female only. The short, saucer-shaped corolla has five lobes and contains three stamens. Mountain valerian might be confused with bedstraws (*Galium* species) but differs in size and dissected leaves.

Valerians are edible and the roots were used by some Indian tribes in soups and stews after long cooking in a fire pit or by boiling. Cooked roots were also dried to make flour. The roots have been used for centuries as a tranquilizer and sometimes as perfume. Cats are attracted to the smell of the plants and will dig them up and roll on them. Hunters have used the plants to mask human odors.

HABITAT/RANGE: Prefers moist to wet soils, often found below snowbanks, in open woods and meadows from the foothills to montane zones in west and central Montana.

Sitka Valerian   *Valeriana sitchensis*

The stem of Sitka valerian is 1 to 3 feet tall. Two to five pairs of pinnately compound leaves with three to five oval, toothed leaflets, the terminal one largest, are attached mostly opposite on the stem. Many white to pinkish flowers form a rounded, dome-shaped cluster on the stem tip. Five fused petals enclose three stamens and a style, which extend beyond the petal tube. The numerous extended stamens over the entire flower head resemble a pincushion. The calyx is at first not apparent but later unfolds into numerous feathery bristles for airborne dissemination of the plant's fruit.

Sitka valerian is eaten by wildlife and was used by American Indians for food and as an antiseptic for treating wound infections.

HABITAT/RANGE: Prefers moist soils in meadows or open forests from middle montane to alpine zones in west and south-central Montana.

Mountain valerian in late June along Sheep Creek in the Little Belt Mountains north of White Sulphur Springs

Sitka valerian in late June in the Flint Creek Range on the north side of Georgetown Lake

VERVAIN FAMILY   Verbenaceae

The vervains share many characteristics in common with mints, such as a stem that is somewhat four-sided, opposite leaves that are usually toothed or lobed, and fused petals. The flowers are usually bell-shaped or tubular, with a flaring corolla of five fused petals. There are usually four fertile stamens and a sterile stamen is sometimes present.

Bracted Vervain   *Verbena bracteata*

Bracted vervain has hairy, horizontal stems that are 4 to 24 inches long and spread along the ground. The opposite leaves vary in size and are deeply divided into three lobes with jagged toothed margins. The middle lobe is the largest. Inconspicuous blue to pink or sometimes white flowers are arranged on terminal spikes and are buried among the bracts. The tubular flower has five lobes, which are slightly flared, and four stamens attached to the upper half of the tube. The style of the single pistil has two lobes.

> HABITAT/RANGE: Grows on waste soils along roads, in pastures, and in open fields in valleys, on the plains, and on hills across Montana.

VIOLET FAMILY   Violaceae

Members of the violet family, with a single genus (*Viola*) and fourteen species reported in Montana, are easily recognized by their pansylike flowers and the presence of a backward-projecting, nectar-containing spur from the lower of the five separate petals. Each flower has five sepals and five stamens, alternating with petals and held on short filaments. The style is often club-shaped with a simple stigma turned to one side. The calyx has five usually separated sepals. The leaves are alternate, simple, and sometimes deeply lobed.

Fresh violet leaves are edible in salads or can be cooked and used as flavoring in jelly, jams, and preserves. Violets are rich in vitamins A and C and in salicylic acid. Medicinal teas and salves for treating skin sores have been prepared from violets. The plants have a laxative effect and may stimulate urination.

Blue Violet   *Viola adunca*

Blue violet is about 4 inches tall and bears mostly basal leaves on short petioles. The dark green, egg- or heart-shaped leaves are 1 to 2 inches long and finely toothed. The flower has five petals, the lower three with white and dark purple lines at their base, and the lowest petal extending backward into a spur.

> HABITAT/RANGE: Grows on dry to moist meadows, prairies, and open woods and slopes from low to subalpine zones in west, central, and east Montana.

Bracted vervain in late July along
U.S. 12 east of Miles City

Blue violet in early June in open woods bordering Lake Alva north of Seeley Lake

Canada Violet   *Viola canadensis*

Canada violet closely resembles stream violet (*V. glabella*) but is easily distinguished by its white rather than yellow petals, although there is some yellow at the base of the petals. Canada violet has 6- to 12-inch-long, leafy stems with smaller leaves near the top. The short-stalked leaves are broad and heart-shaped with a sharp tip. The flowers, which arise from upper leaf axils, have five whitish petals that are often purplish red on their back and yellow at their base. The lower three petals have fine purple lines that direct pollinating insects to the nectar pouch located at the rear of the bottom petal. The two side petals are hairy at their base.

HABITAT/RANGE: Grows in dense patches on moist soils in aspen woods and on shaded slopes in west, central, and east Montana.

Stream Violet   *Viola glabella*

The stems of stream violet are 6 to 12 inches long and bear leaves on long petioles only on the upper part. The broad, glossy leaves are heart-shaped with finely toothed margins and a sharp point at the tip. Smooth stems that originate from the upper leaf axils support the showy, bright yellow flowers. The lower three petals have fine purplish lines at the base, and the lateral two petals are bearded.

HABITAT/RANGE: Grows in moist soils on roadsides, on streambanks, and in shaded woods in west, central, and northwest Montana.

Nuttall's Violet   *Viola nuttallii*

Nuttall's violet, also called *yellow prairie violet*, has a yellow flower that resembles other *Viola* species, but the leaves are distinctive. The conspicuously veined, slightly toothed leaves are 1 to 4 inches long, are oval to lance- or heart-shaped, and have long petioles. The flowers are nearly stemless when they first emerge, but over time the stems grow 5 to 20 inches long and develop leaves. The lower three of the five bright yellow petals have purplish veins on their inner surface, and the upper petals are tinged with red on the back.

HABITAT/RANGE: Prefers dry soils on southern slopes of foothills or forest edges and on dry prairies in west, central, and east Montana.

Canada violet in early May at Sluice Boxes State Park west of U.S. 89 and south of Great Falls

...eam violet in ...rly June near ...ke Alva north ...Seeley Lake

...ttall's violet ...late April ... an open ...cky hillside ...Missouri ...eadwaters ...ate Park near ...ree Forks

Round-leaved Yellow Violet   *Viola orbiculata*

Round-leaved yellow violet, which blooms early and has less-conspicuous flowers than other yellow violets, is rarely over 2 inches tall and has leafy stems. The round leaves, many of which are basal, have finely toothed margins. The leaf petioles are nearly as long as or longer than the leaves. The lower three petals have distinct purple lines, and the two side petals have yellow hair. The tip of the style is also hairy.

> HABITAT/RANGE: Prefers moist soils in woods and forests from montane to lower subalpine zones in west and north-central Montana.

WATERLEAF FAMILY   Hydrophyllaceae

The small waterleaf family has many representatives in the western United States. Many of the showy flowers are arranged in spikes that resemble a bottlebrush, with the stamens representing the bristles. The flowers have parts in fives—five fused, lobed petals that form a bell or funnel, often with scales in the throat, five united sepals, and five stamens that often extend beyond the petals. The compound pistil has a two-cleft style or two styles and a superior ovary. Leaves are often hairy and usually pinnately compound.

Ballhead Waterleaf   *Hydrophyllum capitatum*

Ballhead waterleaf grows 4 to 15 inches tall, with spreading stems and leaves. The large leaves, held on long petioles that are usually attached underground, are pinnately compound, deeply lobed, and coarsely toothed on the margins. The ball-shaped flower head is sometimes hidden by the large leaves. The head contains numerous cup-shaped, five-petaled flowers that are bluish, lavender, or white. Five stamens and a two-lobed stigma in each flower extend beyond the petals, so the flower head looks like a pincushion.

> HABITAT/RANGE: Blooms on soils wet from melting snows in thickets and open woods, and between sagebrush and aspen groves, from low to middle elevations in west and central Montana.

Franklin's Phacelia   *Phacelia franklinii*

The erect, 6- to 18-inch-tall stem of Franklin's phacelia is usually unbranched. The foliage is glandular hairy. The basal leaves and alternate stem leaves are $1\frac{1}{2}$ to 3 inches long and pinnately divided. The bluish purple flowers have a white throat, arise from leaf axils, and are arranged in a dense, coiled cluster. Each flower has five petals fused into a tube that is divided about half of its length. The five sepals are linear and hairy. Franklin's phacelia resembles silky phacelia (*P. sericea*) but has shorter stamens that just barely extend beyond the petals.

> HABITAT/RANGE: Prefers disturbed gravelly soils from low to middle elevations in west and south-central Montana.

Round-leaved yellow violet
in early June in the Rocky
Mountain Front west of Choteau

Ballhead waterleaf in late May
in a wet brushy area bordering
U.S. 12 east of Townsend

Franklin's phacelia in late June on the
west side of Georgetown Lake
west of Anaconda

Silverleaf Phacelia
Phacelia hastata

The spreading stems of silverleaf phacelia are usually 6 to 15 inches long but can vary greatly from a few inches to nearly 3 feet. The basal leaves are lance-shaped, have entire margins and prominent veins, and are attached by short petioles. The stem leaves are much smaller, and are, like the basal leaves, sometimes lobed at their base. The leaves are covered with silky, white, flat hairs. The dull white to lavender flowers are arranged in tight coils. Five hairy stamens in each funnel-shaped flower extend well beyond the length of the petals.

HABITAT/RANGE: Grows on dry sandy or gravelly soils in open areas, especially among sagebrush, and on the plains and foothills up to treeline in west, central, and southeast Montana.

Threadleaf Phacelia
Phacelia linearis

The single or sometimes branched stem of threadleaf phacelia is 5 to 20 inches tall with narrow, simple leaves, which may have two lobes near their base. Each stem bears several pale blue, lavender, or pinkish flowers. Five petals with round lobes are fused at their base to form a bell-shaped corolla. Five stamens extend beyond the length of the petals. Threadleaf phacelia can be distinguished from other phacelias by its narrow leaves and a rather large, spreading corolla.

Meriwether Lewis collected a specimen of threadleaf phacelia in 1806 at a place called "rockfort camp" on the north side of the Columbia River.

HABITAT/RANGE: Found in dense patches on dry prairies, grassy fields, or sandy soils on foothills and lower elevations in west, central, and east Montana.

Silky Phacelia
Phacelia sericea

The several stems of silky phacelia grow in a clump and are 5 to 16 inches tall. The deeply divided, alternate leaves are covered with grayish silky hairs. The basal leaves on long petioles form a cushion, whereas the stem leaves are fewer and smaller. The bluish purple flowers grow in small coils that are clustered in a terminal column resembling a brush. Numerous slender stamens with long filaments and yellow anthers extend far beyond the petals.

HABITAT/RANGE: Found on open rocky and gravelly exposed slopes and meadows, especially on disturbed soils, from montane to alpine zones in west and central Montana.

Silverleaf phacelia in early July in the foothills
of the Gravelly Range south of Ennis

Threadleaf phacelia in early June in Corbley
Gulch near Springhill north of Belgrade

Silky phacelia in early July on
a windy, rocky site in the
Gravelly Range south of Ennis

WATERLILY FAMILY   Nymphaeaceae

Members of the waterlily family have flowers that float on or are held above water on long stalks, surrounded by round or heart-shaped, basal leaves. The simple leaves are alternate or basal. White or yellow, solitary flowers are held on long stalks. Each flower usually has three to nine sepals, three to many petals, many stamens, and one to eighteen pistils with one or no style.

Yellow Pond-lily   *Nuphar polysepalum*
N. luteum

Yellow pond-lily, also called *spatterdock* and *cow-lily*, is an aquatic plant with a thick round stem, up to 6 feet long, which connects the floating part of the plant to the roots in the bottom mud. The broad, heart-shaped, leathery leaves are 4 to 16 inches across. The large waxy flowers are yellow to reddish tinged and about 3 to 5 inches wide. Each cup-shaped flower has several sepals and petals, numerous reddish stamens, and a pistil with a short broad yellow stigma that has lines radiating from the center. A related rare species called **yellow water lily (*N. variegatum*)**, reported only in northwest Montana, has slightly smaller leaves with flattened petioles, yellow rather than reddish stamens, and yellow to greenish petals. Some authorities consider both of these species to be subspecies of *N. luteum*.

American Indians harvested the pods from these plants and fried the dried seeds until they popped to give a product much like popcorn. Indians also used the dried roots, which are edible raw but have a disagreeable flavor, to prepare meal and flour. Muskrats gather the roots and store them in their lodges for sustenance during the winter.

> HABITAT/RANGE: Restricted to shallow waters of ponds, lakes, and slow-moving streams from lowlands to montane zones in west and south-central Montana.

White Water Lily   *Nymphaea odorata*

White water lily has fragrant flowers that are 3 to 6 inches wide with twenty to thirty white petals. The flowers open in the morning and close in early evening. The 10-inch-wide leaf blades are attached at the base of a deep notch on submerged stalks that are 2 to 4 feet long and buried in bottom mud.

> HABITAT/RANGE: White water lily is a native of the eastern United States but now grows on ponds throughout the West. Reported only in the northwest region of Montana, where it is not widespread.

Yellow pond-lily in early June on a roadside pond north of U.S. 2 east of Libby

White water lily in late July at Placid Lake west of Montana 83 and southwest of Seeley Lake

Appendix: Wildflowers Reported in the Bitterroot Region[1] and in Glacier National Park[2]

(Only the species described in *Wildflowers of Montana* are included here.)

FAMILY	GENUS	SPECIES	BITTERROOT	GLACIER
SHRUBS	*Amelanchier*	*alnifolia*	x	x
	Arctostaphylos	*uva-ursi*	x	x
	Artemisia	*cana*		
	Berberis	*repens*	x	x
	Ceanothus	*velutinus*	x	x
	Cercocarpus	*ledifolius*	x	
	Chrysothamnus	*nauseosus*	x	
	Cornus	*stolonifera*	x	x
	Crataegus	*douglasii*	x	x
	Holodiscus	*discolor*	x	x
	Kalmia	*microphylla*	x	x
	Ledum	*glandulosum*	x	x
	Lonicera	*utahensis*	x	x
	Menziesia	*ferruginea*	x	x
	Paxistima	*myrsinites*		x
	Philadelpus	*lewisii*	x	x
	Phyllodoce	*empetriformis*	x	x
	Physocarpus	*malvaceus*	x	x
	Potentilla	*fruticosa*	x	x
	Prunus	*americana*	x	
		virginiana	x	x
	Rhamnus	*alnifolia*	x	x
	Ribes	*aureum*	x	
		cereum	x	
		inerme	x	x
		montigenum		
		viscosissimum	x	x
	Rosa	*woodsii*	x	x
	Rubus	*parviflorus*	x	x
	Sambucus	*racemosa*	x	x
	Sarcobatus	*vermiculatu*		
	Shepherdia	*canadensis*	x	x
	Sorbus	*scopulina*	x	x
	Spiraea	*betulifolia*	x	x
		douglasii	x	x
	Tetradymia	*canescens*	x	
	Vaccinium	*membranaceum*		x
ARUM	*Lysichitum*	*americanum*		x
BLAZING-STAR	*Mentzelia*	*laevicaulis*		

279

FAMILY	GENUS	SPECIES	BITTERROOT	GLACIER
BORAGE	*Cryptantha*	*celosioides*	x	x
		flavoculata		
		interrupta	x	
	Cynoglossum	*officinale*	x	x
	Echium	*vulgare*	x	x
	Eritrichium	*nanum*	x	
	Hackelia	*floribunda*	x	x
		micrantha	x	x
	Lappula	*redowskii*	x	x
	Lithospermum	*incisum*	x	x
	Mertensia	*alpina*		
		ciliata	x	
		lanceolata		
		oblongifolia	x	x
		viridis		x
	Myosotis	*alpestris*		x
BROOMRAPE	*Orobanche*	*fasciculata*		x
BUCKWHEAT	*Eriogonum*	*flavum*	x	x
		ovalifolium	x	x
		umbellatum	x	x
	Polygonum	*amphibium*	x	x
		bistortoides	x	x
	Rumex	*paucifolius*		x
BUTTERCUP	*Aconitum*	*columbianum*	x	
	Actaea	*rubra*	x	x
	Anemone	*drummondii*	x	x
		multifida	x	x
		nuttalliana	x	x
	Aquilegia	*flavescens*	x	x
	Caltha	*leptosepala*	x	
	Clematis	*columbiana*	x	x
		hirsutissima	x	
		ligusticifolia	x	x
	Delphinium	*bicolor*	x	x
		occidentale	x	
	Ranunculus	*acris*	x	x
		aquatilis	x	x
		flabellaris	x	
		glaberrimus	x	x
	Thalictrum	*occidentale*	x	x
	Trollius	*laxus*	x	x
CACTUS	*Coryphantha*	*missouriensis*		
		vivipara		
	Opuntia	*polyacantha*		

FAMILY	GENUS	SPECIES	BITTERROOT	GLACIER
CAPER	*Cleome*	*serrulata*	x	x
DOGBANE	*Apocynum*	*androsaemifolium*	x	x
DOGWOOD	*Cornus*	*canadensis*	x	x
EVENING–	*Clarkia*	*pulchella*	x	x
PRIMROSE	*Epilobium*	*angustifolium*	x	x
	Gaura	*coccinea*	x	x
	Oenothera	*albicaulis*		
		caespitosa		x
		hookeri		
		pallida		
FIGWORT	*Besseya*	*wyomingensis*	x	x
	Castilleja	*hispida*	x	x
		linariaefolia	x	
		lutescens	x	x
		miniata	x	x
		sessiliflora		
	Collinsia	*parviflora*	x	x
	Linaria	*dalmatica*	x	x
		vulgaris	x	x
	Mimulus	*guttatus*	x	x
		lewisii	x	x
	Orthocarpus	*tenuifolius*	x	x
	Pedicularis	*contorta*	x	x
		groenlandica	x	x
		parryi		
		racemosa	x	x
	Penstemon	*albertinus*	x	x
		albidus		
		confertus	x	x
		cyaneus		
		eriantherus	x	x
		laricifolius		
		lyallii		x
		nitidus	x	x
		procerus	x	x
		wilcoxii	x	
	Rhinanthus	*crista-galli*		x
	Verbascum	*thapsus*	x	x
	Veronica	*americana*	x	x
		cusickii	x	
		wormskjoldii	x	x
FLAX	*Linum*	*perenne*	x	x
GENTIAN	*Frasera*	*speciosa*	x	
	Gentiana	*affinis*	x	x
		algida	x	
	Gentianella	*amarella*	x	x

FAMILY	GENUS	SPECIES	BITTERROOT	GLACIER
GERANIUM	*Erodium*	*cicutarium*	X	X
	Geranium	*richardsonii*		X
		viscosissimum	X	X
HAREBELL	*Campanula*	*rotundifolia*	X	X
HEATH	*Chimaphila*	*umbellata*	X	X
	Pterospora	*andromedea*	X	X
	Pyrola	*asarifolia*	X	X
		chlorantha	X	X
		secunda	X	X
		uniflora	X	X
HONEYSUCKLE	*Linnaea*	*borealis*	X	X
	Lonicera	*ciliosa*	X	X
IRIS	*Iris*	*missouriensis*		X
		pseudacorus		
	Sisyrinchium	*angustifolium*	X	X
LILY	*Allium*	*brevistylum*	X	
		cernuum	X	X
		geyeri	X	X
		schoenoprasum	X	X
		textile	X	X
	Calochortus	*apiculatus*	X	X
		elegans	X	
		eurycarpus	X	
		gunnisonii		
		nuttallii		
	Camassia	*quamash*	X	X
	Clintonia	*uniflora*	X	X
	Disporum	species	X	X
	Erythronium	*grandiflorum*	X	X
	Fritillaria	*pudica*	X	X
	Leucocrinum	*montanum*		
	Lilium	*philadelphicum*		
	Smilacina	*racemosa*	X	X
		stellata	X	X
	Streptopus	*amplexifolius*	X	X
	Trillium	*ovatum*	X	X
	Triteleia	*grandiflora*	X	
	Veratrum	*viride*	X	X
	Xerophyllum	*tenax*	X	X
	Yucca	*glauca*		
	Zigadenus	*elegans*	X	X
		venenosus	X	X
MADDER	*Galium*	*boreale*	X	X
	Iliamna	*rivularis*		X
	Sphaeralcea	*coccinea*		

FAMILY	GENUS	SPECIES	BITTERROOT	GLACIER
MILKWEED	*Asclepias*	*speciosa*	x	
		verticillata		
MINT	*Agastache*	*urticifolia*		x
	Dracocephalum	*parviflorum*	x	x
	Mentha	*arvensis*	x	x
	Monarda	*fistulosa*	x	x
	Prunella	*vulgaris*	x	x
	Stachys	*palustris*	x	x
MORNING-GLORY	*Convolvulus*	*arvensis*	x	x
MUSTARD	*Alyssum*	*alyssoides*	x	x
	Arabidopsis	*thaliana*	x	
	Arabis	*nuttallii*	x	x
	Capsella	*bursa-pastoris*	x	x
	Cardaria	*draba*	x	
	Chorispora	*tenella*	x	
	Draba	species	x	x
	Erysimum	*asperum*	x	
	Hesperis	*matronalis*	x	
	Lepidium	*perfoliatum*	x	
	Lesquerella	*alpina*		x
	Physaria	species	x	x
	Sisymbrium	*altissimum*	x	x
	Smelowskia	*calycina*	x	x
	Thlaspi	*arvense*	x	x
NIGHTSHADE	*Hyoscyamus*	*niger*	x	
	Solanum	*dulcamara*	x	x
		rostratum	x	
ORCHID	*Calypso*	*bulbosa*	x	x
	Corallorhiza	*maculata*	x	x
		mertensiana	x	x
		striata	x	x
		trifida	x	x
	Cypripedium	*montanum*	x	x
	Habenaria	*dilatata*	x	x
		viridis		x
	Spiranthes	*romanzoffiana*	x	x
PARSLEY	*Angelica*	*arguta*	x	x
	Cicuta	*douglasii*	x	x
	Heracleum	*lanatum*	x	x
	Ligusticum	*filicinum*		
	Lomatium	*cous*	x	x
		dissectum	x	x
		foeniculaceum		x
		macrocarpum	x	x

FAMILY	GENUS	SPECIES	BITTERROOT	GLACIER
PEA	Astragalus	alpinus	x	x
		crassicarpus		
		drummondii	x	x
		gilviflorus		
		kentrophyta	x	
		vexilliflexus		x
	Coronilla	varia	x	
	Dalea	candida		
		purpurea		
	Glycyrrhiza	lepidota	x	x
	Hedysarum	boreale		x
		sulphurescens		x
	Lathyrus	ochroleucus	x	x
	Lotus	corniculatus		
	Lupinus	argenteus	x	x
		laxiflorus	x	x
		pusillus	x	
		sericeus	x	
	Medicago	sativa	x	x
	Oxytropis	besseyi	x	
		campestris		x
		lagopus		
		sericea	x	x
		splendens		x
	Pediomelum	argophyllum		
	Psoralidium	tenuiflorum		
	Thermopsis	montana	x	
	Trifolium	nanum		
		pratense	x	x
	Vicia	americana	x	x
		villosa	x	
PHLOX	Collomia	linearis	x	x
	Ipomopsis	aggregata	x	
	Ipomopsis	congesta		
	Microsteris	gracilis	x	x
	Phlox	diffusa	x	
		hoodii	x	x
		kelseyi	x	
		longifolia	x	
		pulvinata	x	
	Polemonium	pulcherrimum	x	x
		viscosum	x	x

FAMILY	GENUS	SPECIES	BITTERROOT	GLACIER
PINK	*Arenaria*	*congesta*	x	x
		hookeri		
		nuttallii	x	x
	Cerastium	*arvense*	x	x
	Dianthus	*armeria*	x	x
	Lychnis	*alba*	x	x
	Silene	*acaulis*	x	x
		vulgaris	x	x
	Stellaria	*longipes*	x	x
PRIMROSE	*Dodecatheon*	*pulchellum*	x	x
	Douglasia	*montana*	x	
PURSLANE	*Claytonia*	*lanceolata*	x	x
	Lewisia	*pygmaea*	x	x
		rediviva	x	x
	Montia	*perfoliata*	x	
ROSE	*Fragaria*	*virginiana*	x	x
	Geum	*rossii*	x	
		triflorum	x	x
	Ivesia	*gordonii*	x	
	Potentilla	*anserina*	x	x
		arguta	x	x
		diversifolia	x	x
		flabellifolia	x	
		glandulosa	x	x
		nivea		x
		palustris	x	x
ST. JOHNS-WORT	*Hypericum*	*perforatum*	x	x
SANDALWOOD	*Comandra*	*umbellata*	x	x
SAXIFRAGE	*Heuchera*	*cylindrica*	x	x
	Lithophragma	*glabrum*	x	x
		parviflora	x	x
	Parnassia	*fimbriata*	x	x
		parviflora		x
	Saxifraga	*arguta*	x	x
		oregana	x	x
		rhomboidea	x	
	Tellima	*grandiflora*		x
	Tiarella	*trifoliata*	x	x
SPURGE	*Euphorbia*	*esula*	x	x
		marginata		
STONECROP	*Sedum*	*lanceolatum*	x	x
		rhodanthum		
		roseum	x	x
		stenopetalum	x	x

FAMILY	GENUS	SPECIES	BITTERROOT	GLACIER
SUNFLOWER	Achillea	millefolium	X	X
	Agoseris	aurantiaca	X	X
		glauca	X	X
	Anaphalis	margaritaceae	X	X
	Antennaria	anaphaloides	X	X
		microphylla	X	X
		neglecta	X	X
	Arnica	cordifolia	X	X
		latifolia	X	X
		sororia	X	X
	Aster	campestris	X	X
	Balsamorhiza	incana		
		sagittata	X	X
	Carduus	nutans	X	X
	Centaurea	maculosa	X	X
		repens	X	
	Chaenactis	douglasii	X	
	Chrysanthemum	leucanthemum	X	X
	Chrysopsis	villosa	X	X
	Cirsium	arvense	X	X
		scariosum	X	
	Echinacea	angustifolia		
	Erigeron	compositus	X	X
		ochroleucus		X
		pumilus	X	
		speciosus	X	X
	Gaillardia	artistata	X	X
	Helianthella	uniflora		
	Helianthus	annuus	X	X
	Hieracium	albiflorum	X	X
		aurantiacum	X	X
	Hymenopappus	filifolius		
	Hymenoxys	richardsonii		X
	Lactuca	pulchella	X	X
	Liatris	punctata	X	X
	Lygodesmia	juncea		
	Matricaria	matricarioides	X	X
	Prenanthes	sagittata	X	X
	Ratibida	columnifera	X	X
	Senecio	canus	X	X
		triangularis	X	X
	Solidago	canadensis	X	X
	Sonchus	arvensis	X	
		asper	X	X
	Tanacetum	vulgare	X	X

FAMILY	GENUS	SPECIES	BITTERROOT	GLACIER
	Tetraneuris	*acaulis*		
		grandiflora		
	Townsendia	*hookeri*		
		incana		
		parryi	x	x
	Tragopogon	*dubius*	x	x
	Viguiera	*multiflora*		
	Wyethia	*helianthoides*		
		scabra		
VALERIAN	*Valeriana*	*dioica*	x	x
		sitchensis	x	x
VERVAIN	*Verbena*	*bracteata*	x	x
VIOLET	*Viola*	*adunca*	x	x
		canadensis	x	x
		glabella	x	x
		nuttallii	x	x
		orbiculata	x	x
WATERLEAF	*Hydrophyllum*	*capitatum*	x	x
	Phacelia	*franklinii*	x	
		hastata	x	x
		linearis	x	x
		sericea		x
WATERLILY	*Nuphar*	*polysepalum*	x	x
	Nymphaea	*odorata*		x

1 Lackschewitz, Klaus. 1991. *Vascular Plants of West-Central Montana—Identification Guidebook.* U.S. Department of Agriculture, General Technical Report INT-277.

2 Lesica, Peter. 2002. *Flora of Glacier National Park.* Oregon State University Press, Corvallis.

Glossary

alternate. Leaf arrangement in which each leaf occurs singly, usually on different sides of the stem.

annual. A plant that completes its life cycle in one year.

anther. The upper part, or head, of the stamen where the pollen occurs.

axil. The angle formed where the leaf and stem are joined.

banner. The large upper petal on a pea flower.

basal leaves. Leaves at the base of the plant.

biennial. A plant that completes its life cycle in two years, the first year having leaves only and the second year complete with a stem and flowers.

bilaterally symmetrical. Refers to a flower that has identical left and right sides (mirror images) if divided vertically.

blade. The broad or flat part of a leaf.

bract. A small leaflike structure usually located just under the flower or flower cluster.

bristle. Short stiff hair or hairlike structure.

calyx. The sepals, usually green and separate or joined, collectively.

calyx lobe (tooth). A free, not fused, upper part of fused sepals.

chlorophyll. The chemical in plant leaves that mediates photosynthesis and imparts the green color.

compound leaf. A leaf that is divided into two or more leaflets, each looking like a small leaf but lacking a bud.

corm. Short, solid, underground stem having papery leaves.

corolla. The petals of the flower, separate or fused, collectively.

corolla lobe. A free, not fused, outer part of united petals.

corolla tube. The cylindrical hollow part of the united petals of a corolla.

cyme. A convex or flat-topped flower cluster in which the central flower blooms first.

disk flower. The small tubular flower found in the center of the flower head on plants in the sunflower family.

entire. An undivided, unlobed leaf with no teeth on its margin.

filament. The stalk supporting the anther on a stamen.

gland. A lump or projection that secretes oily or sticky substances.

glandular-hairy. Having both glands and hairs.

herb. A plant without a woody stem and with herbaceous stems dying at the end of the growth season.

hybrid. Offspring resulting from a genetic cross between different genera, species, or varieties.

hypanthium. A cup- or tube-shaped receptacle, located at the base of the flower, to which the sepals, petals, and stamens are attached.

inferior ovary. An ovary that is attached below the other floral parts.

inflorescence. The flowering parts of a plant, collectively.

involucre. The whorl of bracts located below a flower head or cluster.

keel. Two fused petals forming a lower lip in flowers of the pea family.

lance-shaped. Shaped like a lance tip—widest at the base and tapering to a point.

leaflet. A distinct leaflike part of a compound leaf.

lip. Refers to one part of a bilaterally symmetrical, two-lipped corolla or calyx.

monocot. A class of plants having an embryo with a single cotyledon, a leaf that emerges upon germination.

node. The point at which a leaf or flower cluster is attached to the stem. May be called a *joint* when swelled.

opposite. Leaf arrangement in which leaves occur in pairs or opposite sides of the stem.

ovary. Part of the pistil that contains the ovules and will, after fertilization, form a seed-containing fruit.

palmate. Having a shape like fingers on a hand, as are leaflets or veins that spread from the tip of the leaf petiole.

palmately compound. Leaves that are divided to the midvein with leaflets attached at the same point and spread like fingers on a hand.

panicle. A compound raceme in which the inflorescence is repeatedly branched.

pappus. The modified calyx of the disk flowers present in members of the sunflower family; usually containing hairs, bristles, or scales.

perennial. A plant that lives for more than two years.

petal. The often colorful, leaflike parts of the corolla of a flower.

petiole. The stalk of a leaf.

pinnately compound. Leaves that are divided to the midvein with leaflets arranged on both sides of the petiole.

pistil. The female, seed-producing part of a flower including ovary, ovules, stigma, and style.

raceme. An inflorescence with an unbranched stem bearing multiple flowers, each with a stalk attached to a central axis.

radially symmetrical. A flower with similar parts arranged around a central axis.

ray flower. The strap-shaped, petal-like flower present in members of the sunflower family, usually located on the outside border of the flower head and surrounding the disk flowers, if present.

receptacle. The terminal, expanded part of the flower stalk supporting the organs of the flower.

rhizome. A horizontal stem that grows underground and sends up new stems and sends down roots.

rosette. A flat, circular cluster of radiating leaves at the base of the stem.

sepal. A segment of the calyx, usually green in color.

serrate. Margin of a leaf that is toothed like a saw, all teeth pointing forward.

simple leaf. A leaf that is not divided into leaflets.

spike. An elongated inflorescence with flowers that lack stalks.

spur. Hollow, slender, saclike structure of a petal, sepal, calyx, or corolla.

stalk. A supporting structure such as a flower stalk.

stamen. The male, pollen-producing organ of a flower, composed of a filament and an anther.

staminode. A sterile stamen that does not produce pollen.

stigma. That part of the pistil or female organ of the flower that receives the pollen.

stipule. A bract or leafy structure, usually in pairs, located at base of the leaf or leaf stalk.

stolon. A horizontal stem, a runner along the ground, with roots at the nodes and a new plant at the tip.

style. The stalklike part of a pistil between the ovary and stigma.

succulent. Fleshy and juicy like the stem of a cactus.

superior ovary. An ovary that is above the flower parts; the flower parts attach to the receptacle below the ovary.

tendril. A slender and coiled outgrowth, from the tip of a leaf or stem, that the plant uses to attach to another plant or a fence for support.

tepals. Identical petals and sepals.

throat. The expanded region of the corolla between the lobes and the tube.

trifoliate. A compound leaf with three leaflets.

umbel. A flower cluster or inflorescence where short flower stalks arise from a common point, giving an overall flat or umbrella shape.

variety. A taxonomic subcategory of a species or subspecies.

whorl. An arrangement of leaves, flowers, or petals where all radiate from a single point.

wings. The two side petals on flowers of the pea family.

Selected Bibliography

Booth, W. E., and J. C. Wright. 1962. *Flora of Montana. Part II—Dicotyledons.* Bozeman: Montana State College.

Dorn, Robert D. 1984. *Vascular Plants of Montana.* Cheyenne, Wyo.: Mountain West Publishing.

Fagan, Damian. 1998. *Canyon Country Wildflowers: A Falcon Guide.* Helena, Mont.: Falcon Publishing Company, Inc.

Kershaw, Linda. 2000. *Edible and Medicinal Plants of the Rockies.* Edmonton, Alberta: Lone Pine Publishing.

Kershaw, Linda, Andy MacKinnon, and Jim Pojar. 1998. *Plants of the Rocky Mountains.* Edmonton, Alberta: Lone Pine Publishing.

Lackschewitz, Klaus. 1991. *Vascular Plants of West-Central Montana—Identification Guidebook.* U.S. Department of Agriculture. General Technical Report INT-277.

Lesica, Peter. 2002. *Flora of Glacier National Park, Montana.* Corvallis: Oregon State University Press.

Phillips, H. Wayne. 1999. *Central Rocky Mountain Wildflowers: A Falcon Guide.* Helena, Mont.: Falcon Publishing Company, Inc.

Phillips, H. Wayne. 2001. *Northern Rocky Mountain Wildflowers: A Falcon Guide.* Helena, Mont.: Falcon Publishing Company, Inc.

Phillips, H. Wayne. 2003. *Plants of the Lewis and Clark Expedition.* Missoula, Mont.: Mountain Press Publishing Company.

Taylor, Ronald J. 1990. *Northwest Weeds: The Ugly and Beautiful Villains of Fields, Gardens, and Roadsides.* Missoula, Mont.: Mountain Press Publishing Company.

Taylor, Ronald J. 1992. *Sagebrush Country: A Wildflower Sanctuary.* Missoula, Mont.: Mountain Press Publishing Company.

Schreier, Carl. 1996. *Wildflowers of the Rocky Mountains.* Moose, Wyo.: Homestead Publishing.

Strickler, Dee. 1986. *Prairie Wildflowers.* Columbia Falls, Mont.: The Flower Press.

Strickler, Dee. 1988. *Forest Wildflowers.* Columbia Falls, Mont.: The Flower Press.

Strickler, Dee. 1990. *Alpine Wildflowers.* Columbia Falls, Mont.: The Flower Press.

Strickler, Dee. 1993. *Wayside Wildflowers of the Pacific Northwest.* Columbia Falls, Mont.: The Flower Press.

Other Sources

Montana Native Plant Society
P.O. Box 8783
Missoula, Montana 59807–8783
http://www.umt.edu/mnps/

Montana State University Herbarium
408 Lewis Hall
Department of Plant Sciences and Plant Pathology
Montana State University
Bozeman, Montana 59717
http://Gemini.oscs.Montana.edu/mlavin/herb/herb1.htm

Montana Plant Life
http://Montana.plant-life.org/
An online database with photographs and descriptions of Montana plants.

University of Montana Herbarium
Biological Services
University of Montana
Missoula, Montana 59812
http://herbarium.dbs.umt.edu/

Index

❧ About the Author ❦

Donald Anthony Schiemann received a Ph.D. in Environmental Science and Microbiology at the University of North Carolina-Chapel Hill following service in the military, an undergraduate degree, employment with the Food and Drug Administration, and work in preventive medicine with an oil company in Saudi Arabia. He then taught environmental health science and microbiology at East Tennessee State University, served as a laboratory director in environmental microbiology in Canada, and finally joined the faculty of Montana State University in 1981. After retirement in 1996, he embarked on nearly a decade of travel and outdoor photography in Montana, pursuing a passion for natural history that began during his youth in Minnesota.

We encourage you to patronize your local bookstores. Most stores will order any title that they do not stock. You may also order directly from Mountain Press by mail, using the order form provided below or by calling our toll-free number and using your VISA, MasterCard, Discover, or American Express. We will gladly send you a complete catalog upon request.

Some other titles of interest:

____ Birds of the Northern Rockies		$12.00
____ The Bloody Bozeman: *The Perilous Trail to Montana's Gold*		$16.00
____ Discovering Lewis & Clark From the Air	paper $24.00/cloth	$40.00
____ Edible and Medicinal Plants of the West		$21.00
____ From Earth to Herbalist		
An Earth-Conscious Guide to Medicinal Plants		$21.00
____ The Journals of Patrick Gass:		
Member of the Lewis and Clark Expedition		$20.00
____ Lewis & Clark: *A Photographic Journey*		$18.00
____ The Lochsa Story: *Land Ethics in the Bitterroot Mountains*		$20.00
____ The Montanans' Fishing Guide		
Volume 1: Montana Waters West of the Continental Divide		$18.00
____ Mountain Plants of the Pacific Northwest		$25.00
____ Names on the Face of Montana		
The Story of Montana's Place Names		$12.00
____ Northwest Weeds		
The Ugly and Beautiful Villains of Fields, Gardens, and Roadsides		$14.00
____ Photographing Montana, 1894–1928		
The Life and Work of Evelyn Cameron	paper $35.00/cloth	$60.00
____ Plants of the Lewis & Clark Expedition		$20.00
____ Raptors of the Rockies		$16.00
____ Roadside Geology of Montana		$20.00
____ Roadside History of Montana		$20.00
____ Sagebrush Country: *A Wildflower Sanctuary*		$14.00
____ Watchable Birds of the Rocky Mountains		$14.00
____ Wild Berries of the West		$16.00
____ Wildflowers of Montana		$22.00

Please include $3.00 per order to cover shipping and handling.

Send the books marked above. I enclose $_____

Name_____

Address_____

City/State/Zip_____

☐ Payment enclosed (check or money order in U.S. funds)

Bill my: ☐ VISA ☐ MasterCard ☐ Discover ☐ American Express

Expiration Date:_____

Card No._____

Signature _____

Mountain Press Publishing Company
P. O. Box 2399 • Missoula, Montana 59806 • Order Toll Free 1-800-234-530
e-mail: info@mtnpress.com • web site: www.mountain-press.com